WRITER
as
CRITIC

MEMORY
SERVES
ORATORIES

WRITER AS CRITIC SERIES XIII

MEMORY SERVES

ORATORIES

LEE MARACLE

EDITED BY SMARO KAMBOURELI

NeWest Press

LIBRARY AND ARCHIVES CANADA CATALOGUING IN PUBLICATION
Maracle, Lee, 1950–
[Essays. Selections] Memory serves and other essays / Lee Maracle.
(Writer as critic ; 13)
Collection of oratories delivered and performed over a twenty-year period.
Includes bibliographical references.
Issued in print and electronic formats.
ISBN 978-1-926455-44-0 (pbk.).
ISBN 978-1-926455-45-7 (epub).
ISBN 978-1-926455-46-4 (mobi)
I. Title.   II. Series: Writer as critic ; 13
PS8576.A6175A6 2015   C814'.54   C2015-901819-6   C2015-901820-X

EDITOR: Smaro Kamboureli
BOOK DESIGN: Natalie Olsen, Kisscut Design
COVER IMAGE: Susan Point, *Salish Path,* 2010, Serigraph.
AUTHOR PHOTO: Columpa Bobb

NeWest Press acknowledges the support of the Canada Council for the Arts the Alberta Foundation for the Arts, and the Edmonton Arts Council for support of our publishing program. This project is funded in part by the Government of Canada.

201, 8540 – 109 Street
Edmonton, AB T6G 1E6
780.432.9427
NEWEST PRESS   www.newestpress.com

No bison were harmed in the making of this book.
Printed and bound in Canada   1 2 3 4 5 17 16 15

To my teachers

CONTENTS

PREFACE   When Smaro Kamboureli suggested that I gather together my speeches and lectures into a book, I thought it was a great idea. Having already written some of them down and published others, I thought it would be an easy book to put together. It turned out that fiction comes easier to me than non-fiction. Early in the revision process, I became aware of how often certain themes and concerns were recurring in the talks that I had presented over the course of many years. It is impossible to give a lecture or speak on any serious issue in the Indigenous world without placing it in the context of colonialism and our need for decolonization. In collecting these speeches together, I was then faced with the challenge of how to maintain the necessary emphasis on colonialism while still attending to its particular aspects in relation to individual talks. Also challenging was revising speeches and oratories that I had presented over twenty years ago. A talk always reflects where I am at in any given moment. We are called upon to continuously grow from the realizations that we come to when we speak. So revisiting the speeches that I gave years back has involved engaging with my growth since then, and fleshing out how I have evolved by travelling more deeply into a subject.

Sometime during the seventies, I was having a conversation with Haida feminist Lavina Lightbown. She told me this story: When we came out of the clam shell, the men got on the back of a shark, who took them to killer whale, who took them to land. The women came out of the clam shell and saw a woman at the bottom of the sea in an ocean river. They went to exchange pleasantries with her. She asked where they were going. They told her they were going up on land to become human. "Here, you might need this," she said, and handed them some brains. It dawned on me that, in order for us to achieve clarity, we had to go back to the bottom of the sea, through all the layers of green to dark, to consult with the mother of thought who lives there.

I love speaking. I love our orality, its rhythm, its ease, the way we can slip into poetry, story, even song and dance, break the tedium with a joke, particularly an anti-colonial joke. I love how the speaker gets to wander around and through a subject with the audience. On paper, though, the words can lose much of the personality of the speaker, jokes don't fit, and the sidebars, the off-the-cuff remarks, detract and can even trivialize the thoughts shared. When you speak you deliver a voice; everyone knows that what you think is also what you feel. In speaking, there is no problem delivering the integrity of your emotionality. But in writing you evoke, instead of expressing, your feelings. When the immediacy that links speaker and audience is absent on the page, you must find other ways of sharing the feelings that give rise to your thoughts.

My elders always called me *paxim — sweetheart*; some of them still do. I thought that it was because I was a little sweetheart, until one day my daughter was drifting from the family fold in a direction that was dangerous and ill-disciplined: "Just call her *sweetheart*," one of my aunt's said, "worked for you." As a child, I was not disciplined. I have struggled to find the discipline of non-fiction in the course of revising these speeches. I have struggled with order, organization, structure, and clarity without losing my own sense of presentation and orality. *Memory Serves* reads like a new kind of prose, what is fashioned when oratory is written down.

I have struggled to write these speeches respectfully, without losing my voice in the process. Some complex thoughts are unraveled in the pages of this book. Some of the concepts have not yet been articulated in English or in our original languages. I have struggled to deploy *the way* we do things, the processes we use to come to a clear understanding so that they can be articulated in writing. This is especially the case with the essay "Oratory on Oratory." It is difficult enough to write non-fiction without trying to articulate something that is so ordinary for us; it is like breathing, oxygenation and expiration, detoxification. We do it every day, so it should be easy.

Each oratory turned-essay here stands on its own, but read together they create a journey through our world and the underpinning thoughts, theories, and logic that drive that world *as I see it*. I say "as I see it" because I have gleaned concepts contained in stories, stories that I have interpreted in accordance with the direction we are all obligated to travel in — toward the good life and the good mind — and that too requires that I interpret what the good life and good mind are, and map out the direction to determine what will lead us there.

I do not use the word *teachings* in the same way others might. Teachings are not dictums to be blindly followed. They are meant to be the beginnings of the development of governance or theory, but the individual is expected to interpret them personally. I try hard to use the word sparingly. I prefer words that are co-equivalents to how Europe names itself, rather than the diminished words assigned to us. For instance, our knowledge keepers are referred to as elders, while European knowledge keepers are referred to as intellectuals, academics, professors, teachers, experts, etc. In Halkomelem the word is *si'yam*, which does not mean elder, so I don't use it. A *si'yam* is recognized as a knowledge keeper, thinker, law keeper, spiritual logician, historian, and so forth. *Si'yams* know something, and we recognize their knowledge.

Indigenous people have historically hesitated to create books such as this because they express the views of the individuals presenting thoughts on the whole. The individual cannot represent the whole in that way in our communities. We don't assign anyone that kind of authority. I derive my understanding of social theory, of our logic, our processes for thought, discovery, consultation, and learning from the stories I have heard and from having witnessed thousands of oral discussions with youth, elders, middle-aged people, even children. As a witness I pay attention to how these discussions unfold, how each individual engages the whole, the subject in question, and how they play with it. I have been witnessing for as far back as my memory serves, but this does not make me an expert on our people.

What makes my words valuable is the thousands of Indigenous people who have said to me: *You just articulated everything I was thinking.* Firstly, this response makes me a witness who has the people's direction and thought at heart. Secondly, it shows that I am recognized as one of our foremost witnesses, *si'yam*, or, to put this in English, I am recognized by Indigenous people as someone who can capture common thought. This carries both responsibility and honour. I must respect the words I use and articulate what I have learned from what I have witnessed.

I strive in my speaking and writing to articulate my thoughts responsively. I believe my community needs this book just as surely as they need to drink clean water. I also believe Canadians need this book. There is another way to be, to think, to know, and when Canadians witness another way, perhaps the colonial domination can begin to end. I believe, too, that each time any one of us has a thought, others do so as well, and it is in this way that the journey to collective consciousness continues. Writing those thoughts down hastens our journey toward a common consciousness.

Since I started working on this book, many new scholars have begun to articulate thinking that comes directly from our stories. I acknowledge Jo-ann Archibald, whose book, *Indigenous Storywork*, affirmed so much of my thinking that unfolds here. Though I do not cite Jo-ann directly, I believe that her book picks up some aspects of the same understanding I have acquired over the years of interaction with the *si'yams* listed at the end of this book and my own struggling with stories I heard as a child, and carries them a step further down our common road. I also acknowledge Sean Kicummah Teuton's *Red Land, Red Power: Grounding Knowledge in the American Indian Novel*. Again, I do not cite Sean directly, but his book preceded mine and made this one just a little bit easier to write. I am affirmed and informed by the hundreds of conversations I have had with thousands of Indigenous people over the years. I cannot possibly acknowledge everyone. But the works listed at the end of this book name the key people with whom I have engaged under various circumstances and who have become leaders, knowledge keepers in their own right, and with whom I still have a relationship as a West Coast woman.

Lee Maracle
TORONTO 2015

ACKNOWLEDGEMENTS   A short version of the title essay in this volume was presented at a conference on Creative Non-Fiction organized by the En'owkin Centre, and was published in *Crisp Blue Edges: Indigenous Creative Fiction* (2000). "Who Gets to Draw the Maps: In and Out of Place in British Columbia" began as a short panel presentation at the Border Blur Conference hosted by Canada House and Gary Geddes in the spring of 2000; an expanded version was published in *Border Blur: In and Out of Place in British Columbia and the Pacific Northwest* (2003), and it has been revised again for this book. "Understanding Raven" began as a panel presentation at the International Conference on Native Literature held in Krakow, Poland (1999). Parts of "Arrest this Memory," originally published in *My Home as I Remember*, an anthology I co-edited with Sandra Laronde (2000), have been integrated in various parts of this book. "Notes on a Life" was solicited by Thomas King and published in "First Voices, First Words," a special issue of *Prairie Fire* (Fall 2001). "Oratory: Coming to Theory" was solicited by Caffyn Kelly, published as a monograph, and reprinted in *Give Back/First Nations Perspectives on Cultural Practice* (1992). "Post-Colonial Imagination" was written for my daughter Columpa Bobb and published in the *Vancouver Sun* on the occasion of George Ryga's 25th anniversary production of *The Ecstasy of Rita Joe* at the Firehall Arts Centre (1992). I wrote it because a number of Indigenous actors thought she should not play Rita and that Firehall should not mount the work. "Peace," presented at the Stein Valley Festival that occurred during the Oka Crisis of 1990, was solicited by Chief Ruby Dunstan who asked me to speak on peace without betraying the Mohawks; it was published in the Ottawa newspaper *Womanyst* (1991). An earlier version of "Mapping Our Way through History" was written for *The Journals of Knud Rasmussen: A Sixth Sense of Memory, History and High-definition Inuit Storytelling* edited by Gillian Robinson (2008). "Salmon Is the Hub of Salish Memory" began as a presentation to Pacific Northwest Historical Society's conference (2003). The "Lost Days of Columbus" was solicited as a counter word to the Columbus Day Celebrations of 1992 and published in *Trivia: A Journal of Ideas* (1992). "This is Personal: Revisiting Gloria Anzaldúa" was solicited by AnaLouise Keating as a tribute to Gloria Anzaldúa; it was delivered at the 2004 Surviving the Battles, Shaping Our Worlds: Honoring the Work of Gloria Evangelina Anzaldúa conference and published in *Entre Mundos/Among Worlds: New Perspectives on Gloria Anzaldúa* (2005). "Oratory on Oratory" was first presented at the TransCanada One conference (Vancouver 2005), and published in *Trans.Can. Lit: Resituating the Study of Canadian Literature*, edited by Smaro Kamboureli and Roy Miki (2007). "Toward a National Literature" was first presented at Toward a Native American Critical Theory, a conference organized by Jace Weaver in 2003, and was published in *Across Borders/Across Cultures*, edited by Paul Depasquale, Renate Eigenbrod and Emma Larocque (2009).

MEMORY
SERVES

ORATORIES

MEMORY
SERVES

MEMORY SERVES. It is directed by condition, culture, and objective. It is conjured by systemic practice. It is shaped by results. By the time humans are seven years old, the commitment to remember is shaped, and they remember from the point of view of their social milieu.

In a society, which relies on a trial process, memory serves as evidence, as objective proof based on facts. Evidence and facts are collected with the intent to prove some hypothesis or thesis. This proof then becomes the basis for judgment, decision or action.

This is a simple system that fails to count humans as variable, as spirited, creative, and emotional beings. It is a simple system that fails to account for catastrophe, social and personal trauma, and how humans fall off track.

In a society, which is hierarchical, held up by armies, police, punitive deterrents and authoritarian-based respectability, the human as variable does not need to be considered. What needs to be known to humans before a decision is made is who has the authority to make it; what the law or policy governing the decision is; what the place of the author in the decision-making ladder is; and what the parameters of the author's decision-making authority are. People are expected to obey the decision or be punished for their disobedience.

The proof then returns full circle as the basis for conviction or alienation of the dissident. Memory does not exist for any other social purpose. Facts are defined as objective memory. The rememberers strive to record evidence and achieve objectivity. Recorded objective memory is embraced as the only valid memory. The realm of spiritual intent, creative motive or human emotion is relegated to subjectivity and persuasion; the art of engaging others in dialogue, embracing their emotional spiritual and intellectual sensibility, has no place.

Each witness becomes part of the argument between defense and prosecution. Justice is not a consideration. What happened, the activities of the humans, the facts surrounding the case and the law, is all that is considered.

When humans give breath to life, give voice to their perception of life, this is a sacred act. They are taking an event that has already been committed and they are re-membering or reconstructing it in their minds.

Memory serves. In a society governed first and foremost by spirit to spirit relationships to all beings, memory serves much differently than in a society in which property possession determines importance. To re-member is, first, directional. Indigenous people commit to memory those events and the aspects of those events that suit the direction we are moving in or the direction we want to move in if a shift is occurring. I choose to remember what happens to Sockeye because that is the direction from which Salish people move. We re-member events; we reconstruct them because we are aware that they have already ended, are dis-membered, gone forever, and because they affect us and are directly connected to who we are as a people. We may wish to achieve a new direction, secure an old direction, or mark the path travelled so that others may find the path easier to follow. Our memories serve the foregoing.

Who or what is important does not figure into it. This is what governs our lives and shapes our oracy. Memory is also the governor of native literacy.

Creative non-fiction is bound by the original foundations handed to us by ancestors, ceremony, laws, and our relationship to creation. We place our obligations before us when we re-member. To what end do I wish to re-create this moment? What direction do I wish this memory to travel in the future? In so doing we hang on to memories of those things that assist us in conjuring and travelling in the direction charted by the culture that has shaped us. We let go those things that will impair our journey or thwart the courage required to secure our path. We determine the direction we believe we wish to travel before we speak or make a truckload of decisions. The direction we are travelling shapes our memories whether we are conscious of this or not.

Our intent governs our choice of words in recalling events. The winds are our uncles. Our cultures name them and define their relationship to us. Wind, breath, and voice are about where you want to end up, not about what happened or what facts you have assimilated to bolster your thoughts. Facts are mathematical things, quantities intended to persuade the thoughtless and the spiritless. Our direction is rooted to the imagined relationship between two or more beings from the beginning of the relationship to the end of their journey. The winds breathed life into our bodies. We share the winds, and reflect their directional qualities. It is our breath, our spirit, and our heart that are articulated when we open our mouth. Where you are going with this is the question we all recognize.

I love the bones that are stones...

Stone is our oldest grandfather. We refer to the stones that keep our songs and stories as grandfathers. Our grandfathers give us the

3

rock on which we stand, but our grandmothers move us from that stone in the direction of relation with others. They are the keepers of the stories that teach us about relations; they are the flesh of our bones that are stones. *I carry them, willingly.*

I am in my room, about to indulge in another old habit, a bad one; I reconstruct the insult and persuade myself that it is not about me being offended but rather about the other being, the offender. I hesitate; this is my daughter after all. Some little soft voice whispers inside my mind: remember. To what end? This question rolls about for a long time. I have no way to answer it, and for the first time since I was a child I am forced to take my own advice. I pick up the stone on my dresser and ask this old grandfather to help me answer the question: to what end?

Memory serves. It is re-membered by our imaginations. A long time ago we were instructed to hear stone's songs of law and being. What misdirected wind sang so loud in your ears that the songs of your stones that are bones went unheeded? Right this minute we are remembering our past. Every day thousands upon thousands of us are remembering our past.

Some of us are remembering to dismember our relationship with one another, with earth, and with all our relations here; others are remembering to re-member our relationship with one another, but we are all, on some level or other, remembering. It doesn't matter which direction we choose. What matters is that we do so consciously, with the end of the trail in plain sight. It is conscious decision-making determined by our chosen path that we are called upon to enact.

Our culture expects maturity. Such phrases as *I don't know, pass it on, he made me, it was because* are not acceptable reasons for having committed actions. Our maturity is defined by our ability to consciously choose our path, make every act we commit deliberate and our own, turn every lesson we learn to account, and internalize these lessons. We are expected to create relationships based on the establishment of personal direction that arises out of our commitment to and ownership of our actions. For this reason memory can betray the rememberer's desire.

If the words you choose take on a challenging direction when what is desired is re-connection, you will conjure memory in one way and your response to your own conjuring will betray your distant desire.

I watch my daughter, hear her voice rise. She marches back and forth in front of me. The words tumbling out are sharp and full of insult. Her thin arms punctuate every sentence that splits the breath between us. Her eyes flash fire.

I do not always accept what she says. In my shock, I retreat to an old game. Watch the speaker, grocery-list her moves, turn my listening volume down low, just record what I see. Try not to listen. Try hard to remain aloof and amuse myself with the activity of the speaker that I am committing to memory.

Memory serves. Once we understood order, natural order. First comes the crying, and then comes the laughter. Babies cry for months after birth. Babies' tears are their first language. This language was understood by grandmothers who were proud of their grandchildren's capacity to create language of the original voice creation gave us — crying.

Original sound.

For months, dozens of humans create ridiculous images, make faces, and talk foolishly in a desperate attempt to get their child to

5

laugh. Every adult wants to be the first to inspire laughter in a child. Laughter is conjured from relationship. Crying is natural.

Memory serves. Sleep came as it does even when life presents more agitation for my soul than I necessarily desire. Stone sang as he does:

These bones, these stones are you. I remember them, gather them up, dust fragment by dust fragment, bone chip by bone chip, pick them up, reconstruct the old you. Your flesh will not be there. You will emerge decrepit, reshaped, and odd looking, but you, you always were and were forever meant to be there and I shall sing.

My song will breathe new life into the bones. You will wobble free of these other breaths, crumbed between your flesh that rang so loud you couldn't hear your ancient self, couldn't hear your first shame, couldn't hear the screaming sound of your first song of commitment to re-membering me and our modest family.

"Good intentions and love are not enough," Columpa whispers.

"We must have our discipline," Tania murmurs, "and a clear path to embrace it," she adds, and the rush of tears was so great we nearly put out the fire inside us.

Memory serves. Our culture gives us no permission to accept victimization or exploitation of our selves or anyone else. We must re-member to learn, to connect, and to validate ourselves and others in the process. We must re-member to share joy, grief. Our re-membering serves our growth as human beings.

Memory serves. We re-member hundreds of thousands of relationships — to wind, to flora, to fauna, to humans, to the dead, the star world, sky world, sea world. Everything from the humble snow flea on a glacier to the glacial age is re-membered for today and for tomorrow. There is no time differentiation in the conjuring of memory. Future is a remembered thing the very moment I give voice inside my mind to my imagined participation in tomorrow.

Salish remembering depends on the place and perspective of the viewer; the images take on meaning. The place and perception of the viewer influence the direction of the imagined events. This colours the reconstruction of memory. Western doctors have a solution for the newborn that does not cry at birth. We know what it is. We know this solution intimately. We fear it. We abhor it.

I carry your bones now that you're gone these bones that are stones gleam clean white in my apron I walk carefully not to make any sudden moves so as not to jar you or add any new sound to them I want only pure sounds of you and me when we were a we to echo back to me in those long nights when alone and the night's snake-filled dreams find me wondering if I am going the right way did I choose words with the sacred upheld I still miss you after all this time

Memory serves. There are a myriad of angles to the same image. I could have chosen another, one not so rife with emotional depth. There is a lighthearted side to our funeral process. After the grieving, after the wailing song comes the clown. From the clown's perspective, the process looks much different. Both acts come together and form life – first the crying, then the laughter. We are re-born. If we do not cry, we do not breathe; we do not survive. Our cry is the first expression of our life. This cry guarantees life. We understood that once – first the tears, then the laughter.

7

Now this new leaving is upon me. It was not me who chose it. You simply left. I dig around old bones, re-gather them, re-search them for knowing, for understanding. I stare at this old apron for some word trail, some breadcrumb trail of how we ever got turned around. What story breathed into your bones? These bones that held a thousand-year old memory of law inside them were betrayed when you left. What discouraged you from re-membering bones, my bones, my bones that are stones?

Once we burned every dead person among us. Those with no one to carry them were never denied an apron. This apron holds you next to my womb. This womb will purify you and ready you for the next world. I burned you, my breath, and collected your ashes, wrapped your bone fragments in cedar. The pillar of smoke you made flickered between alluring bits and pieces of our lives, and majestic plumes saluted me.

Memory serves. We are called upon to remember the past and re-determine our direction. If we had a difficult past we are expected to let go of the governing feelings of that past and remember the losses created by the difficulty so that we may create a different path. In the process we become intimate with both the difficulty and ourselves in the context of this difficulty.

There was a war. The warriors were called upon to dance themselves to death in a fire of their own making. They asked us to carry their bones, to purify them, and stir them with our bones after a year. Each woman carried a set of bones — her husband's, her father's, her brother's. After the war, we — women and the old men and children — chose to leave. I am re-membering that day as I stare at my paxim's bones. And I search for word clues — breadcrumb trails we say today. The earth wept torrential tears grieving our leaving. We didn't want anyone to know why we left.

There, in that village, were the bodies of women and children bleeding from the bones of their hands. It was our first secret. This secret knowing came upon us in the wake of our first shame, that over-whelming desire to heave up the food inside our bellies, going mad inside our stomachs. The families tried to understand, tried to appreci-ate what they saw. My body wrenched every piece of me, wanted to run in all four directions. I remember the images. Owl brought the message of carnage our warriors had committed. War is fought among men.

The spirit world gathered. Raven, in her largest and most glorious self, delivered the verdict. Burn the flesh of these men. Women and children cannot become participants in war. *You could not raise your face to look at me until you agreed with the decision and the fire rose majestic. Every piece of wood in our homes was thrown onto the pyre. You strode forward head up and walked into the inferno, turn-ing but once to wave goodbye. I loved you even then. My sisters and I gathered your bones. We reached inside the stone memories of our bodies—for song, for depth, for knowing. We pulled from every dir-ection of our past so that we may find some kind of future. We sang. We couldn't stay there without you. We wept with earth as we con-jured the plan to leave.*

These bones, shaped from our ancestral bones, stared sound-less while we wept and walked away, surefooted and so fearless. I wince now for the aloneness of these ancestors. *We came upon a valley when the walking burnt the grief from our feet and we started life anew. New men arrived. We built our world again. We sang the memory of the warriors to the fire. This secret was the first shame that visited our men and children. You look so funny, wobbling, twisted and obviously re-constructed like that. But you are there with me still. The memory that sang so many songs of love, of romance, of struggle, of victory is still there in your old bones. I breathe new life into this dead, made-up being. We wobble toward future, these bones and I.*

9

We begin as memory. Inside the body of a child, a girl child, the ovum is a complex manager and arranger that remembers to transform from a fertilized ovum to a human being. It does not know what to do with the sperm until years have passed and the body of the girl holding it has nurtured it and fed it, helping it to mature and develop the capacity for systemic memory and planning. Inside the ovum are its original instructions, the call to create the complex systems required to program the birth of a human being. The capacity to remember is there from the beginning. The memory is sparked by the transformation of the girl from a child to a woman. The ovum knows it is responsible for doing this. It is there at birth, but it takes twelve years for this girl child to be ready for the transformation, for the ovum to be able to act on its original instructions, for its memory to become this amazing institution of regenerative reproduction. We also end as memory.

Like the ovum, our communities operate in the same way: we have a centre, which incubates our systems and nurtures and recreates those who must carry out our original instructions and manage the systems – the *si'yams* – who hold the re-membered story and oratory, ceremony, knowledge and who have come to understand how to ferret out the word – the directions – that will guide us all on the journey to the good life where we will be transformed into spirit beings or "hidden being." Our memory is an emotional memory. We remember the emotional effort it took to travel in the direction of the good life during difficult times. We remember the days in which we fell off the path to the good life. We remember the stories, the healing modalities, ceremonies, and knowledge we gained from the fall. We remember the efforts we made to return to the path and the thought/feeling we gleaned from the experience. We have a spiritual memory of the processes that became ceremonies that we inherited to heal the spirit and restore our fire so we could return to our path. In our spiritual memory, we come to recognize those with whom we share a spiritual journey. This is felt. We recognize kindred spirits.

This is Personal: Revisiting Gloria Anzaldúa

Borderlands, border blur, bordered fabric and loose weaves come to mind. Old cloth, collared cloth, cotton, and dog and goat hair cloth full of intense familial design that seems to want to adorn a woman's back. De Nîmes, the makers of denim, a town in France: it usurps the markets of the world — creating a disordered, maladjusted diversity in which the center becomes the periphery and the designer falls from the map. Western lingo dominates and supplants language, communication, and metaphor. Gringo conquers language, annihilating humanism, humanity, and boundaries of decency. From below the map, under all that historical cloth, barely covered in an old woven blanket so full of holes the design blurs like the borders of our dignity, I peer out at Gloria Anzaldúa.

I etch word designs onto the cloth of my story with her.

We have a physical memory of the medicines and food required to restore the body and mental memory. We know memory has direction. What we remember and how we remember is dependent on the direction we are travelling. We hold that we are all travelling toward the good mind, the good self, and the good life. It is a responsibility to stay travelling in this direction: we call it our path. We remember knowledge, we work with what we know and we hold up the knowledge that keeps us from falling off our path. However, we are not afraid to fall. We know we have the knowledge that can restore our human journey to the good life. We train our children to remember this knowledge. We train them with story.

Good stories don't take long. I Am Woman was incubating itself in my womb, in my musculature, in my mind, outside my mind, in the wombs of every blurred barely visible Indigenous woman on this Island long before the International Feminist Book Fair. I had spent years resisting writing this work. She had spent years wanting to be born. On January 1, 1988, she insisted on being born. The labour of birth is a strange borderland, slightly asinine, somewhat ridiculous, and just a little too intense for summer conception. Best to weave stories in winter. She came, full term, beautiful and well woven. I dropped her on the world long after the phone call came inviting me to this Book Fair. I tend to like pushing the envelope particularly when a dead line is inside it. As the phone rose in my hand and Diana Bronson's voice invited me to the fair she listed the names of those Indigenous women who would be there ... Gloria Anzaldúa ... I hope you don't mind. We have invited her as an Indigenous woman. Do you consider Mexicans and Chicanos Indigenous? *It was my turn to pause. My blanket drops. I am back on the White Male Euro map. I never wanted to be a party to this map.* Some people, Diana, are not in the habit of presuming to name the place, position, or belonging of others. *The softness in my voice surprises me. It suggests that some piece of me privately forgives her. What is that?*

Our medicine is gathered from the experience of our falls from the path and from the discoveries of the medicines that revitalize the remembering required of us to return to our responsibilities and hold up the knowledge gained from those historical moments. We walk with our *si'yams* who identify these medicines. They let us know how to work with them. They show us how to hold them up. They teach us what our relationship is to them and how we care-take and honour them. Our memory is committed to the context of respect, dignity, honour, and continued relationship with all beings. Memory is imagined and it is imagined for whatever purpose the rememberer imagines she or he exists for. We do not use medicines that we do not have a relationship with; we do not transform, isolate, mutate, or alter the medicines wantonly. The medicines are there to transform us from pitiful weak and sick people to strong, resilient, healthy people who can challenge themselves to stay on the path.

(Nervous laugh) Good...uh, yes, well, good, well...we will uh...send you an official invitation. *The sun fights with the clouds here in winter, each struggling for command of the sky. By nightfall the sea water usually wins. Now I have to write the book. No, I don't have to do anything. The book insisted. I wrote the words* to I Am Woman *while the name Gloria Anzaldúa slid around chaotically in my mind. Who is this woman? Who is this woman whose cloth is woven so tightly out of such stern thread that the organizers of an International Feminist Book Fair would go ahead and invite her without any consultation with the rest of the Indigenous delegation? They invited her despite the fact that they weren't sure we considered her one of us. She must be powerful. She is such a force that the center must contend with her from a momentary periphery. More than that, the periphery they established was positioned somewhere to the left of my old blanket.*

We are called upon to own our emotions, to own our spirit, and to establish relation with others. We know that exploitative relations are short-lived. We have memories of how that is done. Humour introduces us to others. We honour the simple humanity of others through humour. Humour is not intended to ridicule: we remember the story of the peacemaker who was ridiculed for his disfigured face and so fell out of favour with his community, but managed to stay on the path to the good life and bring peace to others, despite his disfavour and neglect. Our memory of humour is intended to play with our folly, our fragility, our moments of

13

foolishness in which we were humbled to the greatness of others, so we poke fun at the ludicrous in society, the ridiculousness of conceit, our moments in which we can use our humour to level the playing field between ourselves and others.

For Salish people, re-membering is not a simple act of recall. All minds have pathways — dendrites — travelling to all parts of our memory. When our spirit is fully awake, the business of pulling the parts together to direct our memory is complicated, layered, and at the same time power-directed and relationship-based. The whole of me needs to be fed, spiritually, emotionally, intellectually, and physically. But our minds are also capable of imagining thought, looking into the future, evaluating impact and measuring affect. Our stories remind us that we are responsible for remembering from within our original context. Remembering is a process of being fed by the past, not just my past but my ancestral past, the earth's past, and the past of other human beings. We are responsible for pulling the best threads from our past forward to re-weave our lives — together. And this, too, is the act of remembering for the *si'yams* of my nation.

It was not so much a moment of forgiveness, but a re-opening of a door Diana had inadvertently closed. Recognizing this was inadvertent, a spiritual intuition, a reading of her emotionality, and a belief in her humanity. I remember what being human looks like. I believe in the being of humanity in others when I see it, because I have experienced this knowingness before in myself. This kind of knowing has never failed me.

Thought has emotionality. It has a spirit, an intended outcome that is never isolated from history, from story, from aspirations. We remember this when we experience something new. *Sqwa: lewel*, which means felt ideas, felt thoughts, take us to a felt knowing, and it feels more reliable than an idea arrived at by instruction, deduction, reduction, simple arithmetical reasoning, or any other such objective analytical process. It feels trustworthy. I feel close to Gloria and the women who will be at the conference. I feel indomitable. We are moving forward together, I can feel it. This is a defining moment in our forward story.

My turn to laugh. This should be fun.

Events occur, humans respond or react, mindlessly, thoughtfully, unreasonably, reasonably, despairingly or spiritedly; whatever drives the reaction or response matters little. The point is we react or respond; we are so rarely apathetic. Even the business of ignoring the despair of others is active; it is not without its sentiment, its memory or reactive emotions, and sometimes it is reasoned out carefully. And reason, sentiment, reaction are all hosted and driven by our memories.

Gloria sits particularly straight, arranges papers, and tags her book, orders up her speech. Mestiza must mean she reads and speaks her presentation. Jeannette Armstrong too is arranging her papers; this surprises me. She mumbles that she had written down her talk so as not to miss the power handed to her in this moment. I know what she means, but am too cheeky to comply. I sit with my hands folded and just wait. Maybe I should not be so arrogant. I have no papers to arrange. Too late now, Anzaldúa is looking up; she leans into the audience like she is preparing to forge a storm. She is. The moat between the audience and us is filled with our dead. The divide sings with destruction. The distance between Native women and the newcomers is measured with our losses and their gains. Anzaldúa knows this; I feel it just like I can feel the texture of the heat and the rough edges of the listening these women will have to do. I will always recognize her.

I like realizing this. I roll the memory about, taste it; I like the edges of it as it titillates my lips. I swallow, savour it going down; each word commits itself to my memory. Anzaldúa looks back at

15

me like she knows me, knows my grandmother. She could have been
any other Indigenous woman, strolling down any downtown core
in Canada or the U.S. We could have been standing on the corner of
Main & Hastings, exchanging new comments about our favourite old
subject, these people ... *Or we could have been in some laundromat,*
saying, Hello, how are you, how's your mom? *and finally getting to*
Old people are just that way, *and laughing till our sides hurt.*

The room blurs. My mountains come into view. I watch as the
newcomers erase my being. I don my old blanket and rise again. I
picture Anzaldúa's relatives resisting the same Catholic and colonial
forces. I erase the room and let the words rise of their own. We are
alone for this moment, each of us behaves as though we are in some
old kitchen, soup bowls in front of us, tea behind us steeping, and
we are about to launch into the beautiful kind of gossip about what
Indigenous women get into — Girl, left her man...good for her. One
of our women had a husband and a wife...she was something else.
Ruby has a new woman. *We know that borders are illusions. We*
also know that these borders are critical to those who benefit from the
illusions. We understand. Gloria knows something about something.

Let them be. I re-member what lives underneath Cynthia
Wright's words — French conquest, French colonialism. *Shxwisox*
w t, conquest and colonialism are her word/direction markers. She
generally speaks from them, but I am thinking of being French at
this moment and, while French conquest is true, being French is
necessary. And these two things, while not the same, cannot be
remembered from the same evaluative direction or recalled in the
same way. And that is what makes all our memories feel crazy. On
the one hand, we have no interest in sending anyone who is here
home, nor do we wish to deprive anyone of those bits of wealth
they have amassed, but we do not wish to have the colonial project
continue either. How the future will look, then, is a fearful mystery

to the settlers. Let them be is not part of their collective memory in their relation to us, but they so want to have relations, the path to this relationship – the ramparts – seems a tangled web for them.

I am a weaver. We must learn to physically weave our blankets before we can know how to weave story into the fabric of our lives. When the weaver's threads get tangled, unravelling the knot depends upon which strand of the web we tug at. We are encouraged to sense it: "Don't touch it yet, my Ta'ah says, wait, the key thread will show itself to you." I wait, looking at the knot, and eventually the thread presents itself to me just as my Ta'ah said it would. Some deep part of our memory knows the future depends on us and what we choose to remember. Cynthia pulls at the colonial memory, while I tend to hang from the non-existent future and the dictums of our laws regarding being and hope. Something presents itself to me. This does not make me pro-colonial. On the one hand, I resist colonialism while, on the other hand, I support being so long as the restrictions placed on us by the colonial order are lifted and their being does not infringe upon mine.

I am an orator. Before I know what I am about to say, I need to read my audience.

I have to think about the word read. There is no equivalent in our language, but in English we use it to talk about the weather – read the weather, the ocean – read the sea, and read the people in the room. It is part of how we re-member what to say. Si wi:l – spirit power, to read phenomena in their silent movement. Once we have read the room, we pull the best threads from our oratorical past forward to feed the room. The faces begin talking. I can see the hunger. It is evident in everyone, they are hungry to see us, to hear us, to imagine a relationship with us and, at the same time, they already know something about themselves but they are not sure what it is. They all have this look on their faces that tells me they have an inkling that they are settlers who have ignored us. We are all women, but the settler women know they have not always regarded us as women. Their reference material about us is clanging about in their heads: "We must support native people and women," as though we did not have women among us, as though patriarchy did not apply to us, as though equality between (white) men and us is out of the realm of possibility. They are remembering the poetry the conference organizers played on the radio to advertise the Book Fair for three months before this conference began — it was mine. There is a faint feeling of trepidation in the room. I imagine they have all read Gloria Anzaldúa; they worry for themselves and wonder about the relationship between the English speaking Natives and the Spanish speaking Mestiza — Gloria. They don't know what is going to happen here. We do. We have had all the necessary conversations, thoughts and feelings, to make this an historic moment, and we know it.

Jeannette and I clasp hands under the table; this ceremony gets us through moments like these. I look at Gloria again. Her forever-brown eyes look like they recognize me. She is so Chicana, so Indigena, so centered yet at the same time declines to leave the border of her periphery for all that is in front of us. I will never forget her.

Our bodies' ancient memory is fully awake. I can feel the ancestors in the room, their memories in my body, and the knowledge of the past awakening in each cell. When we are completely centred in our historic being, we can know things. We can feel one another's connection to our common beginnings here on Turtle Island. Jeannette and Gloria exchange the same ancestral remembering/knowing glance and we face the crowd — we are unified and ready. Our bodies have remembered our stories from origin to the present. Our body memory has identified us to one another. Our bodies have assured us that we are on a common path.

The room is full. More than full. There are women in the hallway, women lining the walls, women seated in chairs and women seated on the floor. I notice Betsy Warland, though we have not met.

Gloria is seated next to me on my right; Jeannette is on my left. From the middle where I sit I wonder about position. No one told us how to arrange ourselves; we just sat down. The hosts are frenzied; there are too many people in this room for the fire regulations. They keep telling people they can't sit on the floor, or block the aisles. No one listens. The organizers do not have the audacity to pitch anyone out, but they can't seem to stop telling them not to sit in the aisles. I look at Gloria. We both wear a sweet smile – very Ravenesque, naughty, transformative and powerful.

I have feared these foreigners before, but this fear has never silenced me, it has never paralyzed me because I remember that the dead are more powerful than the living (Chief Seattle, oratory). It is the sort of fear that someone who has survived a flood knows – it is there, but so is the memory of survival, bucking the tide, swimming upstream, climbing mountains, foraging for food under seemingly impossible circumstances. My fear is a warning to myself to be careful, full of care, not so much for myself but for our ways. In dire circumstances Salish women return to our beginnings, so our oldest remembering will come forward to guide us, to get us unstuck. We have a kind of "Bring it on" attitude when the situation becomes dire. We fought the tide. We won. We remember that thousands of years ago we earned the right to be.

I can hear murmuring from the women who are attempting to declare that the chaos we are surrounded by is unacceptable. They try to order everyone up, but the women have minds of their own and cannot be ordered like pizzas. The three of us know this and turn to smile at one another. From inside our own intellectual territory we share a common sense of humour. It is not the chaos we find amusing, but the futility of believing you have the authority to order it up that strikes us as funny. We are in Quebec now. Algonquin and Mohawk breath still whispers from across the river. This old breath snakes its

way around Montreal Island. The ancestors still breathe some other
sensibility into the hearts of the women who now occupy this land.
As a result, the Quebecoises have their own way of reconciling them-
selves to speakers. I return my gaze to the commotion and enjoy its
sweetness. I will always savour this moment.

I hesitate to use the word Memory. It is a bag holding so many
other words, images, and concepts that it almost tells us nothing.
Our emotions want our bodies to focus on something specific.
Unless we remember something specific th of memory is a bright
blinding light. There is no adequate translation for it. It is thought;
thought can be forever. It is story; story can be forever. It is events;
the impact of events can last almost forever. Still, we remember.
It is safer to steer clear of bag words. We have so few bag words in
our language. Bag words are still, lifeless, yet bloated with stories,
sometimes so bloated that we need to make comedy so we can
empty out the bag and sort through the contents. We make comedy of the propensity of Western society to indulge in bag words.

I savour this moment because I know I will be heard, seen,
and considered for the first time in our common history together.
Generations of Salish women have worked hard for this moment. The
entire story of our being here on Turtle Island has prepared me for it.
The bag I carry is full.

My body is struggling to sweat. Jeannette is shaking from the
heat. I worry. Jeannette gives my hand one last squeeze. I look at
Gloria and she nods. We are ready. I take charge of this gathering
and announce that we are going to get started. Without another word,
Jeannette begins, as though we had planned it this way and not at all
as if it just felt right for her to begin.

She remembers to feel her way through this moment.

I can feel the power of Gloria's listening, can almost feel the open-
ness of each of her cells as Jeannette's words sing inside her.

Listening is an emotional, spiritual, and physical act. It takes a huge emotional commitment to listen, to sort, to imagine the intent, to evaluate, to process and to seek the connection to the words offered so that remembering can be fair and just. Spiritually, words are sacred; this makes listening a ceremony. And because it engages our imagination it is also an art form. Our best selves, the oldest thread of our remembering processes, are invoked and we seek connection with a will.

I imagine hearing Gloria's mind clicking across the words; she is careful not to be considering any other sound but the one she is hearing. I know this kind of Indigenous discipline. I feel her steady, even breath over my shoulder as she leans into Jeannette's conversation, deepening her commitment to listening more and more carefully as Jeannette speaks. I am caught up in watching this listening that is so old, so clean, so innocent and so very intense, and so full of the kind of remembering that is required of the women of Turtle Island. I like the feel of hearing Gloria listen.

I am not the same kind of listener, though my body is deployed in the hearing of Jeannette as well. My listening is sentient, a total body experience. I trust my body to imbibe the words, to swallow them, commit to them, take the words on a journey through my body and then discipline my response to them. I trust my mind to follow Jeannette's words from the place they reside in my body. There is a multiplicity of ways to remember. Each individual brings their own gifts to the banquet of ways to remember. There are no standard ways to remember. No single methodology. Our remembering is so connected to our emotionality, our physicality, our spirituality, and our mentality that we dare not standardize the process for fear of leaving someone's excellence out of the mix. The goal of our learning is excellence in all of us. Competition is one strategy for ensuring that all of us learn. It is not used as a weapon to leave others behind.

I begin after Jeannette finishes. Gloria and Jeannette's listening feels like a blanket — a dome of protection. As it warms, strengthens, and blurs the border at the edge of all our cloths the words inside gain power. The warm isn't like the heat wave rattling Montreal, threatening to bleed us of whatever sanity we came here with, but warm in that spirit way, when you know "We all speak the same language" — Stó:lō, Okanagan and Chicana Anzaldúa. Our backs begin to straighten. An old load is removed. I feel light even in this claustrophobic, wet, mean heat. I am lighter for having sat next to Gloria.

Remembering begins with listening like a lover, listening like a mother, listening like a child, listening like this may be the very last thing I ever hear. Like speaking, listening is a brook of words streaming from ancestors for generations. Like seeing, listening is a flower unfolding, capturing light, trailing webs of experience, weaving them into the body and igniting our best thoughts. Like hearing, each one of us listens in our own way. The words enter the body, pass through it, fuelled by our feelings, through our mind, and are considered from the origins of our people to the present and from the present to the future of our grandchildren. We pull the moments of our story together, search for its possibilities, imagine how this story, these moments can contribute to the good life and create a picture from them. We cast the picture in the direction of future before we speak, so that when we speak we are speaking the same sense and sensibility as our remembered ancestries. At the same time, we are speaking for the sense and sensibility of our unified being in the future. We do this well, or not well, but always it is our desire to remember in this way.

Gloria is next. "Sin Fronteras...Sin Fronteras." It rolls off her tongue not like its Spanish, but like a well-loved woman whom we all want to know. She looks at us, we look at her. Sin Fronteras not like it sits between us, but like we are in the center of it and in front of us is a well-loved Gramma. Jeannette and I nod. Go ahead, Gloria, the ceremony is taken care of and now we know who we all are. We have dispensed with the proper formalities, fulfilled all the necessary protocol, so now begin and talk to these others on the periphery of this fire. Gloria lives forever in my heart.

Gloria spoke of borderlands, not the ones we usually think about. The borderlands we know begin "Sin Fronteras." We begin with paradox. We begin entering the heat during winter with story hot on our tongues. We came to this place, this mountain, in summer. We now wander about each other's cool comforting gaze in the brassy glare of the worst heat wave in Montreal's puny white male history. We come into the world well-loved and screaming and we go out well respected, our voices resonant, full and lyrical, booming and knowing how young humanity's sense of itself is. We are familial. *Family.* The borders of our fabrics fit so neatly in our hearts. The weave suits our spirit. The design that appears so keenly arranged is not. It arises organically from a common beginning, and the memory of the design arranges itself like the ovum. Our bodies navigate these weaves with grace and agility between Sin Fronteras and the borderlands Gloria now defines. We got that from Gloria before she even spoke, the uttering of Sin Fronteras was our affirmation, not her instruction or advice. No one but women from this place can speak like this.

We remember who we are and who we will always want to be.

Sin Fronteras means so much more than that. The blankets we weave with their geometric patterns are comprised of border series, layered one over the other. This layering both acknowledges borders and renders them irrelevant. Borders are silly and at the same time so powerful. Borders and your position within them teach respect, bind knowing to being, move you; borders are slippery, and they glide between thought and imagination. We can create them with a look, dismantle them with a smile, and embrace them like an old lover. Sin Fronteras is without tangible lasting frontiers.

There never was a frontier. We were never on the edge of anything. We have and always will be in the center. The center is remembered. Borders are determined by where our imagination takes us in the moment. There is no white male center in our memory and so we cannot live on any kind of periphery. Women are the heart of our nations. Women erect and dismantle borders at will, but we will never acquiesce to someone's illusion of Fronteras.

As Gloria speaks, tiny beads of perspiration form in my armpits, freeing me of the need to be sick from this heat, sick from the crowded muggy room. Perspire, inspire, and expire — my breath returns. I float between the markers of history, time disappears, and we are here forever as we have always been with neither beginning nor end.

Gloria affirms that the place we take is our own.

I recognize Gloria. I don't pretend to know her. I have no wish to comment on her work, but it felt good to recognize her at that book fair so long ago. I acknowledge Gloria. She, along with every other Indigenous woman who reads this, knows how big that is for all of us. We are not assigned place, position or borders; we do not assume them. We relinquish assumptions or we contrive and respect the borders others take on, but no one but ourselves can define place, position, or power for ourselves. But in order to be remembered, others must recognize the place, position, and power we have established.

Haitchka, Gloria.

We have a spiritual memory that guides us to honour others. This spiritual memory drives us to seek the intellectual quarterback that can lead us from one moment to the next. We are searching inside ourselves for the oldest thread of our memory, not because we want to shine but so that we can contribute to the future of others through the brilliance we have acquired from the world and the stars and those beings inhabiting them. Before we can remember, we need to be able to recognize value. We are taught to recognize fish, see and consider its relationship with bear, and this leads us to the medicine ways of bear. We watch bear fertilize the mountains and the berries and understand bear's value to the earth. We watch mosquitoes rise from the swamp and become food for birds and bats, and their waste becomes food for berries, and berries become food for us, so we honour them. We understand that we have a relationship with these mosquitoes, these berries, these fish. They are medicine, and we honour that relationship and continue to learn from it. We recognize the plant beings and their relationship with fish, with birds, with animals, and with water. We honour this relationship and permit these beings to teach us to acquire the necessities of life in the least obtrusive way possible. Even stone can teach. We will cultivate oysters on the stony ridges of the descending tide, but we will not move camas from where it chooses to grow. We will not turn over soil, already covered with some other plant, to convenience our food collection. We would never have filled the soil around our villages with grass that needed constant cutting. The cutting of a plant requires ceremony, for it is impairing, painful, and insulting. We would never grow a plant that causes pain for the sake of aesthetics. Grass is intrusive now. It has replaced the medicines, the food, and the animal life that grew here in abundance.

Memory is like this for Stó:lō people. Our memories stretch back for thousands of years, but we don't think about them until the condition for the use of memory ripens and calls us to remember. All the pieces have to be ready: the body, mind, heart and spirit all have to be ready. Every cell needs to be hungry for the food of memory the ancestors provided us with. The community will not remember until it needs to know. This business of bothering the memory, testing its skill, makes no sense to us. The community remembers the healing processes when sickness occurs. The community remembers the food necessary to prevent illness from occurring. We share these memories as we see others travelling toward illness. Constantly proffering the memories of others on children, testing them and then permitting them to forget, alienates them from the significant business of remembering.

Memory is tricky. It emerges in those moments when the imagination activates and makes the rememberer wonder if what they are seeing is fiction, or will last forever. It emerges in those moments when we see that the words that have directed us have unlocked a storehouse of remembering. Memory is always connected to the individual and their specific path.

Khahtsahlano's beach rolls before me, steel slate gray, water slightly choppy, waves gentle, tide forthcoming. The water looks warm, inviting. You swing out of the car, look both ways, and prepare to bolt. "Wait." "No," the sound you make is not rebellious. Plain voice. Simple sound "no." "How will I find you?" I hope my logic works. "Easy mom, I'll be the only black kid on the beach with long straight hair wearing red shorts," and his running body recedes into the distant park.

This horrible feeling of panic surges from my womb to my guts. I bellow "Sid, Jaret," but they are squealing and yelling with delight as they run for the beach. Not only do they not hear, but they are too fast for me to catch them. Besides, I am standing there with a picnic basket, four towels and two bags, which is way too much stuff to drop and run and way too much to carry and run. Trapped, I look at my eldest girl. She shakes her head so very slowly and says in a voice far too grown up for her eleven years, "You know that he's right." The panic subsides or maybe I pushed it down, swallow it and refuse to permit it passage.

Memory is slippery. It slides between perception dictated by birthright, upbringing, philosophy and environment and an actualized event. It calls us to re-look at the parts, the significant moments, commit to them and recall them or not, based upon the direction our reality has moved us. It opens doorways or closes them, depending on our emotional dynamic, inertia, caring or apathy. Memory often angles its way into our world as if by accident.

The remembering of an event relies on the ability of the imagination to slip from the disgrace of the useless aspect of something and into acknowledging the grace of useful significance to community of the very thing we remember. "I remember how much you hurt me and I froze...I chuckle, the hurt others offered has slipped to some junk file, I no longer choose to bring forward. Instead, I watch for the ploy to hurt, see it coming no matter whose face it wears." I do not need to dismiss or forget those who have betrayed me to render someone who is indulging in the effort to betray me irrelevant and ultimately useless. I need to remember that the proffering of hurt does not require that I accept it. It is not a gift I can use. Memory depends on the rememberer to deploy imagined being, take it into future and render the remembered new thing significant and appealing. Each aspect of a remembered event – teaching, story – becomes a teacher, a motivator. If we imagine emotions related to an event, hold them close and play with them long enough to become conscious, then memory cannot threaten, paralyze or overwhelm.

Further, we can use this memory to create story, to conjure fiction.

I imagine my daughter, in my womb, my ovum's gray matter, and cells splitting, forming and shaping her. I imagine bequeathing her the memory of all time. I wonder which direction these memories will call her to travel. Will the hopes of Salish women or longhouse power

concepts call up old songs, inspire her to approach the fire at her cen-
ter, lean into the multitudes seated above in the sky world and push
out new story, or will the multitudes leaning into our villages, sur-
rounding our creative spirit, encroach upon her desire to imagine, to
conjure story, to recreate myth? I reach inside for some old story about
an ancient river, a crisp clean dawn, and a silver light dancing at the
river's edge, and begin to speak to this bulge that is my child. The story
emerges; fresh new and so old I want to weep. Salmon dances, bar-
racudas smile, and shark carries us from that old clamshell to killer
whale that carries us to shore. Cedar rises to touch the sky, swells her
trunk to the size of Sequoia, ages gracefully under the care of men who
imagine carefully cultivating a mother tree to safeguard the future
of Cedar's children. Masks float in the spaces between the mundane
moments of life strung together to nurture life.

She squirms as the stories I tell unfold, night after night. I can
feel her wrestle with growth, with transformation and with pending
birth. She almost quits; perhaps the sounds of this city terrorize, sirens
screaming, cars howling, men hollering, lights humming and humans
mumbling of trouble, of strife, of things that annoy the mind, perhaps
they discourage her. Was it all too intense a beginning? Did the sounds
of this city nearly drown the old memories, the old stories rolling around
in your watery home? Never mind, I lay down, hips tilted: "Best to abort
and start again," the old white man in his gynecological coat says and
turns to leave. "That's right. Get out of here," I holler. He turns back
to face me, tries to explain you away, but it's too late, I already know
who you are and won't give you up. He thinks you are already dead.
I know different.

She remembers my fight for her. I know she does. It is in every cell
of her body. She becomes a fighter, someone who is convinced that
she is entitled to reciprocal and fair relations. When trouble besets,
when wonder overcomes, when the joy of just being rises up, I hear

her remember: "You always brought the country to this terrible urban beginning. You never left us at home; you brought us everywhere, to political meetings, literary readings, to the Native Centre, to feasts, you never left us at home like we didn't belong out and about in the world. It was as though you knew we belonged anywhere in the world and you meant for us to experience the whole world as big as you lived it. I remember some people wondered about that, some of them even made comments, but I never felt like I didn't belong." I can hear her trust that I would fight for her that she belonged exactly where I placed her, in the middle of the Third World People's Coalition, the World Assembly of First Nations, the anti-imperialist women's movement or the Native movement or inside my beloved family. She understands her courage, her confidence and the world from the point of view she chose, but she tells me it began with me.

"Old people love me. Why do old people love me?" I remember telling her to sit in front of Grandma, just sit until she says you can go. "I remember that," she says, her voice excited. "She told us the news, or a story, or some such valuable life lesson. It never took long, and then she'd say, you can play now. I remember that, and now old people love me. That's how it happened."

I remember imagining her. Not imagining how she would look, but imagining what kind of woman she would become. I never imagined her career, or sought to funnel her in the direction of a career I chose. Instead, I knocked down walls, created space, so she could find her own direction and become the governness of every memory the world handed her, make each one an opportunity to grow no matter how terrible it was in the moment. She has this extraordinary imagination, she is philosophically fit, sociologically clear, poetically pure, so real and so creative all in the same moment, and she is so loving and so loved. She is resilient. At the same time, she is sharp, just and courage-ous. Loving and sweet, don't try to breathe her air, shrink her space or

29

cheat her, though. "Don't blow up my nose and tell me it's windy," she once told some white man who tried to cheat her. (Can't believe they are still doing that but there you go.) She knows how to plan a battle and win, not just the skirmish but also the whole damn war. She picks her battles carefully. Her memory and imagination work that way.

Memory and imagination are not disconnected. We imagine memory, we remember what we imagine. Events occur, we see them, engage them, and they dissipate into disconnected corners of our mind. The images file themselves in disconnected parts of our brain. Some memories sink into our very cells. We hold parts of the images from these events in cells, in the body, in the mind, in the spaces between our cells. But it is our imagined direction that calls us to re-conjure old events, redraft them, pull the parts together from their disconnected places in our mind and our bodies and decide which ones are connected to the thread of direction we are determined to travel in. In so doing, the imagination reshapes reality and it becomes purposeful fiction.

Salish people endured a terrible flood. We could have remembered the horrific death, the horror of mammalian destruction, the loss of millions of relatives, the hunger, the horrific struggle to eat, to live. Instead, we remember three women, seducing the same man and having him give us all children, build us a longhouse, so that we could begin again. We recall what we need to know to travel in the direction we choose or do not choose. This is the work of conscious remembering.

My children chose to travel toward freedom in the context they inherited. They know they have to alter this context in order to fully accomplish that. They rely on those memories that will plunge them into center stage of the arenas they will have to engage in this country and battle like gladiators, like warriors, like priestesses, like demons and like gods for just a few seconds of freedom. They know this country is heading for hell in a hand basket unless they do something to alter the course of its history, even for just one second. They know this is hell, they remember the tight fitting glove of abuse and the hand that hauls back for a swing at them every time they take a step in the direction of freedom. Still, they move forward, cougar-like, with sockeye's determination, armed with bear medicine stories as though they were indomitable. They retrieve every memory of the challenges they rose to, the challenges their ancestors rose to and the victories our family has achieved. They know how to retrieve the memory of the ancestors of other people, make story from it and then work with that story to brighten the future of their children. They remember every courageous act, every spiritual moment of reversal, of oneness, of connection, and they grab it like intellectual/spiritual and emotional quarterbacks and run for the finish line with grace, elegance, and alacrity.

Memory is powerful. It can twist us in knots, but the imagination can untwist the knots, unravel the memory, rework it into blankets that protect, designs that promote, carry, and create new being. Remembering is significant, holy in its duty, recollecting bits of engagement, social interaction, success and failure. The imagination can transform memory from depression to a simple incident, from a substandard normal to an impotent string of events, from perverse to natural or from failure to opportunity if you are moving toward the good life. It can inspire us to re-evaluate our intervention, alter our course, and create a new beginning.

I re-member courage in the face of awesome fear and haul up the courage from every cell, transform it into desire and push it with a will toward freedom. I re-member rage and dig underneath its hoary cap in search of the justice moving me to rage and then I determine to stretch this rage into some kind of energized force and

31

transform it into justice. When I am successful this will become a moment that will live for all time because others will choose to re-member. I re-member dark, its seriousness, its sobriety, its sacred ability to hold my life still and call me to alter my conduct, change my direction and commit to participating more fully in my life. I come to the table full feast. I offer the host, the multitudes, the dead, the living, and the unborn this food.

I remember the body is made to move, that life is always worth engaging, that fear is a beautiful friend cautioning me to take care, and that courage is there to mediate this fear and is ever willing to be summoned that this old friend will not capitulate and become some beast that no longer serves me. I move as though sure. I fear no decision as belief in my memory grows; it has always served my spiritual path.

My memory begins with an imagined world – my vision. A world in which I dream and see peace: *freedom from war, freedom from strife and freedom from conditions, which annoy the mind.* In my imagined world my body engages concepts of war, strife, and the very specific conditions that annoy my mind. I remember that no one volunteers themselves up for slavery. I remember no one sets to sleep and dreams of war. I make a map. On this map legions of bodies engage an imagined peace. They desire to concatenate, to link together, and to make this common dream roll forward. I envision a tidal wave of different beings. These people clean rivers, save trees that purify our air, clutch desperately to recycling, to writing letters, calling their governments to stop the slaughter. They write poems that may be heard by children who will never stop dreaming of peace.

Humans face choices daily; they choose the events life presents to remember. They engage our desire for peace or they do not. They remember to engage in travelling on this rocky road to freedom or they do not. I link myself to those who travel toward peace and freedom.

Behind me, stones dot my pathway, sharp and numerous. I watch myself dance my way through the stones, toes barely touching the tips. I smile as my face moves from the soft smoothness of youth to the crows-foot-wrinkled age; each year the creases of my smile grow deeper, the very depth of feeling under it becoming more meaningful, more childlike and excited as I traverse the stones to my journey's end.

I danced my way to this moment, this sensibility of peace and freedom. I remembered my imagined world even in my worst moments, when hunger threatened survival and survival coloured my sense of peace in confusing shades of dismal gray. I remembered my children and their consistent love even as my twisted consciousness threw me off track and I left my path behind and caused them pain. I remember it was my children who inspired me to struggle to return to this path. I remember the heroic and excruciating effort it took to manage to return to this path of peace. "We can do this," my uncle says, "hell, we survived a flood." He helps me to remember that I am perfectly capable of heroic struggle. I faced the down side of my beginnings; I faced the down side of my conduct. I fought for the imagination that would reverse the direction I sometimes miss-travelled in, but I always returned to this path, this path with its gorgeous light and sacred dark, this path with its colours of green flora, its fauna, its water, sun and moonlit midnight dark blue hues.

Our memory serves to reflect on the path. The imagination exists to serve this memory. It compels us to move outside our hidden being (mind, heart, spirit) and engage the world. It inspires us to see beyond the wrinkles in the earth, the darkness of the sky and seek the sacred, the lovable and the courage that earth and all her beings share. It evokes desire, blood red, beautiful, resilient and heroic. It compels. It speaks to glory, to wonderment, to creation, and bestows the new and the worthy.

Remembering Memory

The shrill sounds of an old voice
thick with desperation
vocal chords stretched tight squeeze truth
signals the death of peace

Sometimes voice haunts
the dense air
sound loss
wanders through the body
looks for an exit
from the acid scrape of desperation
truth leaks out through
high-pitched throat sounds

My muscles tighten
pull at the lies my skin oozes

The voice of peace muted
memories hold tight
locked to skin cells
force appropriates courtesy
confines manners to boxed sounds
my skin peels off clipped short phrases
renouncing war

We are sometimes so focussed on simple immediate recall that we often fail to consider the total concept of memory from our ancestral points of view. We have a lineage. We have our memory for all time, it lives inside our body. Our body hosts the capacity to organize all of the systems of the body and to function under stress and duress. Just as the ovum remembers to connect each cell to the appropriate companion cell and to organize those cells so that they create systems that work together, so we remember how to create systems of appropriate companions, person to person, so that all the persons together work as a community, as a nation. This is a magical process. Our original lineage memory is the seat of our personal memory. Our oldest memories from the beginning of time live inside the very cellular structure of our bodies and refuse to be ignored.

Stories govern us.

Memory is powerful. It permits us to change the course of our lives by alerting us to deep interests and powerful feelings for a new direction, but it can also keep us still, victims of emotional or spiritual stasis. This stasis is tantamount to spiritual death. When we forget, we fail to learn. Memory is to be played with, my grandmother used to say, so that we can gain in our wit. However, the pain centres of the body need to release the dangerous and hurtful memories so this play can be safe. The body's job is to hold onto the memory until we are safe, then our spirit, heart and mind's job is to let go the governance of the memory that we may be free. Vibrations release the hold this danger mode has on the body, so the hurt of the memory can be released. Song is all about vibration from within the body. Healing through song is a major medical treatment in our communities.

How we remember affects the body as well. Song is lyricism, and poetry is its main expression. Utilitarian language — *I was in a*

35

car accident the other day and broke my arm — is disdained by the body, but if we visualize the accident —

a careening metal monster
tore down an asphalt path,
attacked my being
snapped my bones
and forced me to take care

— the memory becomes poetry replete with the lesson to be learned. That makes the memory work on our behalf. Poetry as images that are lyrical actually strengthens the body when we read it out loud. The strength of the body fires up our courage. The memory then becomes a springboard releasing the spirit and freeing the person to muster their courage to go out and about in the world free of fear.

The fastest road to healing is to metaphorically express the memory in poetic form and draw lessons from it. Our languages are lyrical, image-filled and rich in metaphor. The language of poetry lives in the body and we are always hungry for it. Our elders, even when speaking English, open with prayers that are poems that bring peace to our bodies, and we know, we just know, that we are at one with the world.

In our bodies live the original instructions we received when we came to this earth: *go out and about in the world and create oneness with creation.* When we live in contradiction to this instruction a kind of madness (the split mind) overtakes us; our bodies weaken (autoimmune disease develops), our hearts become saddened and our spirits become overly cautious.

Clear the path, our elders teach, *make memory work for you.*

The body will make us hesitate if we do not release the memories holding us back. One of our elders called the current absence of movement in our communities *colonial hesitation* (Jim Dumont).

Some of the ancestral memories that have a hold on our communities are the memories of illness (epidemic death), war, prohibition (potlatch laws). These are traumatic colonial memories. We need to transform them into lessons that will free our bodies, but many of us are unaware that these memories live inside us.

When we connect through ceremony (sweats, the pipe, the longhouse winter dances), these memories sometimes emerge and we sing and dance our way to freedom from the hesitation they sometimes create inside us. The memory then becomes valuable. It serves the future instead of paralyzing the present. The poetic passages of *Daughters are Forever* and *Will's Garden* are examples of what can be learned and how memory can serve us.

We imagine that we don't want to hear sad stories, but it is our sadness that cradles our love. When we are sad for someone, it is a measure of our empathy. When we are sad for ourselves, it is a measure of love and justice in our lineage. When we dodge that sadness, we also negate the empathy, justice, and love. All emotions have a place in a healthy life. We cannot prevent hurt; we can only gain from it if we allow our bodies, our minds and our hearts to re-member in a way that brings us away from the past and forward into the future, full of courage and optimism.

When settlers tell us to "forget the past," they are asking us to remain powerless. Without memory, we can never be any more intelligent than we are at that moment. No growth can occur. We cannot imagine justice without evaluating the past. We cannot understand the nature of the human world without examining the past. When settlers tell us to "forget the past," they are also asking us to remain stupid. There is much to be learned from our behaviour — both our successes and heroism — but the well of learning from our misbehaviour is bottomless.

Stories are the keys to the endless oratory, the teachings, and

37

the knowledge of our people. It is not all we are, but when we remember the story, the flood of knowledge locked behind it is let loose. Story satisfies the need for connection as it opens the door to the oral knowledge that underpins it.

We plant seeds of memory for the young.

Because force was never used to maintain internal discipline, choice, cooperation and individual obligations must be regarded as sacred by those who are our caretakers. Our creative self must be actualized in order for our beliefs to become sacred inside of us.

Our remembering has an attitude. We remember events from the position of re-connection, community building, relationship restoration, and an ever broadening and deepening of our humanism, not from some bogus factual accuracy or fabricated objectivity. We remember events as obstacles to connection, community, and relationship, rather than from a position of blame, excellence, exceptionality or success.

This is my journey — my personal journey. It is a journey through my memory. I story it up for posterity. I know you are dead, but I also believe you aren't far from wherever I am. I picture you floating about the breath space of the earth, following me occasionally, whenever my life gets interesting or my behaviour catches your eye.

The radio is on. Some man is talking. The car moves.

Sometimes the walls here move. They appear dark, the wood paneling is cherry, stained in the way cherry wood always is, dark, almost foreboding. Not much light enters. I crawl up the stairwell, hauling books and papers, and hoping that I can be of some use here. There are photographs on the dark stairwells and in the hallways. I am not in them. It is a little unnerving. I have been here three years now. I mention this to my director. "My apologies, this is our fault"... "Didn't send you an e-mail, I know she posted it"... My daughter isn't in them either. She's leaving. This year we will both be absent.

The condition of disconnection led to the development of poetry and stories in a language that refused to direct the listener to answers but, instead, stimulated thought in the listener on a given condition, perception, or direction, and the history of events that led to disconnection.

We have positions in accordance with our original instructions. We cherish and we protect these positions. It is not the individual that is important but the position. A director is a modern world visionary in whom we place both trust and responsibility. We have an obligation to contribute to the direction through speaking in the circle, through imagining our position in the whole, which spoke in the wheel we are attached to and from which we are speaking from: manager, organizer, facilitator, teacher, collaborator, cooperator, self-actualizer, independent, or dependent, wolf trail blazer, bear healer, raven transformer. When our director seeks to facilitate the direction of the whole, we muck about inside our teachings, our stories, our understandings, and we seek guidance while holding fast to our connection to our past. We trust others will be there to hold up our best thoughts, our best memories, our good direction.

We have endured crises before. Crises that shook our faith, tarnished our beliefs, drove us from our original path. We reclaimed our beliefs, restored our faith, and returned to our communitist beginnings. I re-member this, every time I experience an event that becomes an obstacle to communitist beginnings. Personal response to language and experience becomes memory, which becomes art and is connected to concepts of choice that is tempered by the social value of cooperation. The listener then becomes central to the story, the memory, and the experience and is engaged in the process of imagining, building, constructing and responding to the speaker's art.

Transitional Year — 2001

It is a transitional year for me. I stopped working full time this year. I choose to work smart, not hard.

I find it curiously odd that I work for a transitional year program at a university. You know the kind of oddity I am talking about. The kind of oddity we always recognize when a plum seems to have wanted to be a twin, because there is this additional bump, a not quite fully realized extra plum growing out of the original. We would hold those ones up to the sunlight and watch the light sprinkle itself on the table near the window where we worked sorting out plums for sale, for eating, for give away and canning. The perfect plum was sold. It made me strive for some slight imperfection — who wants to be sold? The plums with freckles were for give away, the ripe ones for canning. We would eat the imperfect ones, the ones trying so hard to be twins, you and I. Plums are delicate. They are to be handled with care. Their deep dark, almost black, purple, with faint hues of mauve dancing on the prominent curves of their almost apricot shape intrigued me — did I tell you? I don't wish to be sold, or eaten anymore.

Transition: To move across distance, time, space, or being into some other sensibility.

The presence of the speaker has always been a part of the story, song or poem. In the case of remembering, it is our own voice that is heard as we embody the words of the speaker; the choice of our language directs us to our place in the community, to our relationship with the community, or to our dissonance, disconnection, and isolation. Voice, choice of words, sound, tone, diction, style and rhythm characterize the attitude attached to the speaker's memory. A huge array of physical metaphors, developed out of the experience of the collective and its relationship to its environment, is transmitted to us. We embody these movements. We understand their meaning. The concepts of governance and meta-phor must be understood by the listener and interpreted in a way that keeps us connected to the whole in order to understand the significance of the memory. If the thread guiding our re-mem-bering is self-centered, exploitative or dissonant, then it leads us to isolation and we get sick. We feel the isolation despite the efforts of the community to continue to keep us in the center of their good will and affection. No one is entitled to ostracize an individual. The moment an event is over, it is done with and gone. Feelings of vengefulness are not permitted, not in the sense that anyone will tell you this, or object to your vengefulness; it is more that no one in your adult world exhibits them. Instead, we hear *Oh, she is just that way* or *do you open peanuts with a sledgehammer as well?* In rare cases, we watch aberrant, non-communitist behaviour in children and tell them stories that show them that their internal world will be upset by non-communitist behaviour, or they will be transformed in an odd way should they continue on this path.

Because our memory is community based, the use of physical metaphor is understood in the context of the wellness of the whole. The personal interpretation becomes the way in which the individ-ual can contribute to the whole. We exalt the cooperative and the collaborative, the consideration children naturally exhibit, and we exalt their desire to make choices, to self-actualize and relate to community. We respect shyness, the children's desire for per-sonal space and for establishing boundaries.

I am sitting on my daughter-in-law's couch and my grandson sits beside me, leans against my ample frame, puts his arms around me, and I hold him. We sit like this for a long moment — it is the first time that he has chosen to express his affection for me. Until this moment I waited. I waited, and so this moment is so full of joy that

I feel like I will burst. I speak softly to him about my appreciation. He listens quietly and I know he will always be held up by this memory of himself choosing the moment of communion between us — he will be strengthened by it.

Over time interaction of the individual from within the culture deepens both the individual's and the community's understanding.

6:00 a.m.

July 2, 1950

This has been a hell birth. First the ride here was hell. The woman drove herself. In a fishing village, no one is home in July. She arrived at the NV General all dark-skinned, black eyes flashing, dark brown (light black if there was such a word) hair all wild and just slightly wavy hanging down on her shoulders with no blue paper. She insisted she didn't need one. They sent her to Saint Paul's, the Indian hospital.

She talks to herself all the way to St. Paul's. "These people don't want Indians here, it is as simple as that. Bastards." Bastards: illegitimate offspring. In a way she is right. Canada is the offspring of an England that never really had permission from the original people to be here. No one called them here; they just arrived, killed a lot of people and set up housekeeping. Well, not much housekeeping; they dirtied the place up mightily, and they do not want the original home-owners in their sight.

Thunder, lightning, and hail intrude on the woman lying on the hospital bed desperately trying to hold back this birth. It is too soon. Three weeks early, the last child had been late, three weeks late — the word balance crosses her mind.

"This baby is determined to come," the nurse says. "Now," and she came. I became a Catholic moral bastard, an illegitimate child,

a secret daughter, a beloved daughter, a step-daughter of a partially absent step-father and a near non-existent father, almost fatherless, a lives-in-that-old-RCMP-boat-shed-not-quite-homeless daughter, the granddaughter of a grandfather who would become famous and the great-granddaughter of a woman whose life spanned the entire history of our colonization all in one lifetime, all in a moment.

Once memory is stored, it is up for discussion by the community. We share with others what we have heard and it is discussed by other members of the community, evaluated and committed or not committed to. Each person struggles to build upon the thought/ memory of every other person. Two speakers may re-present the same story from opposing points of view and both are considered valid, just as the listener's interpretation of the memory is valid despite the fact that it may be different from another listener's version. At the same time, the individual is expected to find a collaborative point of understanding with the whole. This leads to a tremendous diversity of understanding a single event or memory or thought. It also leads to new thinking.

The first month of the new millennium is drawing to a close. The first half-century of my life is also drawing to a close. My mother is long dead. My children grew up and left. I see them pretty regularly. Most of them live in Toronto. I hop in my little purple car and hoof it down there at least twice a week. I live alone. Well, not really, the characters from my stories wander around this house, getting themselves up to all kinds of mischief. My ancestors are not far away either. My granddaughter's dog Jim lives here with me. Jim's so lively that sometimes I can barely stand his enthusiasm. Every now and then one of the characters dies. Not many, I can't bare killing them, not even the mean and hateful ones.

43

Inherent in our remembering is a non-instructional subtext. The teaching power of the kernel at the center of a wheel of experience becomes a poem. We know it achieves oneness because its journey to understanding engages all time.

Adults have obligations and responsibilities. Children have rights.

The sun dappled its light over what was left of my momma's body. The blankets covering her did not fold or ripple the way blankets over bodies usually do. Momma asks how I did it. How did I eat what those naturopaths told me to eat when cancer threatened my youth? How did I refrain from eating their white sugar, white bread, white rice, their pork?

"I had small children; I would have stood on my head and tried to spit nickels if they had told me it would help," I said aloud. Inside I wept. I felt what she meant. We can't seem to get up enough caring for ourselves to do what we need to do to live.

The room closed up. The air stilled. Her body was disappearing. After that I stopped watching. Instead as she lay dying I determined to see her as she always had been — indomitable, willful, resilient.

December 17, 1999

The dark is contrived. We turned the lights out, so I suppose it isn't really contrived, but we aren't going to sleep. Instead we get ready to speak. It is a small circle, just me and three of my children. DPI's, Dis-Placed Indians. Well, we would be except we aren't Indians anymore but for the purpose of "the meaning of the Indian Act." The pale light of candles warms the faces, carves the cut of them, reminds of the beauty of their ancestry, and reminds me of myself, their father, and those few magic moments when together we conceived these three human beings.

"I pray my elders find a reason to live a long time. My grand-mothers died before I became a man. I wanted them to be here when I had my first child. They could have been, but they died young."

I haven't found that reason yet, but I commit to looking for it, daily.

Our memory directs us to community by overcoming dissonance inside ourselves. This means, first, tracking back to the beginning of the dissonance in ourselves and, secondly, inviting others to join us in examining our dissonance and sharing the origin. We once had slaves, so some of our dissonance begins with that system of slavery. We must as ex-slave holders commit to overcoming masterhood, for we know that the attitude that permitted us to enslave others persists long after the slaves have been freed. We are vigilant. We question ourselves: are we speaking from our masterhood or from the notion that we are all the same height?

You are no more important than a snow flea on a glacier...I had been collecting crabs to smash them. I gathered them in a jar. I was 23 months old, was not even sure I wanted to do this. I tripped. The jar spilled, I grabbed a log and pulled myself up. The crabs scattered. My legs got stuck in the mud. I pulled one out. My shoe came off and remained stuck in the mud. I failed to get the other leg out. I failed to recover the crabs. I couldn't speak, but my brother told my mother what we were doing. "You are no more important than a snow flea on a glacier," she said. The timber of her voice was so beautiful, the words floated elegantly into my memory. Her embrace was so soft, so sweet, I wanted to feel it forever and so I remembered the words, so they would bring up that embrace, that moment of exquisite love that inspired so much kindness and such absolute good will from her. 45

The masterhood is new here and we have barely left behind our own slaving history. We have come up against the new masterhood without fully transforming from our old society. Sometimes, we are like abortions. We were not fully human when the new masters came. This incomplete transformation confused us for a while. They were sent for a reason — nothing happens without a reason. What reason could have brought them here? We imagine them in a land so full of people they had to leave, and some must have fallen into the sea to inspire them to come all this way. Maybe their animals died. We watch them for a while and wonder if they killed their animals out of avarice and greed. We warn them, in words, in story, out loud and on paper. Nothing seems to work. When we speak with them, they argue, disqualify our memories as though they had a monopoly on remembering. Only their memories are correct. They talk to paper, write things in books, and show us the books. We sometimes want to laugh. Their memories are ludicrous: savages, headhunters, cannibals are how they remember us. Primitive, barbarian, dumb, ugly — their images of us tarnish us. *Pre-historic* — we have no story, no memory, no being outside of becoming like them: avaricious killers, squashers of crabs, way more important than snow fleas on a glacier. They begin to look like me as a less than two-year old — incredibly immature, operating from some hedonistic place, outside of consequence, community, love or affection. They have no concept of time. Time is money. I know that the only time worth remembering is generations away when my footprint will be evaluated by my grandchildren and the earth's condition will be held up and those children will weigh my contribution to protecting the earth or failing to.

The spirituality of the orality, story, song and poetry of First Nations peoples is extremely misunderstood. Mistranslations of songs, story and poetry spoken to white, mostly male, scholars prior to our mastery of the English language arose sometimes from well-intended intellectuals who attempted to fuse their extrinsic sense of the spiritual aspect of their story and their poetics, with the poetry and story of Indigenous people. This filter shortsights their understanding of us. When they found the correlative they were looking for, they stopped exploring. This is dangerous when dealing with someone whose English is deficient. Thus the concept of God intervened and our relations with the sun, the moon, the stars and the natural world became worlds of sun gods, war gods, animal deities, etc. This poses huge obstacles to understanding the nature of our oratory more frequently than not. Because the sense of the spiritual is expressed simply the complexity of Native concepts of spirituality are often misunderstood and/or reduced to simplistic interpretations by scholars.

"All things possess spirit, creation is sacred, transformation is being alive, oneness with all creation is human" — all these have become tenets simplistically interpreted and applied to any and all circumstance, rather than explored for their range and complexity and placed in the body politic and culture of the people. If all creation is sacred, then words as created entities facilitate oneness. If oneness with all creation is valued, then words are intended to achieve oneness. The speaker then seeks oneness on the spiritual level with the audience. Through artistic presentation of the sacred the speaker orchestrates the community process of spiritual concatenation. Voice, diction, tone, style, rhythm and physical metaphor are intended to present the spirit of the poet, elicit the spirit of the listener, and conjoin all spirits into a single powerful sense of oneness with creation. Thus the choice of words, the sound of language, the essence of meaning, the attitude of the poet must all be carefully, and prayerfully, considered and transformed before the poetry of the poet can or will achieve spiritual concatenation.

The influence of speakers is dependent upon their personal capacity for eliciting oneness on the spirit level with the listener,

47

their commitment to the sense of community, and their exceptional sense of the desire for the good life that lies within each member. The remembered poems then remain treasured moments of spiritual concatenation. Spiritual concatenation between poet and audience has no co-relative among Europeans.

The object of European story and poetry is not spiritual concatenation between the self and listener but rather self-expression. This is not to say that European poetry does not evoke concatenation, but rather that it is not the goal. Spirit and spiritual concatenation cannot be understood mechanically or in terms of formulae, standard practices, basic characteristics. It cannot be understood from the above perspective because it is a single view of a single wedge in a circle of understandings. Further, poems, stories or art may or may not be connected to an event that affects everyone and whose impact threatens that concatenation of the whole. The subject of story, song, poetry, etc. in European society is a free choice matter. It is not that I do not support freedom of expression, I do. But in the creation of art, my freedom is found in my connection to community.

In order to understand original oratory, First Nations speakers must gather together (and in fact, they did so historically), engage the oratory around the poem or story, remember the circumstances that birthed the words, and engage each other in discovering meaning (new, contemporary and old) from them. They must do so in a manner that facilitates spiritual concatenation with one another and the natural and spiritual world. Story, poetry, word art engage the imagination of the community, the heart of the nation, and the spirit of the present, past and future. Word art must move people from where they are to where they need to go to ensure community concatenation. They must activate the community-based thought process of the listener without prescribing a response.

The stories that have been told many times change with each generation as mythmakers reform them to serve the moment. Even as we return to the good life ways, we will need to study the stories that will guide us in our concatenation with the newcomers. Our stories and poems will show us how to create oneness between ourselves and the world.

My daughter studies World Literature at the University of Toronto. She is in her Bachelor year. The sun dropped gently behind the trees on our balcony as she read from a presentation she intended to deliver to her Italian literature class. As the words fell from her lips and wrapped themselves around me, I slipped into a comfortable reverie. As she drew conclusions from her experience, it struck me how utterly absent we have been from Canada and alienated from acknowledgement in the education process.

I attended school for nearly 18 years and I do not recall recognizing myself in anything being mentioned except once, and then only as a cannibal. It is as if we had been completely vanquished from all things Canadian. Today there is a radio station in Toronto called Aboriginal Voices, but none of the news, the music or the subject matter of that station ever makes it onto any other station in Toronto. There is a television station and occasionally some program crosses over from mainstream television and is picked up by Aboriginal People's Television Network, but the street never crosses the other way. Every now and then a few actors or poets like Lorne Cardinal or myself makes it onto a CBC program, but since the death of North of 60 there are no Aboriginal programs on CBC. My throat caught as I realized how painful those years of so-called education were for me.

SALMON I
OF SALIS

SALMON IS THE HUB
OF SALISH MEMORY

9 MILLION SOCKEYE HAVE DISAPPEARED. *They didn't run upstream. We have a story about that. Sockeye were sent to Salish women to assist us during times of hunger. We were asked to honour sockeye and take care of the waters. We were told that if we take the sockeye or their habitat or the women for granted, they would not return. The story does not say that if we lose our fishing rights, we are not responsible for caretaking the fish or the women. It does not say that if we allow the newcomers to desecrate the waters, we are relieved of responsibility. It says that if we don't take care, they will not return.*

History, according to *The Canadian Oxford Dictionary*, is defined, firstly, as the "continuous chronological record of important or public events"; secondly, as "the study of the past, especially human affairs"; and lastly, as the "systematic or critical account or research of a past event, development or movement, etc." Importance implies a level of worthiness. Worthiness is, on the one hand, religious and, on the other, socially or culturally driven.

It was in the summer of 2001 that a run of sockeye committed suicide. It was after the 9-11 attack of the World Trade Center Towers in New York City. Humans in Canada and the United States were still reeling from that horror when thousands of mating sockeye pairs swam to their death too soon, leaving behind no progeny, in effect killing themselves and the future of their species. Although it was recorded in the media as an unheard-of event, this phenomenon had been recurring since 1995 in one form or another. Scientists have been dissecting and testing salmon since this phenomenon began in the hope of discovering what toxin or illness might have inspired sockeye to do this. They still have no idea what the cause is, nor have they studied the phenomenon from a historical perspective. Compared to the attack on the World Trade Centre, sockeye suicide is considered a fairly mediocre event, therefore not worthy of study. Despite the fact that the commercial value of the sockeye is worth a lot of millions, they are deemed worthy only of toxicity and disease testing in a laboratory environment, the social conditions under which they live or perish being entirely ignored.

At the time that the salmon were committing social suicide, Afghanistan was the object of international invasion. Salish people know that the homelands of the salmon have been the object of chronic invasion by fisheries, pulp and paper mills, the forestry industry, and all manner of toxic dumping. Are these events connected? Is there a connection between Western society's devaluation of the lives of Afghanis and the devaluation of salmon, the degradation of their life conditions such that suicide seems their only option? Are the Afghani people and the sockeye of equal value? Is there a connection between suicidal salmon and suicidal warriors? Should we undertake a historical study to ponder together their life conditions as they unfold? Would a comparative examination of habitat degradation and human degradation help us understand better the suicidal options taken by fish and humans? I think it would. Yet none of the official accounts of the important events that transpired in 2001 attempts to trace systematically the connection between the 9-11 suicide hijack-ers and the suicide sockeye. Traditionally, the scholarly study of history, with its singular focus on a particular object, relies on a researcher's institutional credentials and authority to assign weight and importance on the events examined. Most Western historians do not see suicidal fish and suicidal warriors as connected, and so suicidal salmon are not considered important enough to study.

In the Salish cultural worldview salmon and humans are not separate. The suicide of sockeye is an event worthy of record, worthy of memory, and therefore worthy of study. Both of these events are tied to a single social and economic system that shares the same history of social and physical degradation of human and salmon habitat. Of course, science does not view salmon as a social construct; at best, it considers the suicide of salmon to be an environmental anomaly. In the oral records of Indigenous people, animal, flora, and the business of war and mass suicide tend to travel in tandem. They are connected to each other, and so are their habitats. For us, the habitat of salmon and the habi-tat of humans are a single habitat. Moreover, violence to earth and violence between humans are connected. The last time the salmon did not run upstream was connected to violence against women. (See E. Pauline Johnson, *Legends of Vancouver*, as told to her by Chief Joe Capilano.)

Memory, according to *The Canadian Oxford Dictionary*, is the faculty by which things are recalled or kept in the mind. But in oral societies memory is much more complex than that. First and foremost, remembering requires that human beings assign them-selves the task of observing, selecting, and committing to memory certain phenomena. It also requires that the rememberer possess the acumen, skill, and training for recollection. It is critical that the human recalling an event possesses recall with a high degree

53

of accuracy and that the faculty of the rememberer is recognized and honoured by her or his community. The community needs to have experienced and witnessed the rememberer's skill; they need to know the training she or he has received, and they need to know, too, that the rememberer is able to connect the events recalled to other phenomena, events, and habitats. Because events happen in the moment, it is critical that the human observing commit to remembering the event as it unfolds. Further, rememberers are called upon to consult with others who have witnessed the event, engage them in discussion about the history leading up to the event, and come to a clear and common view of how the event came into play. This is always a selective process. The rememberer must choose what to witness, what to commit to ready and accurate recall, and who to discuss the event with. This process is at once historical, sociological, political, legal, and philosophical.

Both historical documentation and memory require humans to make decisions about what to commit to memory or what to commit to the page for posterity. Either way, both rememberer and historian assign a level of importance to the event and its constitutive parts, and create the necessary processes (documents, dendrites, discussions) in order to recall, examine, and understand it.

This is where we differ. Few, if any, anti-war activists study the connection among earth rape, the dehumanization of Afghanis, the invasion of Afghanistan and salmon suicide. Neither marine biologists nor environmental scientists nor historians have a way to perceive of salmon and human suicide in relation to habitat and human invasion, or earth rape and human rape, let alone do so in the context of our global system, and then connect all to the invasion of Afghanistan.

Further, scientists do not engage in much discussion about their studies or their findings until the study is complete. Historians also study more or less as individuals, even when they collaborate; they are responsible for their personal contribution to a text. There are cases when a scientist collaborates with other scientists, or historians jointly study history, but in general the business of scientific inquiry and historical examination is seen as an individual or a small group enterprise that is isolated from other disciplines. Because even multi-disciplinary studies fail to factor in conditions from different habitats, the findings of Western inquiry tend to be limited and reflect the emotional illiteracy of the inquiry itself. All studies are first narrowed, and then focused, so they can be tested, measured for results, and then tested yet again. Connections are theoretical and culturally constructed, and so they cannot be tested or verified, runs the argument. It is my contention that the business of testing in isolation is theoretically and culturally constructed, and so cannot be fruitful or useful to our understanding.

Both history and memory are subjective acts prefaced by judgment. In European culture, memory is considered to be random and subjective, that is random bits and parts are remembered which may or may not be suitable as historical records. We remember things, which suit our lifestyle, based on our point of view and our belief systems. Thus memory is generally seen as unreliable, and students are not taught to remember in any systematic way. This broad sensibility about memory renders memory itself untrustworthy.

History's judgment is the assessment of what is important. The events, developments and movements being researched, studied and critically accounted for are important in the imagination of white men who have compartmentalized and stratified the importance of individual events. This is why the suicide of sockeye was not seen as equivalent to the bombing of the World Trade Centre.

The world is in dire need of another point of view. We need to embark on studies that will influence literary authors to create the kind of novels that affect a change of heart. It ought to be more difficult for political figures to dodge the necessity for change in social relations with non-human and human beings. We need economists who want to level the playing field by creating opportunities that benefit both humans and other beings in ways that are beneficial to all. In his essay of the same title, C. Wright-Mills called for a "sociological imagination" and narrowed his imagination to humans in the U.S. as though the U.S. was separate from the world. That wasn't the case then and it isn't now. I am calling for a sociological imagination that sees all life in its interconnectedness. Ralph Waldo Emerson, in his speech "The American Scholar" addressed to Harvard graduates, called upon Americans to reconceive of scholarship. We need to reconceive of scholarship beyond our own nations.

The essays of the foregoing two gentlemen are inextricably bound together. The latter influenced the former, and the latter was influenced by Indigenous orators of his time. The common thread between them is the influence of Indigenous thought on the direction humanity needs to travel to augment its humanism and connect itself to the world. Yet we have never been accorded credit. As the newcomers gained power, we lost it. As the newcomers gained voice, we became mute. This silencing is rooted in concepts that have held up the old colonial relations between Canada and its Indigenous people, relations that held in place the sexual inequities between men and women in this country and between humans and other beings in the world. These concepts are bound to all of us like a ball and chain. They cannot be altered without a great deal of painstaking and painful study of this place called Canada, its history and its origins.

Historically, Indigenous people have been left out of what is thought to be important. On the one hand, our knowledge was plundered gratuitously and, on the other hand, we were deemed to be without science or knowledge. Our conceptual frameworks for determining knowledge and scholarly study were dismissed and the knowledge itself was appropriated without citing the source.

The interaction and discourse between Indigenous people and European men led to whole new fields of study, sociology being one of them. Marx credits Lewis H. Morgan for his discourse on tribal communalism. Yet although Morgan studied and lived among the Iroquois for twenty years, Marx did not see fit to credit the Iroquois Confederacy. Morgan's work reflects Iroquoian systems and values. Anthropology is another subject born of discourse and interaction with Indigenous people. Franz Boaz and Thomas Blackburn, among others, studied and plundered Indigenous knowledge on the West Coast mercilessly for decades. Similarly, political science arose out of the discourse around democracy, a notion arrived at through the study of the Iroquois system of governance. Herbology, largely based on the documentation of the use of herbs as medicine practised by Indigenous women, even such things as sanitation and modern drugs like aspirin and digitalis, arose out of the study of Aboriginal medicine and were appropriated at the same time that our medicine, herbology, political systems, intelligence and civility were dismissed as non-existent. This entitled White men to demean us and declare a free-for-all on our land, story, and knowledge. Much of the knowledge expropriated was female-owned knowledge. Fortunately, we have memories. Despite the Canadian government's attempt to separate us from our knowledge through our removal and consignment to residential schools, we managed to cling to threads of memory and we are busy weaving these threads into a new fabric.

In our imagination it is considered unreasonably frivolous to study human history outside of the history of interaction between humans and the other living worlds. It is frivolous to imagine that history is only about humans and their important or public events. It is also frivolous to establish a hierarchy within human society and determine that some are worthy of study while others are not. Every minute of every day, hundreds of thousands of events occur in the natural world and in the human world. We sort through them based upon some imaginative sense of hierarchy and significance and we commit to record or remember them depending on what the hierarchy in our mind looks like. The natural world does not necessarily abide by our imagined sense of order and society.

All living beings on earth have a place in our memory. This memory does not narrow the subject to be remembered, e.g., human or fish, but rather our concepts deploy different means to remember, analyze and recall. Salmon is at the hub of our memory wheel. The health of salmon is directly connected to the health of Indigenous people. If Indigenous people commit suicide, sockeye suicide follows; conversely, if salmon begin to die, Indigenous people too will begin to die. Indigenous people on the West Coast cannot separate themselves from salmon. We cannot disconnect the health of salmon from the health of the ocean, and the health of the ocean is dependent upon how we treat the earth. Salish memory is disciplined by the connections among the ocean, the earth, and living beings.

Memory begins with song. Our songs are prayers and these songs precede decisions. These songs remind us of where our loyalties lie. To sing our songs requires that we open up our bodies, and open up our hearts, our minds and our spirit. After song, stories about the beings and the teachings are the means by which we spark the memory of oratorical decisions made in the past that affect the conditions we are looking at in the present. How such conditions affect us is bound to our philosophical foundations. In discussions about water, we begin with a recounting of our relations with sockeye, whale, barracuda, shark, clams, and so forth. We then move to land, sky, air and human maintenance of the agreements and relations we have to all those beings. Humans are not restricted to who we are ourselves, but include all humans. Suicide, we decide, is hinged to the overall health of the living world and the health of the relations between humans and the living world. The salmon suicide in our communities was preceded by whale suicide — beaching — that occurred in the 1950s. This suicide signified a totally toxic and diseased physical and social condition from which the whales saw no apparent relief or possibility of change. In desperate and toxic-diseased circumstances living beings express despondency and hopelessness as suicide. The suicide of sockeye and that of whales are not all that dissimilar. Habitat degradation leads to despondency and disconnection from the earth, from one another, and from life. This disconnection de-humanizes people and is the foundation for violence between humans — suicide and war.

Our conditions and the health of our bodies are linked to the earth, the sea, the sky and all humans. To imagine we are disconnected is to delude ourselves. Yet Western scholarly practice generally disconnects objects and subjects of study in its pursuit of history. Afghani suicide bombing thus becomes evil, the work of terrorists, not a desperate act of a persecuted people. This is the nature of the mental malfunction of the hierarchy of Western society. This mental malfunction has created all kinds of diseased and toxic constructs: Western Society imagines that commercial interests are above social welfare of other living beings. In its diseased and toxic constructs, it cannot imagine that plant life, berries, bugs and roots and their health are connected to human health, mental

59

wellnesss, and emotional maturity. It took a lot of diseased behaviour to eradicate the plant, animal and human life in North America. In my village 100% of our sea vegetables, 90% percent of our fruit, 80% of our fish and 100% of our edible wildlife – elk, seal, clams, and oysters – were destroyed. Doesn't this constitute genocide for our plant world? It was Western society's commodification of buffalo, salmon and rice that preceded their destruction. Once their commodification was complete, commercial interests overrode all other interests. Commodifying them without assigning connective or living social values to their continuance is a sign of fundamental mental illness. Even today, as some North Americans try to imagine another way of being, commercial interests continue to dominate. The destruction of sea vegetables under the first oil spill (the result of a pipeline being sabotaged) was not worthy of historical inquiry because they had no commercial value. Commercialization and commodification altered history irrevocably, and did so not in good ways.

Indigenous people were reduced to the same rung on the ladder of Western hierarchy as sockeye. Neither Indigenous people nor animals and plants are assigned any capability of discovery, perhaps because they can't commercialize the beings around them. Historians focus on the nation-building qualities of Canada. Wise women are not the primary subject of historical inquiry; they are less important and so the study of them is renamed women's studies. Asians, Africans, and so forth fall in the same boat. In fact, until relatively recently, Indigenous presence before the Europeans' arrival was studied as pre-history, anthropology and archaeology. One practical result of this attitude can be seen in the construction of the Sea to Sky Highway for the 2010 Winter Olympics in British Columbia whereby the commercial interests of the Olympics superseded the food interest of Indigenous people. 13 mountains worth of blueberries were destroyed.

Health-conscious organizations such as the American and Canadian Medical Associations would most likely dismiss ordering a study of berry consumption by the human and bear and the effect of this consumption on the villi of both with the view of determining the value of berries in the treatment of common human diseases. And yet, colon diseases such as Crohn's did not exist prior to the destruction of berry and plant habitats that began in the early 1950s. Almost one hundred years following the historical destruction of ancient plant life in North America, Indigenous people and bears are eating at substandard levels and violence is increasing among them.

Salish imagination requires that the history of the berry, the sockeye, human, and bear be considered together in the formulation of human health directions in determining human conduct and the critical study of public history. Salish imagination considers the suicide of whales in connection with their exploitation.

To Salish intellectuals the mosquito is a significant other in the living world. Consequently, they are called upon to remember the mosquito, consider the role it played and its history before draining swamps, and thus destroying mosquito homes and the lowering of human and animal health as a result of the mosquito swamps' degradation. We also maintain that the lowering of human health increases the mosquito people, despite the lack of swamps. When I study swamp life and human health I determine that the consumptive loss of B1 of the humble blueberry leaves humans susceptible to mosquito bites; since the loss of B1 contributes to the decrease in health, it ipso facto contributes to the increase in mosquitoes. I take B1 in its synthetic form and head for the hills to pick blueberries from the mountains.

Frog has a relationship to mosquitoes, swamps and insects as well as to wolf and humans. Wolf and Frog clans are committed to

61

discourse outside of their habitats to augment understanding and achieve knowledge, so all is not lost. Discourse between rememberers from different clans and animals and even different nations used to occur. A discussion between a Salish Wolf rememberer and a Salish Frog rememberer, as well as between them and the wolves and frogs they are related to, reveals that the relation among swamps, insects, humans and health is critical from a historical perspective in order to understand the decline of swamp life on the West Coast and its relationship to the decline of public and environmental health and human and salmon suicide.

That which is not history is categorized as something else.

Salish people have a story about respecting the dance of the bee. I heard this story and understood it to mean that I should not indiscriminately eat honey, but today I can see it means much more than that. Soil depletion, floral ill health, and land destruction — all this is contributing to the malnutrition and depletion of the bee population. If it continues, in a very short time there will be no more bees. Every food dependent on bee pollination will die; every being connected to consumption of bee-pollinated food will suffer. There are so many animals, birds, plants, insects, and aquatic beings on the brink of extinction, yet still we cannot connect the dots.

Only when we understand the connection between ourselves and all living things, and connect this to the historical direction we are travelling, can we find the means to develop a clear perspective. Only when we have uncovered the places in which stasis cripples development can we free ourselves to develop a rational and inclusive value system. Only when we see ourselves in our relationship to the whole can we master our lives and govern ourselves in a sustaining way. When we understand the connection between the living world and ourselves, we will begin to study history as the connection between humans and the living world.

It is imperative that we become governors in a sustainable world and benefit from holistic historical inquiry. If humans truly had a sensibility of what constitutes history in 1750 they would have studied the history of disease and its relation to sanitation rather than slaughter nearly the entire world of whales for the production of perfume over the course of 200 years because humans smelled. If humans truly had a sensibility of what constitutes history, they may not have slaughtered the buffalo in favour of wheat farms, they may not have substituted white bread for black bread, and they may not have slaughtered some millions of Indigenous people in the Americas. If humans understood which humans were important in a sane way they would not have transported and killed millions of Africans as slaves to produce sugar. If they understood the connection between themselves and the plant world they would not have produced sugar at all, implicated as it is in numerous diseases, not the least of which is violence among adults and among children, and hyperactivity. If humans had an accurate sensibility of our connection to the living world they may have studied the relation between fish consumption and health, and overfishing might not have occurred. But the humans in charge do not have an accurate perception of their place in history.

Belief and authority pre-justify human behaviour. Before we commit an act we have already justified it based on our authority to do so and the beliefs that underpin that authority. Historical conditions grant humans the privilege of examining phenomena, or deny them that privilege. There is a structure and systemic support for those who possess this privilege. Structure reinforces — this is its very nature, its function and its duty, if you will. Systems self-perpetuate — that too is their nature, their function and their duty. The magic of the white man's foot is secure because the structure, shape, form, and content of society ordain it to be so.

The wolf knew where he was when those hapless white men first came upon his trail and sought to kill him. The buffalo knew where he was, when hundreds of hunters sought to murder him. Even the grasses know where they are and they have a perfect right to be. That right to be was occluded by the bizarre sense of history that shaped this continent. The arrogant beliefs that hold up this society are akin to a grotesque mythology; they need to be challenged, not upheld.

We perpetuate this arrogance at our peril.

WHO GETS TO
DRAW THE MAPS
IN AND OUT OF PLACE IN BRITISH COLUMBIA

MISCOMMUNICATION HAS COMPROMISED and distorted our sense of memory. When history books are written, they don't say things like: "The village of Vancouver was incorporated today on June 1, 1835 with the construction of the town hall. We seized 34 or so smaller Indian villages and forced them onto a main village adjacent to the land we wanted. On these former smaller villages we established lumber mills. Just across the water is a convenient Indian reserve where we established the first garbage dump. It is at this site that we decided to deposit the toxic waste of Vancouver's new sawmills. Given the rate of death among Indians, it won't be long before all of Vancouver is going to be ours. We shall have full access to all of their villages by the turn of the century." (Conjured after reading *Conversations with Khahtsahlano*, compiled by James Mathews.) But for one village site, this is what happened.

Not only is the confiscation of the major lands not spoken of, but also the humiliation endured by the remaining villages that were used as garbage dumps is not addressed. Because official histories omit such facts, non-Indigenous people do not question their entitlement to this land.

Recovery and reclamation are a process. Those who are keen on conceiving and re-establishing jurisdiction need to remember that diction is about voice and authority is about authoring or creating story. What sort of story do we want to be telling about this island one thousand years from now? Once we have envisioned the answer we need to find some friends — no matter what race they are — and make that vision happen.

Whether in written form as literature or in oral form, stories clarify humanity and articulate social meaning. They also invoke emotional responses from the reader and inspire transformation. They are internal maps illustrating conduct, direction, governance, and possible future being. They point out obstacles to the realization of humanity and unfold the dramatic direction that the removal of these obstacles may or may not take; they map the impact of successful or failed removal through the actions of characters. In much the same way that land maps illustrate physical travel, stories map the emotional, intellectual, social and spiritual travel of characters within the socio-economic and cultural parameters from which the author writes.

Physical maps point to pre-selected destinations that mark a journey from location to location. They determine the beginning, middle, and end of a trip. The journey is bound inside a frame that ensures the traveller's arrival at her or his destination. The physical context and the pathways en route to the destination are made readable and knowable.

The reading of physical geography and topography, in short the environs, is analogous to the reading of the totality of interaction between characters whose conditions provide the natural, economic, and cultural context contained in story. Topography influences travel just as conditions influence the movement of characters.

Maps can be topographical, geological, or roadmaps, while markers and boundaries serve to locate the individual in a point or place within the bioregion being traversed. This ensures that travellers can locate themselves and evaluate time, distance, and space between current location and the journey's end. The events storied and the responses to the interaction of characters locate the reader inside the journey of the story. Stories are owned by families, which are communities, and so their plots are owned by communities.

Communities are bioregions, their histories contain markers, and a story's plot elements mark the boundaries that locate the individual. Both maps and stories contain plot points. The markers look different, but story maps the time and space between characters and shows the ups and downs (the topography) as it attempts to close or open up the distance between them.

Land maps contain the end, the course, and the destination of a journey in much the same way as story contains the emotional journey and the obstacles to the journey as the characters struggle to arrive at some sort of epiphany or transformation. Maps sometimes imply the history of the land holding the destination just as description and context in story imply a historical time and spatial frame holding the end: growth and transformation. Without land maps humans would have trouble locating themselves during movement through spaces with which they are unfamiliar. Without story, locating oneself in a social milieu and making social interaction or mobility outside the familiar possible would be similarly difficult.

Travel from one locale to another, even within the same country, requires relational, physical, and personal changes as travellers seek to re-locate and establish themselves in the new environment. Migration, as well as change or growth, would be frightening for humans to contemplate but for maps, both geographical and social.

While change may be fearful, humans constantly face it. Stories make change almost knowable, nearly familiar, hence less scary.

In a life of constant variance, growth and development, both land maps and story maps help to stabilize humans undergoing change by directing them to familiar ground. As internal maps, stories show the spiritual, emotional, and intellectual journey of characters in both foreign and familiar social environs, and thus render new directions much more understandable.

Like maps, stories establish the physical boundaries of social interaction. Boundaries act as a human safety net for those risk-takers seeking new relationships. Pre-authorized by culture and class origins, they limit the possibility of invasion and assault on those being storied. The journey of interaction with others is linked to memory and an imagined past, present and future. Because all good stories contain an element of transformation, they serve to chart the future. Movement past these boundaries toward a new destination is connected to both the origin and transformation of the characters, and always takes place in relation to the reader.

The establishment of cultural boundaries, their very existence, indicates prior social authority; whether that prior authority is individual or consensus-based is made clear in the story. Social authority is a kind of permission to manage the present and postulate future interaction in a way that protects the original citizens' belonging, safeguards the fundamental nature or ideals of society, and marks each person's place in that society, while still projecting desired growth.

As an internal map of a society's world, stories illuminate the sources of social authority of the past by either upholding or challenging that authority. Our most prized stories don't merely cover old terrain; they envision the direction humanity might travel.

They contribute to the mapping of a hoped for destination. They inspire empathy for the characters and hope that the characters will remove the obstacle.

Maps don't just locate nation states; they delineate the boundaries of a nation's entitlement and thus demarcate the boundaries and entitlement of citizens as opposed to non-citizens. In the grand scheme of things, the authors of maps represent the authority of the nation state, though they may not be a part of that authority. The boundaries of authority within a nation state are comprised of legal and social entitlements — some of them invisible — that are mapped out by language. For example, the Mayor of Vancouver has a different authority in British Columbia than does the Chief of Musqueam, though they co-exist within the same boundaries and serve a common function. In the sociological map the Chief of Musqueam is lower than the Mayor of Vancouver. What is more, the Musqueam nation is not usually indicated on maps of Vancouver. Stories of both Vancouver and Musqueam metaphorically represent the topography of relationships in both communities, but the stories of Vancouver are the stories that are heard. Stories also indicate a kind of welcome, an embrace. The removal of our stories from Vancouver's sociological map is a kind of erasure of Musqueam presence on both the sociological and the topographical maps of Vancouver.

In a hierarchical society, permission and entitlement travel in a skewed fashion. Interactive boundaries change depending on where an individual's group is on the chain of authority. Entitlement is not rigid between groups of people who lack official authority. Not all individuals within a group lock themselves to the preconceived place on the map. Those on top assume that their map — their world of stories — deserves to occupy a more prominent place. They then apply their internal maps to people lower down who then defy their

69

authority. Intrusive relations then occur between those higher up and those lower down as the differing assumptions and presumptions lead to clashes. In some cases, the people on the lower level seek the same permission as those on top, though they may have no idea how permission or entitlement works or is acquired. Defiance and resistance can lead to social change.

Maps are about boundaries. Social boundaries are marked by linguistic boundaries. These boundaries become symbols or metaphors mapping responses. We are allowed to cross on the green light, but not the red. As we await permission to cross, we need only say "red light" and everyone around us, including the blind, stops. We are aware that the words "come in," or some variation of them, allow outsiders to enter someone else's house. The assumption is that without permission no one but the host is entitled to enter. When I identify as a professor at a conference organized by a university, I have much greater entitlement and authority than were I to identify as an elder. Our word maps are uneven. Professors are European-recognized knowledge holders, while elders are recognized knowledge keepers. Their systems of knowledge acquisition are different. Elders are considered less important in the academic world, thus if I speak as an elder to an academic audience my entitlement to belief is narrowed, and my place in the world map shrinks. However, if I move onto the map of territory my entitlement increases. As my entitlement changes, so do the boundaries shift; conversely, as the boundaries shift the nature and extent of my entitlement to belief shifts. Such shifts are based on cultural maps of entitlement and belief and these cultural maps are articulated by story in oral societies.

We understand the constraints and the opportunities that language maps for us depending on our origins. Visitors lack permission, while hosts administer permission. The exclusion of

Indigenous people in all aspects of the cultural, social and academic maps of Canada reduces us to visitors within the boundaries of our nations.

Words define courtesy, demarcate entitlement, and outline to all members of society what is polite or rude, what is permitted or unlawful, and so forth. The terms "Canadian" and "immigrant" mark the boundaries of different entitlements. Embodied in the term "immigrant" are a number of limitations that, if violated, could lead to the discontinuance of the immigrants' very entitlement to being in Canada. The term bears a different story depending on the persons labouring under it: it can imply the threat of deportation or the absence of the right to be here. It can also imply "Not quite good enough." Entitled Canadians do not have to be concerned with disentitled immigrants; their different entitlement begins with a different story and naturally creates different new stories.

Those above must rationalize and justify the limitations of permission and entitlement of those below as fair and just or see themselves as unjust. Thus when Indigenous people are storied up as Neolithic, without culture, without science, without scholarship, Canadians delude themselves into thinking that Indigenous disentitlement is justified and they conjure stories and myths to verify the disentitlement — the story is we haven't earned the right to be treated in a respectful and equitable way. We become very much like newcomers/immigrants who haven't earned the right to be here. In the colonial condition of white male culture the story of earning this inheritance has a twist: newcomers of colour and Indigenous people must disavow their own maps, scholarship, and culture and submit to the white-streaming Western. That is, they must disavow their own story, belief, and authority. Few people will completely disavow the internal maps coming from their own stories, and so entanglement results.

Cultural boundaries keep Indigenous people from engaging in the Euro-society in an equitable way. European cultural boundaries, such as the presumed supremacy of literature over Indigenous peoples' oral story, make Western literature a superior cultural product over Indigenous modern literature.

In the hierarchy of things a social psychotic form of overstepping boundaries and violating those below occurs; or, to put it another way, the upper classes cross the boundaries of the classes they consider subordinate in undesirable ways.

Indigenous people do not have the authority to curtail invasion and violation by others. Witness the remarks of a man who raped and killed an Indigenous woman: "I didn't think it was wrong. She was just an Indian." This man believed he had permission to engage an Indian woman in a sexual relationship, while she lacked the authority to disentitle him. This man's belief that he had permission to rape an Indian woman was marked by the initial absence of investigation.

Cultural expression, specifically story, indicates and challenges the boundaries of relationships. Our story repertoire is comprised of origin stories, flood stories, transformation stories, as well as personal narratives, and global (community) narratives, ecological, environmental, ceremonial, horticultural, male, female and trans-gendered or two-spirited narratives. They were all oral until recently. This does not mean they are without artistic merit. Oral story is word art. Written story is word art.

To this end I give you a story:

There is a lake called Cultus. It is not too far from the Skagit Valley, which both Canada and the United States share or claim to share. It lies within the territory of the nation in which I hold membership and that also lays claim to the lake. During the last serious flood (a little more than a decade ago) in the Fraser Valley, British Columbia, the Skagit Valley almost joined Cultus Lake in Sardis.

There was a beautiful young woman who lived among the Stó:lō. Two very worthy young men from a neighboring nation fell in love with her. She saw them fighting amongst themselves about who should win her heart and hand. She addressed both of them: It is not up to you. It is up to me, so don't fight for love of me. They didn't listen. She heard from the villagers of the neighbouring nation that they continued to fight over who was worthy to be her husband. She cautioned their relatives to remind them that they were powerless to decide, and so fighting over her was futile, that she alone held the answer to their hearts' desire. They didn't listen. She grew sleepless and upset. Since speaking to the humans didn't seem to help, she addressed the lake. Now at this time flora, fauna, water, and humans all spoke the same language.

"These two men keep fighting one another for love of me. I keep telling them that it is not up to them, that I alone must decide who should be my life-long partner, so their fighting one another is futile. They were also cautioned by their relatives, but to no avail. They continued to fight. I grow upset and sleepless. These two men keep fighting over me. I told them it is not up to them; they should not fight over me."

"Why don't you tell them to come down here?" the lake replied. "Challenge one another to a canoe race."

She thinks the idea is brilliant. The winner would settle her own heart. She wishes she had thought of it first; nonetheless, she tells them to hold a canoe race. They liked this idea. They each set about carving canoes. A year passes and finally they are both ready. All three of them go to the lake. Both men paddle with all their hearts. As they reach the middle of the lake, the lake swallows them.

"What did you do that for? Now they are both dead," the young girl says, horrified. The lake answers calmly, "Sometimes to go forward you have to go back to the beginning."

73

At first glance, this is an amusing story about not fighting over women, but on further thinking this story also embodies the Salish view of the journey from the spirit world to the material world. It outlines Salish sensibility about reincarnation. If you don't get it right on the first pass, you will be returned to the spirit world and sent back to the material world. It directs us to get it right on the first pass. It also teaches us to track back to the beginning in struggling to remove the obstacles to going forward; it suggests that movement forward is the natural or desired direction; and implies that humans desire movement forward. This business of forward is not necessarily technology driven but rather humanity driven. Lastly, the story clearly states that women choose their own partners.

This cultural map of the Salish internal world has value. The story asserts the humanity of the people, and it has value not just for Salish women but also for women in general. It asserts the position of women in relation to men and delineates the boundaries of male behaviour in regards to women. It is up to the women to choose. These boundaries have been continuously violated by the Western devaluation of Indigenous and non-Indigenous women since colonialism began. That is, many men believe they are entitled to our bodies with or without our permission. This makes it an anti-rape story.

Who gets to draw the maps: the land and its claims

At first glance, this question sounds innocuous and not at all controversial. A closer examination, however, shows that it is rich with story. First, it presumes that map makers have authority over boundaries, which of course they do not. The authority to establish boundaries belongs to those who represented the British Empire and to those who represent Canada. Map drawing does not give possession. Drawing a map of a room does not give the map maker

possession of it. In the same way, it suggests that those who determine what makes a story a good story are entitled to map our place
in society. This mapping of place for others has proven to be disastrous. The world has experienced a steady stream of wars over
place, boundary, and social structure for a very long time.

The original cartographers in Canada were Native. They drew
maps for the explorers but they did not give the Europeans proprietorship over the land, nor did they have possession of the land
themselves, even though they occupied it, accessed its wealth, and
established caretaking responsibility over it. At a certain point in
history Indigenous people — those who drew maps for England,
France, Spain and Portugal — found themselves without claim to
the land of their maps. They had become disentitled.

The crowns of Europe claimed authority not merely over
cartography, whether or not they drew the maps, but also the
object of cartography, the land. Once the settlers outnumbered
the Indigenous people, the crown re-mapped the commercial, economic, scientific, intellectual, political and legal relations that travel
with human interaction on this island. The crown also changed the
rules of engagement, proprietorship, movement, and citizenship.
The passed laws were implemented against Indigenous people
restricting movement, the head tax against Chinese restricting
immigration, etc. In fact, England mapped the world in accordance with its interests and dominance, and arbitrarily declared the
boundaries of many nations of the world. It set itself up as the arbiter of facts and fiction, of all that was deemed to be true or worthy,
by dint of the bayonet. Many people have since quibbled with this
decision, skirmished with one another over it, but England's political, sociological, and commercial map of the world continues to
be the base from which boundaries are negotiated. They created a
whole new story for the people of the world.

A map is just a map. But when it is framed into a question it becomes loaded with story, and stories carry meaning. Since maps no longer carry Indigenous stories, Indigenous people must verify their claim on the land.

Stories are cultural products, maps to social being. Western literature recycles its social structure by gate-keeping stories that provide a different map to an alternate social being. Stories that locate the displaced in their own social place are dismissed. We are at a point in our history where we just may need to return to the beginning. At the very least we must re-evaluate how we arrived at the place we are at now. I am speaking of a juncture on a sociological map when I say "place." Maps direct travellers to their destination. Words direct humans to the authorship of their story, while authority assigned to individuals determines the value of the words, spoken or written.

Corporations such as mining companies are entitled to exploit and control its use, but cannot lay claim to it. The Crown owns the land but does not develop it. When we stage a sit-in on lands we are claiming and halt mining explorations we are arrested. It is we, not the corporations, who endure the negative effects of our joint disentitlement. The real map maker, the Canadian State, favours the corporations. In the hierarchy of things, this is what political power is all about: the words mapped by story serve entitlement or, its opposite, adversity, isolation and dismissal.

Choosing to discuss who gets to draw the maps, instead of choosing to discuss what direction the various peoples who now populate this land are travelling, falls short of being fruitful. Choosing to discuss maps rather than global human affection for the earth and each other shapes what we do not wish to discuss.

The internal map to transformation that stories provide is complex. We might desire transformation but we are limited by our lack of authority, so we reduce the discussion to something we can manage. Transformation is emotional but humans tend to fear change. Transformation requires mutual understanding but few non-Indigenous people know our stories. Transformation is about sharing but the individualism and acquisitiveness of Western society may not be amenable to that. Transformation requires that we see others from a clean place, but many of us are loaded with assumptions about one another. Transformation requires a language that entitles all people living here access to the wealth of the country. Transformation is story based. Once we have a handle on the story of our peoples, we can imagine a new story and begin transforming the current one.

Indigenous people do not control the intellectual maps that determine the worthiness of story. To alter direction humans must see that where they have been is undesirable. Humans must be able to speak of and to each other with purpose, which requires a change in their view of one another, which requires, too, altering how humans feel about one another. Humans must want to travel toward the development of a shared common society, but to engage in this process humans must understand both their different and common spirit. This requires a new language map, shaped so that it is free of insult and the unequal power attached to authorship and authority. This is a new story.

A travelling agreement free of coercion must be charted and the re-languaging of Canadian perception of First Nations as fellow travellers needs to be invented. This cannot be done so long as we choose not to discuss the history of North America as a white male Anglo-Saxon dominated colonial settler state that is chronically engineering the re-invasion of the land. It cannot be done as long as the new immigrants continue to be disentitled by previous social maps. Once settler colonialism in modern North America

77

is on the agenda and we have a planned agreement to travel in a different direction, then we can discuss the social and physical maps – internal and external – that we will need to draw to get us moving away from this history.

When the phrase "land claims" is used, images of Indigenous people pop up. The assumption is that Canada's land claims, the settlers' entitlement to the land, is inviolable. Those who hold deeds claim to own that property. From the Indigenous side of the fence, these deeds mean very little. The Crown also asserts that it owns 90% of the land. Indigenous people own nothing. Canada was acquired by hook and by crook and by conquest. Nothing acquired by hook, by crook, or by dint of conquest or special entitlement is sacred. In fact, the assumption of inviolability of settler and Crown land claims is based on the assumption of the violability of First Nations land. This latter assumption is held up by the power of the state – its army, police and courts. But in fact they are all just that, claims. The absence of rights extended to newcomers keeps the privilege of white settlers in place; the disentitlement of First Nations keeps the privilege and power of white settler citizenship in place. And of course the power of white settler citizenship upholds the authority of the Crown. Lastly, the disentitlement of Indigenous people and migrants maintains the privilege of men over women. These three conditions are storied up in the myth of white male superiority. The difference between white settler claims and Indigenous claims is really about whose story is told. Those who hold the power to decide the validity of story claim the land.

I am not advocating disinheriting anyone who owns a home. Rather, I want to draw attention to how the colonial word maps obliterate the capacity for reasoned thinking between Indigenous and non-Indigenous people.

In and Out of Place in B.C. and the Pacific Northwest

Let's think for a moment.

Let's imagine that the Pacific Northwest exists in exactly the location that current maps say it does, just for discussion's sake. Despite the fact that this area already had a name, and despite that its being North and West of a central place called Washington, D.C. may be fiction, it is still an arbitrary decision made by colonial map makers, which renders everything north of British Columbia and the state of Washington as being non-existent or not worthy of being *the* North West. Even by the doubtful standards of those Americans who posit that the North West is the State of Washington we are off kilter. What is excluded from this map is Alaska and British Columbia. Washington State is not the North West; in fact, it is pretty much on the centerline of Turtle Island.

What I am speaking of here is not really about maps, but rather the direction and dominion that the colonial order has established for itself in relation to the power to locate and name the position of lesser beings. The colonial order directed its people to touch the earth in the name of a monarch, rename places, people and things, and establish the monarch's order as the only power broker on this island. That is their story and they are sticking to it.

When things and people are renamed to assert power and authority, ultimately things become misnamed. When a few rename for the whole, no one gets to where they want to go. If First Nations and Settlers agree to meet in the middle of the Pacific Northwest and they don't agree that Prince Rupert and Alaska are part of the continent, they will have a problem. Further, if Canada and the United States are not viewed as being the result of European land claims, these settler colonial states cannot be deconstructed even in our imagination.

Indigenous people deserve to be seen as capable and worthy of charting the connection between our internal map and the external course of colonial society. The determination of direction, distance, and space between the settlers and us must occur with the consent of First Nations people. What complicates this is that some of us have become like the others. We do not assign ourselves permission to be, to direct or to manage. Instead, we chronically seek permission from others. We do not establish institutions and lobby for their accreditation; instead, we seek the permission of European institutions to participate in theirs, under their authority, their sponsorship and their power. This seeking of permission needs to end.

We have become caricatures of these others. Our transformation is incomplete, cartoon-like. Indigenous people need a solid stone to stand on to be able to say, "This is where we are going, this is where we will end up, and this is how we will get there." We haven't found that stone yet. Newcomers also lack that. People of colour lack that. Women — white and non-white — lack that. White men seem to have a monopoly on it. It is called citizenship. We are entitled to citizenship, not the imposed citizenship, but citizenship from within our nations. When First Nations speakers are invited to Euro-settler dominated gatherings, they are exercising a crippled form of participation. Such invitations need to be altered.

Citizenship in all its manifestations has long been discussed at conferences. There are a lot of names for it, but it is about white male scholars coming together at conferences to discuss the direction of their country. People gather to map future. Scholars affect the direction of students. That is the essence of governance held by instructors and teachers.

To speak about what direction Indigenous people must travel, a common subject must be sought that can lead to a common direction. That is, a change of subject and a change in the nature of interaction must occur. The discourse and method of engagement that would naturally occur between Indigenous scholars and Euro-scholars have to change. Inter-Indigenous scholarly discourse is more important to me than the discourse between Indigenous and Euro-Canadian scholars. It is more significant and more crucial, but less fundable because white men have determined it to be less worthy of study. Citizenship is not experienced in our interactions on the Canadian Settler stage; rather citizenship is expressed by charting the course of sovereignty and the recovery of our Indigeneity with other Salish scholars. Despite Canadian government claims, Indigenous people do not have self-government. We have caricatures of self-government governed by people that lack the capacity or authority to cipher the direction of the humans on this land. We have almost become caricatures ourselves. This inhibits our ability to be critical of our governors, or those who extend permission and authority to others.

The ability and opportunity of Indigenous scholars to challenge Canadian settler systems currently in place are lacking. In more than one former colony this condition has led to civil war. Everything becomes polarized outside of intellectual discourse and scholarly challenge. Polarized as things are, decision-making becomes a one-time only desperate act rather than the exercise of power and authority by confident citizens. Without the means to alter itself organically, to shift directions quietly, peacefully, reasonably, and intelligently, society stands at the brink of totalitarian oligarchy or a violent *coup d'état*.

Inside our stories are our laws. Salish people have a law that says we are duty bound to feed our families with the least damage to other life save the one we are taking. This country damages billions of tree people, bird people, four-legged people and plant

81

people every day while it eats. Studying our internal world of story may alter this attitude.

Before the first oil spill in the 1950s, there were 27 riparian edible plants consumed by Salish people living on the shores of Burrard Inlet. Today, not only are the plants gone, but also the shoreline, the space between the water and the land, has all but disappeared. In its place are docks and concrete walls and platforms. Our stories tell us we are responsible for rectifying this situation. Our stories do not tell that if someone abrogates our authority over the territory we are off the hook.

It was the responsibility of Salish men and women to ensure the longevity of our plant, animal, and fish worlds. Our stories teach us that if we do not do this, the fish will not return, the plants will leave, and we will die. We have let go not just of our stories but the responsibility that travels with them. We did this because the Indian Act has infantilized us. Until 1962 Salish people were foreign children in the eyes of that law. But in 1962 they were suddenly declared Canadians. As Canadians they have the right to vote and travel freely within Canada. However, as Salish people, they are still children in the eyes of the law. Their votes must still be sanctified by the Minister of Indian Affairs and their decisions are limited to their villages, the sphere of female authority. Off reserve while voting on Canadian issues we are adults, but on reserve we are children. Nowhere are we permitted to exercise our caretaking role over the land.

Indigenous people are headed for adulthood under conditions that we have not had the time, space or opportunity to study through our original law and culture. This is a dangerous place to be. Commercial fishing is killing the entire industry and whole species of fish are now endangered but First Nations people participate in commercial fishing not remembering their ancestral heritage that tells them this is wrong. Murdering a species for tribute is wrong. It is also a violation of our law.

Overfishing in a capitalist state is about forcing fish to become personal tribute. This is lawless to Salish people. People are led to believe that there are environmental protection laws, yet violating these laws is not a crime. Indigenous people have their own laws, but they are not being adhered to. Canadian scientists are still arguing about whether the earth is warming up or not and whether this is a problem or not. I maintain that we can see the evidence of climate change. The tallest cedars in the world grew around Snauq'w, False Creek, but there are no giant cedars left anywhere in the lower Mainland or the state of Washington. Even if climate change is not happening, what is the problem with a law that says take only what you need and clean up after yourself?

Salish people must address our sense of law on this island. The laws that kept the island pristine and productive must be revisited. The laws that kept this island clean and the laws that kept this island alive cannot be ignored. In the process, hopefully, we can begin a discussion about where we are going because, until we know this, we cannot talk about bridging the gulf between the various peoples in North America. These laws are embedded in experience and articulated by story.

We were once a warlike people. We were clan stratified. Young men were in the habit of going out and plundering other villages. Older men and women would stay home. They garnered booty and dispersed it among their villagers or clanswomen. On one occasion, the men went out and killed the women and children of another village.

Raven came to the women and old men and said, "These men have gone out and killed women and children. They have killed creation. They have destroyed future. They must kill themselves

83

when they return. Only those old men and young men among you now will be spared." The men returned. The women told them what Raven had said. The men talked it over and agreed to do what Raven had said. They built a huge funeral pyre and they were going to throw themselves upon it. Before they did so they asked the women to collect their bones after they were burned and carry them for a year, then bury them individually when their sons approached manhood. They wanted their bones stirred in with the bones of the village's dead. The women agreed. The men threw themselves upon the fire and they were burned. The women collected the bones and placed them in their aprons.

The women were so grieved that they could not stay in the village, so they burnt their homes, gathered their things, and walked east. They walked for fully four seasons when they came across the valley where the land serpent lived. It was so beautiful. They called it Ohio.

The consequence of killing creation, destroying future, is that you destroy yourself. Today, like salmon, we have a really big problem with suicide. These stories have much to teach.

We all need to go back to the beginning. In the beginning, we had a duty to access this wealth disciplined by the land's right to exist in a mutually beneficial relationship with humans and we offered the same access to the newcomers. We need to end the business of inviting newcomers to a humiliating position, off side of the table. We need to repair the damage to the land and our souls and begin to rethink of ourselves and the future of North America from the perspective of the island and all its people, one thousand years ahead.

UNDERSTANDING RAVEN

TOMSON HIGHWAY is credited for launching the movement to revive the trickster in Toronto in 1982. Beginning as a Stage Manager for Native Earth Performing Arts (NEPA), he soon began to write plays, and direct and guide NEPA. His works, *Rez Sisters* and *Dry Lips Oughta Move to Kapuskasing*, are rich with trickster-style characters. Highway deliberately set out to revive Wasakeejak in his work and through NEPA. Upon publication of his plays European and First Nations scholars began to study trickster. As a result Native Literature became categorized as unique because of the trickster figure. The very act of defining is meant to bring the broad scope of a word to a small point. There is always a danger in defining a nation's art through one of its mythical figures, let alone doing so for the literatures of many nations. Characterizing all modern Indigenous literature through a single metaphorical or mythical character is a tad absurd. Similarly, it is ludicrous to study Tomson Highway's work only through the lens of trickster. Highway contributed more than trickster to the world of drama, including the fact that there can be dramatic tension and story without conflict.

Scholars are not necessarily an intellectually energetic lot. To complicate things, the context for debating the business of the trickster is usually narrowed to Native Studies and Native Literature. Rather than debating whether or not First Nations stories qualify as viable cultural products worthy of study, the debate centres on whether or not trickster tales are the foundation and defining point of First Nations stories. Tomson Highway's Cree trickster dominates the scholarly defenders of the existence of Native Literature.

This leads to a strange homogenization of race as opposed to the creative power of individual authors and the story tradition of their nations. The role of story and metaphor are not included often in the study of this literature. As a result critical articles tend to convert Raven, Coyote, and Wasakeejak to near national mascot status rather than seeing trickster as simply a literary device, one among many. Gerald Vizenor, noted Ojibway scholar, has joined the debate and contributed to the elevation of trickster as a kind of iconic signifier in what defines Native Literature.

This tendency to homogenize Indigenous people is not new. It is not new for Indigenous people to homogenize themselves either. The images of the Lakota were applied universally to Indigenous people so that some Indigenous people began dressing like Plains people. Thomas King writes a hilarious account of this in *The Truth about Story*. Some Indigenous people began organizing and participating in powwows even though their original nations had no powwow history. Those who sought to elevate the study of Indigenous literature by writing about the trickster had good intentions, but good intentions are not enough. Those who approach our literary authors from this narrow base inadvertently participate in reducing Indigenous writers to creative forest creatures that possess a single storytelling tradition: trickster makes literature Indigenous.

In Highway's celebrated *Rez Sisters* the trickster helps the audience empathize with Marie Adele Starblanket for having too many children, staying with an abusive husband and eventually dying.

Highway helps us to see that it is the history of oppression inflicted on the Cree and not the failing of Marie that is the problem here. The comedy normally assigned to the Cree trickster is expressed through characters that have trickster-like attributes. The trickster figure is then free to take on a much more complex and sophisticated role: it becomes the arbiter between the oppression of Marie and her friends in the *Rez Sisters* and the audience. Highway is conspiring with both audience and the sisters and he succeeds. His success makes him a transformative trickster. Indigenous people as audience feel this story in a way that makes us want something more from our lives; we want to resist not just the oppression, but also the business of being stuck, being caught between a rock and a hard place. Highway is careful not to become didactic: no one is to blame here; no one wants to turn the clock back. As an audience member, I felt as though I were in the play rather than simply watching it. As an Indigenous woman, there were moments when I felt the women were too comic. But I could still see the brilliance of the revolution Highway was leading trickster on. Trickster became the transformer inspiring a different, less cataclysmic, social relationship between Canada and Indigenous women. No one had ever advocated or created theatre about this before. Highway's trickster did so as though trickster himself believed Canadians and Indigenous women desired a different outcome. But this trickster is more complex than many realize. When Highway took on the totality of Mare-Adele's story, his trickster danced Indigenous women to the edge of their own social elevation and he did so with alacrity.

Despite the danger of nearly caricaturing the women in *Rez Sisters*, the young women who saw that first production in 1985 sat at the edge of their seats, and vowed never again was anyone going to laugh at our death. Hundreds of young Indigenous women have come forward as playwrights, singers, artists, novelists, poets and performers carrying their own tales. I personally vowed to create the kind of stories that showed both our heroic sides and the grit, as well as the determination that Indigenous women need to turn the ship around. I have always declined the victim stories. The stories that have survived our oratorical history do not have victims. Though I imagine the war, the slavery, the natural disasters and the social implosion that goes with all that, our ceremonies are largely a response to implosion and our stories are about our recovery, not our demise.

Indigenous women have been fighting the murder of their sisters ever since colonial murder began. We have become agents, transformers and arbiters of our own existence. We may not have made a lot of progress in eliminating the murder of our sisters, but we no longer accept the low standards set for us by society. In this way, as the audience, we have become the transformers. That to me is the role of Raven: transformation and agency. And that, as Salish mythmakers hold, is the point of story.

Highway revolutionized the trickster from a simple bumbling storyteller to a complex arbiter of social change, but hardly anything has been written about that bit of genius in Highway's work. The *Rez Sisters* brought out both the worst and the best in us.

In struggling to understand life, Indigenous people see themselves as cultural entities and family members but rarely as individuals capable of altering the context in which they live, this despite their understanding of original story. As such we focus on what we have in common with other Indigenous people, so much so that sometimes we lump together concepts, cultural maxims, metaphors and symbols in a single mass as though they were all the same (see Thomas King). In similar ways we strive to find objective correlatives to Western society and scholarship. This is particularly true in recent times as interaction among different nations has led to a great deal of cultural exchange, the result being a blurring of the cultural lines separating us. It is important, however, to cite the difference between adopted cultural practices or teachings and original national culture. What Highway's plays do for me is to show that balance between what is and what we need to do. How we see the world and the power we have to intervene in the way we see ourselves is dependent upon the lens through which we view our mythology in the current context.

Resistance to our common colonial history spawned the internation interaction of recent times. This resistance, which began as a political movement directed at decolonization, ended with the birthing of a passionate renaissance of cultural reclamation that is but loosely connected to our separate pasts outside of our colonial context. This uniformity of cultural being has an air of falseness attached to it. It is a mask that our common colonial legacy has conjured. But as we draw nearer to freedom and liberation, the mask will fall and what lies beneath will show itself. We will begin to see difference, complex and separating.

Referring to our literature as Indigenous rather than Salish, as though the mask were real, permanent and inherent, means participating unwittingly in our homogenization. Yet to ignore our commonalities is to invite isolation. Perhaps the persistence to generalize in this fashion has to do with the endurance of the Western myth about our simplicity. The isolation created by the historic injustices committed against Indigenous people keeps us coming back to fear of simplicity and sameness. Perhaps it is because, despite the destruction of so many stories, the trickster has been enduring in our storytelling tradition that we so revere trickster. Perhaps it is because trickster is more acceptable than the si-siutl's, Tsuniquid, or the stories of incest (see Maracle, "The First World War," *Sojourner's Truth*), the woman who had a husband and a

89

wife (J.B. Joe), war (Joseph Dandurand) and the other darker sides of our history. Perhaps the birth of our new literature is contingent on the narrow scope of acceptable tradition left to us by colonization. Perhaps we are just overdosed with shame, shame and loss. In any case, Highway's work sparked fearless determination among the Indigenous women who sat in the audience and saw their lives played out. There is no going back.

In Canada, Indigenous writing is new, yet the works created seem to be so old. April, in Beatrice Culleton's *In Search of April Raintree*, remembers her original family with courage and fierce loyalty. To an oral culture memory is governance, it is being, and it is the foundation of culture. The narrative of *In Search of April Raintree* slides off the page and the tongue so easily. Its very orality persuades that there has not been a break in our storytelling tradition despite colonial dislocation; yet there is no trickster in this story. Old characters come alive under the pens of Jordan Wheeler, Richard Van Camp, Thomas King and so many others; they are so alive that it feels like we are hearing a story, not reading it. There is a coyote in Thomas King's *Coyote Columbus* and some say Harlan is the trickster in *Medicine River*. Perhaps this is true, but it is not the only interpretation of who Harlan could be to Indigenous readers.

We have a practice in the Canadian west, a contest played when we gather together. "Bullshit story" it's called, and someone like Harlan in *Medicine River* always wins. The humour is intended to have an easing effect on everyone and is designed to bring joy and spark laughter and communion with one another. We have been telling this kind of story for centuries. This kind of humour has an element of challenge attached to it; the stories are told in a competitive spirit, something people have told me Indigenous people are not supposed to have. The stories must ring true and at the same time they must be so obviously and comically false, yet they are not

trickster stories. When we laugh until our bellies hurt and someone is a clear winner, some old person invariably says, "Laughter is
good medicine," and we all know the party is over. King's Harlan is
good medicine, despite his treatment of the romance between the
lead character and the pregnant Indigenous woman.

Comic stories also go with the kind of round robin beat a joke
to death style of humour that finds its way into Sherman Alexie's
works. Although, generally, this practice requires a social context
in which someone starts off telling a story about themselves and
then one of the relatives finds a crack in the logic and the jokes
begin, Alexie does this all by himself, which is why we think him
a genius. Yet there are no tricksters in Alexie's work. This second
type of humour is applied to painful situations to relieve tension,
like government negotiations, funerals, and memorials, or when
new visitors from a different nation come to visit. When the tension rises, someone calls a break and the people gather around the
coffee urn and tell jokes about that or other person, causing them
pain. No trickster there.

In the poetic work of Marilyn Dumont, Louise Halfe and Marie
Anneharte Baker, the humour takes the form of a cultural collision
with Western society; the absurdity and understatements of that
conflict show the ludicrousness of oppressing a people. Again, no
trickster here, just intelligent, powerful, artful and transformative
humour. Sometimes our humour is used to open people up to hard
truths. Drop the joke, open up the inner circle, and pretty soon you
are wondering what you are laughing at as you realize there was
nothing funny about the first joke. *Ravensong* has its share of that
humour as does Drew Hayden Taylor's *alterNatives*. In fact, much
of Taylor's more serious plays follows this pattern: the first act is
rich with humour, but the second act makes you wonder why you
laughed in the first place.

Studying our work from within a narrowly constructed frame fails to garner understanding of the characters in Indigenous story. It also blinds us to the genius of the individual crafting them. We deserve better.

Authors are not always sure what makes them good storytellers or writers. Drew Hayden Taylor does not see himself as culturally an Ojibway writer, but he twists up language without regard to the English language order, social being, and tragedy in the same comic way that old Ojibways played with words, and he uses humour in much the same way Ojibways always have used humour. He does so with such ordinariness that it is hard to tell where his Ojibway being ends and Hayden Taylor's individuality begins. He loves writing about the same story that peppers Ojibway original story-telling, justice, and human folly (*Someday, In a World Created by a Drunken God, The Blues* trilogy). Two of his plays are fearless; one of them is even disturbing, but its disturbance is about what we laugh at and the assault on human dignity through laughter and its connection to oppression itself from all angles, oppressed and oppressor alike. It is layered in its courage to present how we are, *siem*. No one escapes. There are no tricksters in his stories per se, but they are tricky.

The Pan-Indianist narrow view of the scope, depth and lay-ered complexity of trickster as a theoretical modality has made the acceptance of our entire cultural literary chest difficult and has led to scholars asking writers like me who the trickster is in *Sundogs*. It also makes Hayden Taylor wary of the cultural moniker assigned to Indigenous story (see also King's *The Inconvenient Indian* and Daniel Francis' *The Imaginary Indian*). Given that we have been part of the process of creating this pan-Indianist narrowed view of ourselves, the general public can hardly be blamed for not see-ing us as distinct cultural and national entities.

According to Cherokee historian and artist Jimmy Durham, this cultural nationalization of our distinct nations was a direction initiated by our origins prior to colonization. Colonialism simply hastened the process. I tend to view it from a different perspective. The natural process of unified development between us was aborted by colonial oppression rather than hastened. Throughout the world, the homogenization process that colonialism has been is breaking down. Colonialism is a mask obscuring the story of who we are and will always want to be. In our mask teachings, the negative can be a reality only as an always false face. The moment oppression is set into motion it begins to die. This is particularly true for colonialism. Colonialism set to dominate Indigenous people, destroy our connection to the land, and eradicate our culture, our knowledge and our stories. It drove our ceremonies, our teachings, our knowledge and our stories "underground," that is, we wore the mask of colonial society as soon as we left our communities, but inside our communities we carried on. Despite all its efforts it was an abysmal failure – nothing more than a mask, a mask that could be removed or donned at any moment. We were covered with the mask, but we remained who we were underneath it.

From the old comes the new, to paraphrase Karl Marx.

After colonialism killed the majority of us, we were cut loose from our national and cultural moorings. Natural death leaves in its wake the memories of the living. The brilliance, the difference, the philosophical orientation of the departed all is constantly reconstructed, making their departure easier to take. If there are too many dead, the shock never ends. *There is too much to remember.* A general state of terror is left behind.

In the recounting of the holocaust, little is recorded of the individual victim's idiosyncratic behaviour. Their character, their quirks, their odd thoughts are not often conjured by survivors.

What is recalled is the horror of so many dead. In order to move past the loss of a life, the living must be able to re-member the dead according to the Salish people's comic way. The recollection of the uniqueness of the departed launches the process of recovery. Thus, when we remember the epidemics, we remember the constant digging, the boarding up of village homes, the dictum of *don't go in there, we don't know how long the sickness inside can survive* (McDougal, oratory) but we do not remember that Lilt said this about that or how he turned his head to face his own words, or that Slahoot had this odd way of walking like he was always on a mission. We can't imagine what the individual members of the epidemics might have said while doing something as simple as berry picking. We can't picture a single murdered Beothuck mother, child on her back, picking little white berries and singing some old song. We can't picture them laughing at an old funny story while they stitched nets, or built weirs and readied themselves for fishing.

Memories of the dead not only appease the living but they continue to contribute teachings to their descendants. First Nations' survival rates are on the rise. In the past 40 years our average lifespan has nearly doubled from 39 to 66 years. In this state of assurance, we must now review the horror faced by over 500 years of continual attack and death. Life is now an option and, for the sake of our youth, we must make it a desirable one.

In some strange way, memories of death flesh out the living. Grandmothers and great-grandmothers and mothers on the eave of a newborn child's funeral are so devastated that they will never be able to flesh out the loss through their memories of them. The faces of the parents at a child's funeral are different, the hand movements change, and the shaking, the crying, is nearly threatening; even the tiny little box seems to pose a threat. The density of grief at a great-grandmother's funeral provides the impetus to move forward. The coffin is often open, the deceased looks peaceful, and while the grief is immense, the grandparent is memorable and so the grief is expressible and therefore manageable.

We watch our great-grandmothers in their kitchens over and over again. The memories of smells, of woodstoves, of plums and berries are tangible and in the course of recalling these simple things the grandmothers' wisdom hitches a ride with memory, and we are re-educated by their lives yet again. Invariably, the conversation shifts from simple recall to deconstructing their teachings and re-constructing who we are. The words uttered in the original language of the rememberer or in English direct and re-teach over and over.

On the other hand, the dead take much knowledge with them. In their living state, elders pass on information — this story for this grandchild, and that story for that one — such that the death of an individual requires the family to gather together, to articulate all the bits so we can see the whole. Humans gather together to assemble the memories collectively or the lives of the elders would pass on without a murmur. We must aggregate to see ourselves. Our imaginations cannot discipline themselves outside of some form of social context; some sort of peer pressure is required to convert our wildly operating brain into some framework that will provide us with a reliable sense of order.

Epidemic death destroyed our ability to come together to re-create our cultural selves. It challenged our belief in the knowledge of the dead and the living. The shock that accompanied those loses continues to threaten the capacity for clear thinking. Bits of information required to prepare the simplest food perish. I remember camas was a staple food among Salish people, who tilled it and harvested it, until the pre-emption laws removed it from us, so the memory of its preparation is gone. I have no memory of what

95

it felt like to crawl about the wild lands where it must have grown, so I can't imagine my great-grandma picking it. Why would I? If it no longer exists my great-grandmother would have no basis for teaching me how to prepare it. But this does not mean no one knows how to prepare it; someone has the memory and so we congregate in host feasts and ceremonies to re-construct and relearn about our lives.

People articulate themselves in the context of the business of accumulating the means to live and the process of preparing the reproduction of their lives. Their daily ablutions birth whatever knowledge they have about being clean — cleaning agents, the efficacy of this soap over that soap, the scent, even the importance of cleanliness itself. None of this comes into play outside of daily routine. Choosing this tree over that one to build a weir is a matter of knowledge transmission. After an epidemic, the keepers and the infrastructure necessary for this transmission are debilitated.

There is a story of a child being the last child to be alive in a typhus epidemic. All I can picture is her missing her folks, but she lived for days, and she must have eaten. There must have been food. She must have known about it, gathered it. She and all the others died, so the memory of this food collection, preference, and preparation is gone. The land she roamed is still there, but most of it has changed; only a small part of the park was kept in its pristine originality. Some of the plant life there must be edible. But that doesn't mean someone else from nearby doesn't know about this plant life, and so we gather to learn and to teach. But we are disconnected from one another, and coming together to re-gather our knowledge requires that we plough through the fields of our fractured selves and fall in love again.

We believe the old carried wisdom; maybe this was so, and maybe it wasn't. Maybe it was so because their departure in huge numbers was so sudden that it left us with so much grief that we conjured the fiction of dying wisdom to ease our pain in the same way we remember the wisdom of children only when their childhood is gone. I do know that my relationship to knowledge has changed since grand-motherhood: transmission and orality gain significance and my memories are focused on the skeleton of our culture. Perhaps the reverence we accord our elders has something to do with that. It doesn't matter, we believe it, and so as youth we gather knowledge, think about the stories we have gathered, and struggle for depth, breadth and understanding, and we become wise in the process. We make it true.

Following the epidemics was our intermarriage. Some have whispered to me that only the mixed blood survives the white man's diseases. Some say in secret that intermarriage was our one chance at survival. Others believe the mixing of the blood began with mass rape. We don't know. Few white people documented their rape behaviour and few elders preferred to offer up such stories. The records, the journeys, are either missing or unresearched.

In any case, we know our blood is mixed with the blood of others. The mixing of the blood altered our culture. We can surmise this. White people endured a great deal of hardship in the intermarriage process. Their relatives often disowned them. The unrelated freely castigated their choice of *country wife*, shamed them liberally for choosing their partners from among us.

Some of those who married us spoke reverently of our ways. Perhaps this reverence was inspired by white people rising above the shame of marrying an Indian. Some of the Jesuit records indicate the reverence was deserved. Some records indicate the opposite. The dead haven't come back to tell me which version is true, but I suspect that those who articulate our culture best are those who understand the culture of the others. I did not give a single thought to who I was until I was among people who were not like me. Why would I? According to Paul Mannheim, in the study of others, the self becomes understood.

We have gained so much understanding of what it is to be Indigenous through scholarly studies of oratory. The words of great-grandmothers and grandfathers come alive and oppose the colonial intellectual will.

Karl Marx says we begin human history as people in ourselves; it is not until humans effect social change that we become people for ourselves. This process of becoming a person is about becoming a conscious intelligent being. Perhaps change simply has to occur, no matter who or what inspires it.

Death on a mass scale must have changed us. Did it make us desperate? Maybe we clung to whatever remnants of being we have left because we were horrified at the massive passing.

"Our cultures are thinking cultures," Babe tells me. Maybe I insist on my culture's complexity because others are always trying to simplify it. I ferret through memory bits of cultural information and try to reconstruct our whole being. We are so dispersed, so crippled and so dissipated. Maybe we rose, satisfied our appetites, clung to the moment, enjoyed ourselves or did not. Maybe we read so much into the fragments of who we are because there are so few of us left to remember our totality and because our memory is so fragmented. I consider things that appear simple and I see their complexity and I insist on the complexity of Salish being.

The philosophical origins of Indigenous people are different from those of the newcomers. Difference is valuable. Each culture has something unique and specific to offer. The complexity of culture from which I arise is made manifest by the complexity of character and being in my family. Whether it is a result of cultural collision with others, or whether it is a result of our history or all of the foregoing matters little. I imagine original story from my current and historical being. I glean lessons from it and turn them into reality.

I studied Salish story in the same way I was taught to study European story. I ploughed through Salish metaphor with the same diligence and care that I ploughed through Christian metaphors in *One Flew over the Cuckoo's Nest*. Franz Fanon says that Native intellectuals want to return to culture only because they have left it behind. It never occurs to the intellectual that the mass of the people may not have left themselves behind. Amílcar Cabral says that when there is no other way to resist colonization, the oppressed Native resists culturally. I believe both those things are true. No one wants to be like his or her oppressor. In fact, separating ourselves from the oppressor leads us to a greater sense of what it is to be human.

The study of culture and story was born of foreign systems colliding. The European systems collided with the systems of North American Indigenous peoples. One culture oppressed the other. The oppressed resisted physically when they could, and resisted culturally when physical resistance was futile. Out of the collision and the resistance a new body of knowledge was born. Each party in the collision compared themselves to the other and change occurred as a result. The oppressor gained in humanity and the oppressed gained the very tools that gave the oppressor dominance. Each lost something of themselves in the process. Raven articulates our losses as a positive.

I remember Raven. Raven is a harbinger of change and a metaphor for social transformation. She calls us to forever grow and change. There are no Raven stories left rationalizing slavery, internecine war or plunder, though there is evidence of our having partaken in all of that. There are no Raven stories sanctioning hierarchy, though we still endure the remnants in the language of *good family*. The outlawing of slavery stripped us of the ability to muck about the coast plundering one another at will. It ended internecine war among Salish people, though it did not end the tribalism that goes with it. It ended hierarchy even though the remnants still exist in our language, choice of partners and friends. It ended polygamy without leading us to monogamy.

All this change restructured our Raven repertoire of stories. We have carefully preserved and retold the stories that urge us to cherish change. We hung onto those stories that sanction and elevate social change to lofty heights. With the elimination of polygamy, the place of women went up a notch or two. We gained value. We raised our children in the lap of transformative Raven stories.

Women don't miss the Raven stories men must have told as they bragged about how many wives they had. Men don't remember them now because the women who learned to appreciate being the only wife never taught them and the men who might have told the stories had no context for doing so. There are few stories of jealousy in our Raven repertoire. Polygamy to exist jealousy must be subdued. Jealousy is an emotion born of monogamous existence. Modern traditional men caution women not to be jealous but they have no cultural stories to show us this is not a good emotion. Women don't believe them with any depth or commitment. We love our jealousy. It appears to keep us safe. We even love jealous men; they make us feel special. We repeat stories of jealousy to ourselves in the comfort of our kitchen. They aren't Raven stories, but we don't care. Jealousy is tricky, amusing, fulfilling and transformative for us.

We attach Ravenesque meaning to our jealousy. This Ravenesque meaning is powerful. We cherish these modern stories full of love, romance, betrayal and jealousy. The characters in modern stories exhibit their jealousy so subtly and smoothly, so free of rankle, that only an Indigenous woman can see it. It is underneath the musings of Slash in Jeannette Armstrong's *Slash* as he wonders where Mardi is, what she is up to, whether or not she is married. You can feel the yearning; the burning underneath, the jealousy struggling to be expressed, and you can feel its failure. It is there in what Slash never says. He never says he wants her, never admits he loves her, but you feel it. Instead he says he fell in love with the way she spoke, her grit, her determination, her feelings about culture, but never her. He describes everything Mardi does in minute detail, but he studiously ignores what she looks like. This is not a man talking. It is Armstrong avoiding the subject we all love most, jealousy. In avoidance there is prominence and power.

Jealousy is new. It is the product of monogamy, and Salish people were not monogamous until recently. It is fresh. It is so alive because it is so new. It is so new that we can only speak about it around our kitchen tables only in the company of women. Jealousy is our trickster altering social being. Jealousy makes Raven more complex. We jealously safeguard culture; jealously protect our children, our sense of family, and our ways. Raven assists us. We complicate the story even more than we intended in order to safeguard our complexity.

Stacey runs. In every step she muses over her ways. She crunches into the gravel of her *Sundog* journey jealously recalling her mother's pipe and drum philosophy. She imagines Paise Platte and the ghost of some young man finding her irresistible. Irresistibility is bound to monogamy and has jealousy as its faithful emotional companion. We need to feel irresistible to satisfy our burgeoning jealousy. Stacey imagines neglect as the seed of cultural decimation that led to the sanctioning of violence, but it isn't. It is the freeing of woman from the bondage of arranged marriage, polygamy, and the institution of free choice, monogamy, that births the emotionality of jealousy. Raven knows this. She is complex. She can handle change. It is us who find change intolerable, terrifying and unsettling.

Raven cannot be understood outside of change, outside of our context and outside of our history. To refer to her as a trickster is to return to her origin in a kindergarten kind of way. This denies change. It alleviates the effect of death, of oppression, of emancipation, of reconciliation with change itself. It obviates our having become conscious, of having become people, mature and knowing, discriminating and discerning.

Raven can't be understood in her simplicity. We have sorted through so much of our historical being. We have discarded much, clung on too much, and re-evaluated ourselves so much that the stories we now tell would hardly be recognizable by our ancestors. Even their spiritual intent has been altered. When we cling to the past we do so as different people. Our ancestors moved forward into history; they moved into the new world with courage and renewed vigour. Even while their very existence became precarious, they continued to struggle to move forward, to integrate, and to assimilate themselves and their children into the world of the newcomers without much thought for their origins. They sent their children to school, despite the pain of having been there themselves.

When their children threatened to leave those schools they told Raven stories of acceptance of difference. They told wolf stories of endurance. They told eagle stories of vision. And they tricked their children into staying in those places. Raven has become a metaphor for cataclysmic social change. She has brought us from a simple fishing and gathering village life to the computer age. Raven has done so as the paramount engineer of social transformation. Simple trickiness could not do this.

We needed more than a trickster to bring us into the new millennium. Our grandmothers and grandfathers conjured her from the original stories. "I have travelled a greater distance than simply landing on the moon," Chief Dan George says in *My Heart Soars*. Raven brought him from his simple canoe to the horse and buggy, to the automobile and the space age, and did so with elegance and grace. With elegance and grace the old Chief carried me to the pages of my books, helping me to create characters who endured change, who marched themselves toward it with courage and Ravenesque simplicity. Characters who are complex but who in their simplicity realize their complexity is irrelevant can fool you. They can make change look so easy and appealing that readers themselves desire change. Raven removed the terror of systems colliding. She removed the terror of epidemic death. She removed the terror of residential schooling. She removed the terror of racism, sexism and patriarchy. Raven removed the terror of resistance to colonization. Raven has become the ultimate transformer.

Raven is also the ultimate preserver. She teaches us to cling to images of environmental responsibility and spiritual responsiveness. She reminds us that we have spirit-to-spirit relations with all beings. She reminds us that all things have a spirit. They begin with their aliveness and they die. "Are all these rocks alive?" this white man asks. "I don't think so," the old man replies. "Some of them must be dead" (Oratory). Raven calls us to assert our belief inside our own world. She calls us to extend this belief to the outside world. Raven calls us to take on the responsibility of cherishing the environment, nurturing it and ending wanton environmental destruction.

Raven calls us to cherish words, to embrace the sacred and to strengthen our belief. She demands that we become conscious

103

beings, that we police ourselves, become mature thinkers. Raven clutches at the skeleton of our cultures left behind, searches for the significant in our scant memories and inspires us to augment these memories, reconstruct and reclaim ourselves. Raven has become the harbinger of colonial resistance. Despite the newness of colonization, we see this as part of the renaissance of original culture. Raven has matured under the collision of systems. Raven has matured under the horror of epidemic death. Raven has matured under the terror of cultural prohibition.

Colonialism led to social demoralization and implosion. Raven endured the process with us and so she stories it up and leads us out of it. This is especially evident in the novels of Jeannette Armstrong, Beatrice Culleton and my own. Each of these novels exhibits the spirit of transformation that forms the foundation of our remembered repertoire of story. Despite the fact that all of us three writers come from different nations, we all embrace the transformative power of original story (Raven, Coyote and Wolf). The transformer has become a beacon of hope, a call to re-birth and cultural reclamation. She has become a complex metaphor for continuous growth and transformation. We can no longer understand Raven any other way.

Raven calls us to embrace the sacred and to strengthen our belief. Raven is only one source of our vast repertoire of oral story and oral story is but a thin wedge of our repertoire of oral memory. We can claim complexity as the descendants of the orators through our own complex sensibility of who Raven is and what our stories are all about.

We share who we are. Blood leaking blood running blood spilling blood shaping blood pumping blood pounding blood flowing. Blood is so powerful we can't stop thinking about it we can't stop writing about it we can't stop defining ourselves with its movement its stillness its character. Blood chilled blood constricted bloodless and still blood draining from our faces blood draining from our legs blood vessels collapsing the word conjures so much of ourselves in such little space we are so enamored of blood it was the first cell to be seen through some microscope it was the first cell to be photographed and committed to memory at school I remember the blood cell I saw in the microscope I don't remember the skin I remember the picture of blood in the science text no other comes to mind human blood is sweet I look at the man who says this he is a teacher, how does he know he tells us that we would all become cannibals if there was nothing else to eat I can't picture this nothing else I picture that little Inuit boy in the Arctic, plane crashed, the white man with his broken leg he gathers moss and bark eats it till it kills him he could have killed the white man and eaten him he didn't he died without ever knowing that that white man's blood was sweet

POST
IM

POST-COLONIAL
IMAGINATION

CEDAR CALLS FROM EVERY HILLTOP — *not again, not again — not twice. The sound of cedar crawls out from under the burden of the garrisons locked gates, far away from the clang of industrial machines. Her limbs, frocked in green lace, dance, hold up our imagined selves, struggle to remove the burden of forts that locked up our imaginations.*

My own dream space where my words are born:

I feel a little like Zola, making political and now literary proclamations from within a sense of reality that other humans do not necessarily share. Here I am, one of the two non-academics at a conference of English academics on "Post-colonialism: Theory and Practice." I am the only non-degreed teacher ever hired to deliver a university program at the University of Victoria, and I am the most published Native woman author in the country. .

I remember my first words as a child. The sun was gone and rain spilled from the sky. I watched my mother enter, hunkered down into her coat as though hunching her head into her shoulders would protect her from the rain and cold. She slipped off her boots and said, "It is raining pitchforks out there." I saw no pitchforks. Instead, I imagined her discomfort and played about with the picture of her hunching down to protect herself from the rain.

I imagined pitchforks falling from the sky, thin and sharp – painful. To some folks rain is painful, like pitchforks might be to shafts of hay.

"Between cloud and rain there are no pitchforks, only people who think they see them, right Mom?" And my Mom laughed and hugged me. It was my earliest understanding of metaphor and its place in our lives. I was three-and-a-half then. I have memories that pre-date this image, but no words were ever let go of by me, until this moment. In my mind, the image always came first, then the words were layered overtop. This process of thought still lives with me. The images come, then the words. If there are no images, then there are no words. Consequently, I understand mathematics only in terms of physics, chemistry or shopping.

I remember the first time I spoke in school. Ms. C. asked me, "Where did Dick run?" I answered, "Far from the fence posts that locked up the grasses no one wanted to grow," and everyone laughed. It was a different kind of laugh. Ms. C. responded, "Your insolence will not get you far in life." Perhaps it was not insolence that did so much for me as my belief, belief in my dream space where my words are born.

There is a place between the sand bank and the river where silver streaks are born. This place slides along the dream space of the stream that birthed it, unaware of the wonderment of its conception, the miracle of its birth and the tenuousness of its life. Fools see the silver in terms of cost and thus place no real value on it. The wise know that in the thin lines of silver, secrets and truth form a soft whirling knowledge that calls the body to free itself of all burdens and look at the world through the dream space of this silver streak.

Thin is the line along the river's edge but vast is its internal life. This place spins dreams and webs of new life are woven into whole new worlds. I live within the boundaries of this streak. Others live here with me. They are shaped by colour and difference but no one possesses the authority to disempower others on the basis of this colour and difference. In this place all are distinct, powerful and beautiful. In this place we dream new words with old themes rich in human love and promise. We strive to inspire without words, painting our dreams of change. We are the poets, the painters, the dramatists, those who really believe that if we just write this one last poem, paint this one last picture, create this one last character, we can change the world.

In this dream space there are no post-colonial conferences on literature, no conferences on Indigenous sovereignty, and no one asks, "What do you Indians want anyway?" We all know that the human spirit divine requires freedom to blossom, freedom to dream, to create and become whole. This freedom is as basic a need as is food. However, in the real world, colonialism is our condition and so we need to have such conferences.

Unless I was sleeping during the revolution, we have not had a change in our condition, at least not the Indigenous people of this land. Post-colonialism presumes we have resolved the colonial condition, at least in the field of literature. Even here we are still a classical colony. Our words, our sense and use of language are not judged by the standards set by the poetry and stories we create. They are judged by the standards set by others.

With conditions as they are, it is a luxury for me to wander into my dream space and conceive of post-colonialism. A multitude of faces, all white and too numerous to name, gather around the edges of my dream space. If I enter despite them, their words ignite and nearly melt away the thin line of silver housing my ability to dream. Images of screaming squaws, dirty Indians and weeping women write along the rivers of tears we have shed over these images that continue to meet page, print and reader. And still I imagine new words to deal with old dilemmas that still stand on the way to freedom.

At dawn, when the river reaches the sea, my ancestors, before they potlatched, danced and sang. There the sun keeps time with her own sense of music and the surface of the sea transforms. On it I see a tiara of grandmothers and grandfathers. I hear words of challenge and struggle, of transformation and change. I feel my nation's passion for these things. I see future. The voices of George Ryga and some of the citizens who died join the congregation of my ancestors and form an arc; I suffer living and envy the dead.

In the literature of this country is the search for an essential Canadian self. This is an arc created from our common voices and vision. Each new dreamer adds their song, their vision, their story, to this space. The concept of the arc of light, which both binds and separates us, is born of the realization that humans hold a thread of hope – thin, stubborn and resilient – and that the stories they share create new light inside both listener and storier. Watered by the sharing of light and story over time these storiers and old writers fill our contemporary baskets with this hope. This hope is held dear by those who refuse to peer like cowardly voyeurs at the world from behind the fence posts of a colonial fort. I am inspired by all those whose spirit excites literary courage, those who recreate language, and reconceive humanity not as statistics but as creative sacred beings capable of change, capable of bringing dreams from conception to birth and transformation.

In the thin arc bridging my life to the future, the roots of my life are nearly overwhelmed. The industrial revolution, the lie of it, the stagnation inherent in it, the violence and the death culture it birthed become clear. The history of this revolution and its victims has long complex tendrils of industrial waste and death.

This culture that aggrandizes its authors stretches itself all over the world, winding itself around imagination, choking all those whose images have no room for it. Those who stand in awe of this industrialization process are not yet free of it. Even the dead are not free of it. We can't even imagine beyond our common colonial condition because of it.

We are the grandchildren of an abusive industrial British parent, and in fact are nowhere near a post-colonial literature. The dirty waif of Dickensian literature has become the modern Indian waif, but without a name. Canadian writers still hover about the gates of old forts, peek trough the cracks of their protective ideological walls and try to write their own yearnings for freedom from the safety of their intellectual incarceration. The colonized still hover outside the gates, dreaming of coming in while the ideological madness of this ridiculous desire hides our truer aspirations and colours our language in stilted erratic parroting of the mother country's tongues. Or worse, this desire paints images of coming into the fort as equals. The existence of the fort, the laws of this fort, and the humanity of it are rarely questioned. Canadians must get out of the fort and imagine something beyond the colonial condition — beyond violence, rape and notions of dirty people. We must move beyond what is to re-enter our dream space and recreate ourselves. We must get away from the fort's door where the scent of pillage and imprisonment still terrorizes our dreams.

In George Ryga's play *The Ecstasy of Rita Joe*, Rita says, "No child on the road would remember you, mister." Ryga joins the congregation of my ancestors and their dreams of a life outside the fort. "No child would remember you, mister." You, who clutch the gate keys of your colonial master, acquiesced to your colonial imprisonment in language and law intended to dehumanize. You can never be remembered by an innocent child. Children are forward people, they are dreamers and their memories are too innocent to recall the jailed and the jailers. Ryga knew something then.

I want to be able to fictionalize our lives and still hold fast to truth, yet our lives are so rich with death. I fear that in storying this death in numbers so immense, with love so deep, I may not survive. I spiral down into the silvers streak of solitude to find my ceremonial self. From within this bright womb I can spiral out into the world again to reconceive of place. I can stretch time. I can erase the artifice of separation that divides today from yesterday and yesterday from tomorrow. In this place all time is the same time. In this place images speak reality, paint truth in believable pictures.

In this place my self is a significant self, a self that rises, swan-like, to engage the rigours of loyalty and love, a self that, wolf-like, journeys doggedly along old trails with new directions in mind, a self that sees transformation, personal and social, as natural and indispensable to growth. These things inside are not things at all, but songs sung by me, my grandmother, my grandchildren, and men like Ryga.

We conjure new words by understanding our different and common pasts. We cannot resolve this past unless we can come to the silver streak between riverbank and sand without quarreling.

From inside the dream space comes my language coloured by my need for you to see me – really see me. The heart and spirit under my skin animate my need to carve images of myself onto the pages of your books, never to be forgotten. Inspired by my need to experience oneness with you at the crest of an arc of our mutual construction, in a language we both understand, I build my end of this arc, word by word, dream by dream.

This arc becomes the meeting place for our two worlds. The desire for this arc, this meeting place, this oneness, does not negate the existence of both worlds. The arc presupposes the harmony of both, not the invasion or the suppression of my world by yours. It invites sharing between them.

But we are plagued by our colonial condition. Inside the fort, Canadians seem to think this arc can be built despite the disentitlement of our land, our words, and our very selves. Outside the fort, we hear the laughter and feel we must shed our ancient selves, move away from our homeland and give up our words. If Canadians are locked in the fort, we are locked outside of it. Doubt rises huge and fogs the source of our creative voice, making the arc disappear. We search your institutional hallways for evidence of ourselves. But we have forgotten that the trail to our ceremonial selves is in the dream space we once occupied.

In order to resolve this colonial condition in literature we need to have Canada recognize, first, that this is our condition and that, second, Canada needs to view this condition as unacceptable. In literature this means to move over and create a new space for us in the annals of literature in Canada. It means, don't pick up a pen and imagine you need to write on my behalf or that you should. I mean that those who lay claim to a place in the dream space of creativity must come to understand the difference between honest stretching into the world of the imagination and pirating someone else's imagination.

If you conjure a character based on your in-fort stereotypes and trash my world, that's bad writing, racist literature, and I will take you on for it. If I tell you a story and you write it down and collect the royal coinage from this story, that is stealing – appropriation of culture. But if you imagine a character that is from my world and attempt to deconstruct your attitude, while you may not be stealing, you still leave yourself open to criticism unless you do it well.

113

Part of our colonial condition is that we are still too busy struggling in the whirl of paddling through the rapids in the centre of the river, or we stand unsure at the edge of the river, to be able to enter the dream space. So we stand at the edge of it or nearly drown in the centre. Few Indigenous people have had the time to study our remembered story. Some have no memories to ponder, but those of us who have pondered our memorized stories know we have criteria for story.

If the speaker achieves oneness with the listener, then it is a good story.

If the listener is empowered to move to his/her dream space and imagine him/herself, it is a good story.

If the listener is empowered to move to this dream space and re-imagine oneness with the humanity, earth, flora and fauna, it's a good story.

If the story makes the listener want to re-conjure it different but the same, it's a good story.

If the story enters the world from the dream space where all good stories are born, it's a good story.

These are my culture's standards — conscious and unconscious — and, until they become standards alongside yours, colonialism in literature will prevail.

SHARING SPACE
AND TIME

CANADIANS NEED to understand Indigenous law more than they need to understand Indigenous people. Prior to the new millennium this understanding was impossible. Our laws were abrogated, demeaned, and prohibited. More than that, some form of mutual sharing of access to the land must be achieved between Canadians and Indigenous people. At the same time that Indigenous people are aware of Canadian history and its development, whether by force or choice, they have consistently been kept outside of the Canadian experience. The flow of knowledge has always appeared one-sided. To the victor goes the spoils of war, and one of the spoils for the victors seems to be a happy ignorance about those that have been conquered. At the same time, much of the knowledge that exists in modern times has a root or connection to the so-called "lost knowledge." Because oral knowledge is public knowledge, no one has to mention its source. We become an invisible people without knowledge or contribution to Canada.

Colonial relations are not a thing of the past. They still exist. Out of the north Canada receives billions of dollars in royalties coming from licensing fees. These fees go south to benefit Canadians. The Cree, in whose territory the mines are, receive no payment whatsoever. (Consider the De Beers mine in Attawapiskat.) For every dollar Canadians get from the federal government, Indigenous people get 55 cents. We receive nothing from the provinces and the towns, despite our paying property taxes and the millions provinces gain from stumpage fees and mining and tree licenses for harvesting the resources in our territories. Canadians pay some $354.00 for education; our tuition is $10–15,000 per year for grade school. We don't have access to the spaces required to survive. Our spaces serve Canadians.

The Indigenous confederacies living along the 49th parallel were dismembered in the process of establishing Canada. The dissected nations are now divorced from one another. This dissection has crippled the possibility of nationhood for the nations that straddle the international border. Neither Canada nor the United States stopped at separating our confederacies by international boundaries. Instead, both federal governments took it upon themselves to further separate one village from another by establishing reservation borders, setting up a pass system, and limiting movement through violence both legal and illegal. These conditions severed connections to relatives, and continue to impair our economic, trade, cultural, social, ceremonial and political being. The impairment of trade destroyed the original economies and lowered the standard of wealth accumulation for Indigenous people. Wealth is the measure of leisure time. Time is the measure of artistic and conscious development.

Both governments established departments to caretake Indian Affairs whose sole purpose was to limit movement and curtail access to space. This curtailment of space took place alongside the arrest of all systems of governance and exercise of power over health, wellness, the environment, economic development, knowledge transmission and cultural education. As a result our understanding of ourselves atrophied. Recovering from this condition will take time *and* space.

Our territories have become exclusive exploitation zones for the conjured nations of the white settler states of Canada and the U.S. that occupy this space. Their authority to continue to do so is held up by law and the threat of military force. Development in our homelands is exercised exclusively by the American and Canadian states and can only occur with their sanction. The threat of invasion is a violation of our very right to space. Economically, we are confined to reservations without the possibility of annexing the original territories even if we were to purchase them. So much of our being, our governance, and our economy is attached to the space we have access to.

Freedom is inextricably bound and attached to the concept of space, and is realized or not realized depending upon the access or restriction placed on individuals and their communities within the space they are entitled to occupy and utilize. Indeed, incarceration is severely limiting an individual's space and is the height of punishment. We are the most incarcerated people in the country.

Concepts of family were altered more than a century ago, as were Indigenous concepts of citizenship, first, through the restrictions placed upon physical movement and, second, through legislative acts. Along with the insistence on nuclear family living arrangements came male dominance and insistence on a woman moving to the man's village upon marriage. Indigenous people were legally deemed unfit to govern and to vote as they were considered "children in the eyes of the law." What completed this curtailment of space and Indigenous modes of living and being was the removal of children from the care of Indigenous parents through the Residential School System and, more recently, through the various Children's Aid Societies.

These conditions limit authority over family and preclude the Indigenous assumption of citizenship and power. They have obliterated our ability to define family and determine citizenship in our own terms, and led to the general belief that we are not entitled to any space at all. At the same time that our mobility, emotionality, morality, and our concepts of justice, family and being have been altered, concepts of disentitlement upheld by settler society dominate our lives. These conditions continue to threaten and stymie Indigenous survival.

Today, the liaison between the settler state and our villages is primarily maintained by men and women who have no territorial authority or social or clan responsibilities whatsoever. The village has become the seat of government in such a way that nationhood no longer exists. The Canadian government has taken to referring to each reserve as a *First Nation*.

A village is not a nation, no matter what the government or our chiefs say (Ray Bobb, oratory).

The slicing and dicing of the nations and the legal removal of territorial integrity and connection among our villages have secured our confinement. Confinement opposes space, which, in turn, precludes freedom. Only in a free state can time be utilized to effect nationhood. The state justifies the concretized slicing and dicing of a First Nation's territory by pretending that Indigenous people were Neolithic, tribal, had no original confederacy, and thus had to be saved from themselves. The Canadian state has been busy deluding each village into believing it is a nation; it urges them to make real estate and governance deals as individual entities separate from the nation as a whole. The villagizing of our nations is a curtailment of space.

We still have our original cultural bundles. We still have our original concepts of authority, but we lack, first, the space to effect them; second, the time to restore the belief and trust among ourselves to accept them; and, third, the time to reconstruct our systems.

Indigenous people were oral. Knowledge keepers were trained rememberers. They were educated to recall the significant in what is said or done. If an action occurred, which might impact the generations to come, rememberers were schooled to recognize it, track its history, identify its direction, and commit it to memory. Others, thinkers, were trained to examine the action and assure that the direction the nation took in responding to the event did not lead to a divergence from the original path. Indigenous leaders and thinkers accounted to community, clan, and nation in determining what actions to take in response to whatever challenge the nation faced. The confederacies responded to change as a whole. A village had — has — no territorial authority over a nation, period.

In one sense, time is irrelevant. It matters not a whit how long or short the distance between the beginning and the end of a journey is. It matters not a whit what the obstacle to re-connecting with this journey is. Whether or not we are free to take charge of the destiny of our nation, as citizens we are still responsible for it. The time frame between this moment and the resumption of our duties is up to Canadians in their response to Indigenous calls for self-determination. On the other hand, time is critical. Humans require time and space to contemplate, to analyze, to foreshadow, to predict, and to make decisions.

Every human being possesses the capacity for creation, consciousness, concatenation, and curiosity at birth. People have a responsibility and an obligation to think deeply, to consider carefully, and to remain vigilantly curious when someone speaks — whether they do so about change or preservation, about the significant or the mundane. The limited space currently occupied by Indigenous people does not change the space to which we are

119

entitled. Canadians may believe we are no longer entitled to this space, but Canadian belief does not eradicate Indigenous claim to original space.

Sometimes to go forward, we need to return to the beginning.

Many Indigenous societies were grounded in concepts of continuous growth and transformation. Growth and transformation were seen as natural, desirable, and the doorway to the very best in human beings. No people transform without remaining connected to the original path. All people have memories. The uneducated Europeans who moved to North America remained Christian. In the course of their moving Christianity transformed. But even the transformation of Christianity did not diminish Christendom. Holding onto cultural memory makes us both radical and conservative. On the one hand, we find freedom in the context we inherit; on the other, we alter that context in order to expand our freedom. At the same time, we accommodate our sense of duty shaped by our original path and our very history. Accommodating our sense of duty governs our use of whatever leisure time we may have. This paradox of the relation of time and space to the disconnection of carrying out our duties and responsibilities has us stymied – but only temporarily.

We are not strangers to paradox. Disconnection from original pathways led to breaks in our continuum. The difference between the original disconnection and where we are at today is centred on both time and space and our relationship to both. Before colonialism, the conflict arose from within the community, the nation transformed and grew from the challenges it faced, but the conflicts of the past were not accompanied by occupation – the curtailment of time and space. Nor was our access to knowledge and or systems threatened. Our transformation was dependent not upon begging for access to space and time, but rather on our ability to grow and to recreate our societies, different but the same. Wars were fought, but then when they were over, there was a return to access to space and time.

Any attempt by Indigenous people to alter the relationship between colonizer and Native has led to settler violence against Indigenous people. Land is space and access to that space creates a place in time. Time, for us, is a critical illusion. Space is physical to the newcomer, subject to military occupation. For us, however, space is spiritual in the sense that it is there to establish relationship between ourselves and other beings so that we can sustain ourselves and augment our sense of the good life. Space is also political. For human beings to become intelligent, they need time and space.

The land is alive; it owns itself. And it possesses an agenda that assures its existence. The earth came into being and will someday go out of being. This is not our concern. Our concern revolves around our relationship to the earth. We are also concerned about the joint place of newcomers and original people in her life. The place we occupy in relation to the earth is tied to the promise of space made in exchange for executing agreements with her. These agreements are based on equal access to space, not merely for the humans but also other beings. Humans are no more entitled to privatize parts of the earth's body or militarily occupy and subdue her than they are entitled to privatize parts of another human's body. Yet, to Canada the earth is a vast space, a space to be bought, sold, inherited, exploited, and damaged at will; a space to be tampered with without regard to earth's own interests or her willingness and ability to sustain us when we violate our agreement with her.

Time is linear to the Western world and attached to it are assumptions of time as a progressive transformer. Concepts of intelligence are based on linear forward movement over time. There is no evidence, and certainly no proof, that the longer humans live the more human or the more intelligent they become. According to the Western world the farther backward in time people travel the less intelligent the humanity, as though having travelled through two millennia of arbitrary clock ticking somehow makes us more or less intelligent. Space figures into this formula in a strange way: the Neanderthals had smaller brains; therefore they were not as intelligent. It doesn't occur to Western science that perhaps the Neanderthals used their whole brain; it is already a matter of record that current humans do not. While the Neanderthals' brain size may have occupied less space, their realization or thoughtfulness might have been much greater than we imagine.

Conquest of space is thought to be achieved by civilizations more advanced than those conquered. Smarts then are hooked to violence and domination. Indigenous concepts of time, space and change carry no such arrogant mythology. We imagine the past as part of a continuum and at the same time as different from the present. This linear logic of "progress" does not affect our concepts of humanity. Disentitlement of time and space is not allotted to anyone. Raven is a transformer, but not all change is ipso facto good.

Access to time and space has not been our choice for some time. Still, Indigenous people take responsibility for the impact change has on individuals and families no matter who or what has affected the change. This is not the case for Canadians. "All that happened in the past," they say; "I didn't do that, my ancestors did." Or, "My ancestors weren't responsible because I am a recent immigrant." This kind of thinking assumes that their current occupation of our space is justified by patterns of colonization set in the past, that what happens now is not connected to the past, as though time and space could be rearranged according to the settlers' illusions about them, as though once disentitled we can never become entitled. The division of time between present and past becomes irrelevant when we examine the conditions of today. The dismemberment of Indigenous people remains a constant, and our future is governed by this condition. The future space we will occupy is hinged to upholding the mythology of the settlers' past.

Time demarcations do not exist in the consideration of present and future conditions. Space contains access to the means to be. We all have the right to be, but the demarcation of space as land that is subject to private property laws and laws limiting access to space have crippled our right to be. There is no projected alteration in the current system on the horizon.

An alteration in the conditions of life changes everything. It changes our physicality, emotionality, spirituality, as well as our intellect. It alters the cultural precepts and the social continuum upon which culture is rooted. It alters the sense of belief in the surety of future. To accept external control requires submission on the physical level, defeat on the spiritual level, apathy on the emotional level, and disbelief in the very intellect that guides.

Our belief in ourselves as human beings holding up history, carrying science, and possessing medical, social, economic and legal knowledge, as well as the resources that can address, resolve and reconcile us to continued survival, has been corroded. This was not our choice. Not one of our ancestors ever sat down and planned the violation of our families, our ways of life or the relinquishment of control over our survival.

This is the set up: every wave of immigrants faces exclusion and vicious exploitation by those born here. So each new wave is forced to busy themselves with survival. As such this country was built by people whose natural curiosity about others, whose natural concern for others, whose natural sense of social responsibility toward others are diminished by the absence of time – time for reflection, time for consideration, and time to be curious, to explore their new homeland. Further, their access to space is also curtailed in a variety of ways: legal immigrants, visa immigrants, educated but unrecognized immigrants, and cheap labour immigrants. The result is that their commitment to this country as a vast space is determined by these limitations. These limitations capture them inside a frame within which they cannot stand upright. Privilege is handed out in accordance with gender and colour. This keeps Asian and African Canadians fighting for their survival in a country that persecutes the homeless. The newcomers become unnaturally self-interested, not by choice but by condition.

It is in this context that Canada opted to transform those Natives who had survived the epidemics, the headhunting, the slaughter of food, the continuous and chronic appropriation of land and resources into English caricatures. This is now a Christian country. Although the Bible failed to account for our existence and the church doubted our humanity for two centuries, the Christians treated us as potential converts.

By the late 1800s the government determined to educate those of us who chose to follow the ways of Christian Canada. In the beginning school was elective. By 1920 school was compulsory. Residential schools, often viewed as a magnanimous response by the church to the refusal of the provinces to include us in their schools, were more concerned with saving souls than sharing knowledge. There was no space for our spiritual beliefs, our language, songs, relationships, or knowledge. The priesthood stripped us of our beliefs and introduced us to hard work. Our *si'yams* estimate that it took Indigenous people on the east and west coasts eleven and a half hours a week to produce the food, clothing, and shelter needed for their lives so that the afternoon, after the morning's work, was reserved for creative pursuits, thus leading balanced lives. They also recognize that hard work has destroyed us, for it leaves no space for our free and intellectual development. While our languages were forbidden in residential schools, English was not taught. Even at their closure, literature was not a subject taught in any residential school.

Without language humans cannot think or consider the context of their life. Without language they cannot reflect on their historical journey, sum up their thought, and create a vision of future. Without language they cannot view obstacles as surmountable, alter their being to suit new conditions, or strategize on the direction their lives must travel to resolve the everyday problems of life, much less the tyranny of domination. Without language humans cannot possess rational emotions. We have become victims of our own emotionality, not as adults but as wounded, almost languageless, children. Without language humans cannot conceptualize their sexuality, their physical or intellectual desires; their spiritual motivations become confused. Without language, law, moral fortitude, spiritual beliefs cannot serve humanity.

A good citizen once told me that we should just pick up ourselves up by the bootstraps and acquire wealth the same way every other Canadian does. I responded that I could not do that, not just because I lacked boots, but because neither I nor my ancestors came by boat to Canada and so deluding myself that I could retrace someone else's journey here would be ludicrous. Further, I lack the stomach to kill millions of humans, animals, plants, trees, or alter the entire prairies or burn millions of acres of other people's forests or cornfields, to create endless space for myself. I lack the stomach for the creation of a class system as exploitative as industrial capitalism.

125

Canada says it seeks to emancipate its *Native Nations*. It does so from the position of total access and control over space and time. It does so from the position of having military dominance. Indigenous people wish to wrest control of the terms of union from Canada, but many Canadians fear the terms we might establish. It is a conundrum. Fairness and inclusion on our terms are required in order for sharing to take place. And Canadians must desire to include us. But we have not had the time to determine what our terms are, so this dream is far from its realization. We are all severely damaged goods: on the one hand, Canadians are damaged by their history of plunder, the constant rationalization of their preponderant super-sized entitlement over space, and their control of time; on the other, Indigenous people are damaged by the absence of entitlement, so damaged that sorting this out will be a nightmare. But do it we must.

One millennium ago a group of men – correct me if I am wrong, but I read this some thirty years ago – gathered in a former officers' training camp in England and laid the foundation for a university. The intent was to gather together and discover knowledge wherever it presented itself. The goal was to study universal knowledge, to study the world, as they knew it. What a dream!

Western society is an old withered ghost; even as we speak it is continuously destroying itself in one way or another. It is a self-absorbed society that ignores some of its finest dreams. The desire for universal knowledge birthed a new sense of humanity, albeit somewhat perverted by capitalist colonial praxis. It ended with white men seeing themselves as possessing a primary claim to humanness and so they assumed intellectual and fiduciary control over the dream of universal knowledge for women and other men. They became the arbiters of knowledge credibility. This control governs the rightness, the wrongness, and even the proprietary right to the very possession of intellect. This view disables the dream of the universality of universities.

We need to let it go. There is knowledge outside these institutions. We need to open the doors and invite all knowledge in. Universities need to humble themselves to the existence of the knowledge in other people. Move over, create space and time to accomplish this universality of knowledge.

I believe that the knowledge of Indigenous people – resurrected, fleshed out and reconsidered in our new context – has a valuable role to play. I believe that, granted access and authority over space, we could rebuild our nations without anyone's assistance. I believe we are all personally responsible for resurrecting, reclaiming and reshaping the very notions of time and space that will invite the knowledge of others into our fields of study, so that a genuine sharing can occur.

127

INDIGENO
A

INDIGENOUS WOMEN
AND POWER

WE ARE NOT FEMINISTS; WE ARE GENDER COMPLEMENTARY.
Panel presentation, Indigenous Feminisms conference, Edmonton, 2006

I hear these words and I want to roll off my chair, gnash my teeth, and pound my fists. Although I believe the term gender complementary, coupled with the term governance, describes many societies of the past, it does not address our situation today. It unashamedly suggests that because we were gender complementary in the past we should not be feminists today. A different past does not form the foundation for opposition to feminism.

We are besieged by a patriarchal settler state. We have limited self-government at the state's good will. This patriarchal settler state has shown itself incapable of sustaining its good will. It is chronically shrinking our sovereignty, as well as the legal basis for it here and around the world. Furthermore, the position of Indigenous women is decidedly lower than the position of Indigenous men. The reduction of Indigenous women to second-class citizens within their communities includes the refusal of our nations to restore the gender complementary systems of the past. The issues facing women are ignored at both tribal and government levels. The authority of Indigenous women is not gender complementary in our communities. Family violence is about violence against women and children, but gender complementary advocates rarely address this phenomenon.

Gender complementary forms of power existed before patriarchal invasion, but they were dismantled. The boarding school system removed the children who were to be schooled in this system. Because we have not had the opportunity to study the original knowledge systems, they have not been maintained. Tribal leaders, mostly men, are not concerned with integrating the female complement to the original governing systems today, except in a few instances. The current tribal governments and national chiefs' organizations are not lobbying for investigation into gender complementary systems of power, nor are they strategizing to end male-on-female violence in our communities. Our women have been disempowered.

Restoring female positions of power is not what the gender complementary group of Indigenous women is pursuing. Rematriation and decolonization must be our response. Rematriation and the restoration of our original systems would be a feminist activity were the gender complementarists to ensure that our current tribal governments were actually gender complementary.

In 1997, Wendy Grant-John came close to winning the AFN Grand Chief position, but she conceded to Phil Fontaine after a two-hour discussion. I have a memory of some of the women being saddened by her concession, as they feared that women's issues would again take a back seat. How has it come to pass that women's issues exist separate from those concerning men? How has it come to be that the standard of what is normal for women is lesser for Indigenous women? Why have Indigenous women become the most violated, the least educated, and the most overworked and unprotected human beings in the history of Turtle Island? Indigenous Studies does not have a women's component.

Some uncomfortable questions need to be asked of our leadership. How many male chiefs have been elected based on solid knowledge of the past, particularly their personal past, and disclosure of their departure from the good life? How many of these chiefs have a vision of the future that includes women? How many voters know that their elders, long since dead, objected to the electoral process being imposed upon them? Today many of our communities have two sets of chiefs: the Canadian legally recognized chiefs and our original chiefs. The elected chiefs were imposed on us by Canada.

Women held power, were stood up as chiefs, and stood chiefs up — selected them. Today chiefs and councils are not elected after open discussion about integrity, spiritual cleanliness, or the capacity to respond to women. Even fewer ensure no harm comes to women and children. Chiefs are not selected based on our original world view.

At the end of the 1960s a group of young Indigenous people started a national self-determination movement on the West Coast of British Columbia as an alternative to the historic colonial oppression of Indigenous people in Canada. This was not the first movement intent on decolonization. The youth were unaware of history because access to history had been severed. From generation to generation Indigenous people struggle to hang on to threads of our past through repeated losses. For some 150 years on the West Coast of Canada we have survived with little connection to our past. The systematic attempt to decimate our population, disperse us and cut the threads of trade and commerce and social interaction among us, has included isolating us from Western trade and commerce. For a long time, we were denied access to Indigenous and

131

Western knowledge. Today, the first 12 years of education are based on Western knowledge.

Colonization has crippled the politics of governance and the political direction of the struggle to decolonize. Before I take up the banner of what men uphold as the ultimate goal – self-governance, an end to home rule by Canada and the U.S. – I need to retrace my own steps, the steps of my mother, grandmother, great-grandmother, right back to our original selves. I need to re-view their journeys and re-claim the cultural base upon which we organized our communities. I need to know how it came to pass that Indigenous women have become de-valued. I have a commitment to re-building the governing institutions in which Indigenous women held power alongside men.

Indigenous women have been asked to put their issues on the back burner as though the re-matriation of our governing structures – ending family and domestic abuse – were somehow separate and secondary to the nation-building process. We are being asked to stand on the barricades with men who violated our cousins, our sisters, and ourselves without speaking up. We are asked to do so in the interest of national unity, in the interest of the movement for self-determination, as though we are not really part of our national movement. We are being told that someday someone will recognize our loyalty and include us in the process of governance and freedom. We do so without knowing that in order to claim cultural integrity and national identity women must reclaim and take charge of the institutions that form our realm of governance.

Some of us are apprehensive about standing next to men who put violence against women and children on the back burner. Some Indigenous women became diehard feminists, and were ridiculed and ostracized by Indigenous men who have a vested interest in opposing feminism. I respect these women. I am one of them.

I believe we have been lied to not just by Western colonialists but by our leaders as well. It is convenient for the colonial system to hold up leaders that remain culturally blind.

I understand that men did not sit down one day and plot our violation. No one sitting in the living rooms of the villages jumped up and said, "Hey, I have an idea. Let's all get poor, get drunk, beat and rape our women and children." Still, although we committed ourselves to rebuilding our nations, the original governing structures of our communities and the place of women in them were not included in the agenda of political self-determination and economic development. When women bring the place and power of women forward, they are often shamed. The lies and treachery of the government men have uncovered reflect their male perspective. This deciphering of lies and treachery serves to bolster male forms of power and demean female governance.

I listened to an elder unravel the history of economic paralysis contrived by Canada to keep us poor. He named the tricks used by the Canadian legal system to ensure that each time the nation recovered from the deliberate impoverishment of Indigenous people they were slingshotted back into a state of poverty more desperate than before. At no time did this elder ever mention that the original economy was managed by women, that women were the great sociological governesses of the past that held jurisdiction over land and the wealth of families. The matriarchal aspects of our systems destroyed, the door was opened to inequity between men and women, and shame and violence became our lot.

Men from matriarchal societies often control family wealth and its distribution. When they divorce, men may retain the home and any wealth accumulated. If a man doesn't retain the home in divorce proceedings, his fellow men speak of him as having *given his home to his wife.* In a matriarchy, the home and the aggregate wealth of the family are not his to distribute or give. At the same time, these men tout their countries as matriarchal as though their women actually had control over the wealth and its distribution within the nation, as though violence against women and children did not exist.

Many men oppose Western human rights legislation coming into our communities, seeing it is a political invasion from the outside. It is not coincidental that they object to this particular invasion of Western law, which includes the protection and equal rights of women. These same men don't stand up, like the scholar Ron Hamilton did, and say to their fellow chiefs, "Shame on you for taking a post that women have not sanctioned." Unlike Ron Hamilton, these same men have not posited rematriation as the alternative to Western legal invasion.

In the vacuum of protection afforded I understand why women call for human rights to end the violence against them. I do not agree with the women who advocate equal rights for native women under Western laws, not because women do not deserve protection and equality but because human rights legislation will not give us that. Human rights laws mask the consolidation of sub-normative conditions for Indigenous people, just as they mask the entrenchment of substandard conditions for Canadian women. We must be protected. That is the bottom line. I am not in favour of throwing in the towel on matriarchal restoration. The least we can expect is to end, one way or another, the violent conditions under which we and our children live.

I want the best and the fullest life can present. Our past societies created human beings who were self-reliant, self-disciplined, loving, sharing, powerful beings. In our collectivity, we produced extraordinary individuals. In our spiritual maturity we created humans who relied on their own disciplinary structures as social beings, not the Canadian court system. They were subject to public scrutiny, accountability, and their personal conscience to lead their lives. Their systems of organization were cognizant of the smallness of humanity in the general web of life. Their personal spiritual significance in the governance and realization of life was studied and adhered to. Women had dominion over the social relations of the nation and the education of children. We were not merely executors who followed some curriculum estranged from life, but developed processes of education based on our living experience. We commanded the economy of our nations, the pedagogy of the young, and the governance of the relationships among citizens.

Western society, in general, accepts the estrangement of spiritual belief from emotional wellness and physical existence, and knowledge and intellectual development are divorced from the spirit. Although all white people look powerful to us, only a few control their world. Walk around the neighborhood of any white community and ask those you meet exactly what aspect of their society they can say they have direct influence over or manage. Not even the graduates of their cultural institutions manage the education process. We have inherited the castings from an educational mould that has little cultural benefits for us. This inheritance is rife with gender- and race-based inequity along the social, political, economic, cultural and spiritual planes. Canadian class-, race- and gender-based inequities share this history.

In a pyramid society, the lower layers seem to struggle for the benefits of the layer just above them. Many white women want the advantages accorded white men. Many Indigenous men want the advantages accorded white women, and so on. The images we have of white men are distorted to begin with. We believe that white men struggle from a place of power. Yet their power is rooted not in themselves but in their society's economic

entitlement to the spoils of capitalism and their mutual acceptance of their power shared among themselves. This is pretty much
the only power they have. They have more stuff than we do, but
then they had an unfair boost up. The respectability white men
enjoy is connected to the lateral disrespect among us. Even those
who object to our self-disrespect accuse white male power as the
culprit. Like a group of siblings, we holler unfair to one another
rather than eradicate this unfairness. As Indigenous women,
we look at the conditions we are immersed in and view human
rights legislation as our only hope, rather than seeing it for the
cheap knock off that it is. It is dangerous to request something
less than what we need.

Divorce often leaves white women living at a much lower standard than before. If they lose their homes, there is no cultural
tradition that would encourage their relatives to take them in. In
most of our communities it is still assumed that when a woman
divorces her husband she keeps the home and the children unless
she chooses not to raise them herself. It is also assumed in many
communities that children have choices too. Further, the woman's
relatives often take the family in until she is able to stand on her
own feet.

Human rights protect violent men better than they protect
women.

The more Canadian legal sensibilities invade our communities,
the greater the corrosion of the rights of children and women. In
white society whether or not a woman gains custody of her children is often based on her financial ability to provide for them.
Whether or not she keeps her home is dependent upon how much
she paid into it, the credibility of her lawyer, and the effort her
lawyer makes on her behalf. The investment of homemaking has
no dollar value and is not factored in.

Indigenous women are chronically underemployed and under-paid. Almost half of Indigenous women in Canada do not legally marry, nor do they divorce through the courts. Many of the men plead no contest in divorce proceedings and women keep their homes. The loss of the husband's income is generally nominal as most Indigenous men are not high-wage earners. What we lose is the valuable assistance in the rearing of the children if the man was a decent father. The good mother scenario, which invades many white women's futures, doesn't affect our right to our children in the same way. We have more choices than white women do, though we have considerably fewer assets. We have more to fear from the state taking our children than our ex-husbands.

Those who are calling for human rights generally live outside our communities and are educated; they have greater opportunities for employment than do most Indigenous people, be they men or women. The human rights response to inequity will most likely enhance their place in our world. With human rights laws comes the praxis.

The current band and tribal government structures, community agencies and non-governmental organizational structures through which Western power can be acquired exist at the good will and expenditure of Canada. Because the financial capability of Canada to continue funding these structures is imploding, cutbacks to the Indigenous people are and always have been Canada's first response. Funding Indigenous people is always contingent on the leftovers Canada has after it provides for its own people. Canada's capacity for economic recovery after each economic downturn is hinged on imperialism and global economics, not just good will.

Our understanding of the foregoing must be rooted in a clear perception of our current reality. I believed our elders when they said *reality is always false.* I was very young and inexperienced

137

when I asked my grandfather why we promoted kindness and gentleness toward white people when the truth was that they apathetically watched us die or some of them actively promoted or participated in our death. It strikes me as inhuman to watch a people die or promote and participate in their death. His answer was, "The truth is everyone is born with a great ability to connect; they are curious; they are creative, and they are capable of great consciousness. Imperfections and poison fed to them resulted in this reality. Further, underneath the mask the spirit desires to rid itself of the poison. We need to continue to feed them a different meal until they change, and that will alter our reality. The truth remains the same, no matter what the condition of the people."

Reality then is transitory. At the time that I asked this question, I was still burning with rage at the memory of white youth terrorizing our reserves and the many attempted rapes by white men wrought upon my body. Today our children, especially our daughters, face the same violence and rape, but some of the faces have changed. Today, men of colour join with white men to perpetuate violence and rape. The outside world's belief in our lack of value has invaded us, but there is no truth in this belief.

Racism, sexism and underclass conditions, which are culturally based, invade our perceptions. They invade our perception of economic development, of political decisions, of making federal legislation, of governance, education and social development. They create a transitory false reality for Indigenous men and women. Just as we search our past for our original perceptions, these colonial perceptions invade our homes. My response to these conditions is a feminist response.

The colonial reality for Indigenous men is loss of power in their relationship with Canada. The reality for women is loss of power over the social relations inside our families and the internal world of our nations. The reality for everyone is systemic breakdown. This breakdown is held in place by the beliefs we hold about ourselves and the transference of those beliefs onto one another. We can change all that.

Supposing men did not believe in the loss of power in their relationship to Canada. Supposing that they went hunting when it was time to hunt, regardless of the laws Canada attempted to impose upon them. Supposing they decided to simply cut down logs in their national territory to build homes, and controlled access to the logs in our original territories. Supposing they insisted that Canada prove its ownership of the logs, fish, or animals in our territories. Supposing every Indigenous man in Canada ignored the need for a piece of paper proving transfer of title, ownership, or rights to use the land. Should Indigenous men decide to act this way, their action will contravene the central belief that we have dragged home, namely that Canadian law is valid and superior to our own. Canada for the most part cannot prove ownership or jurisdiction over our original homelands. The best it can prove is our defeat through death.

Supposing women decided tomorrow that there would be zero tolerance for violence. Supposing we joined together and informed men that they would be removed from our homes if they chose to be violent. Supposing we decided to remove violent men rather than agreeing to give up our homes and build shelters for abused women and children. We would be in violation of Canadian human rights law. Supposing we said our laws clearly state that the home, the village gardens, the river's fish, the village itself is the dominion of women and we as women are assuming responsibility of dominion over our homes and villages. Should women do this, the need for Canadian human rights legislation and the organizations that advocate such rights will be rendered redundant.

There is a journey to belief but there is also a journey that can lead to that belief's undoing. It is not self-governance to take up another nation's legal system and entrench it in our nations. There is no cultural integrity in guiding our actions based on external world beliefs. There is no spirituality when it is rooted in conditions created by external spiritual beliefs. The restoration of female institutions of power management and authority, choice, permission and jurisdiction and our assumption of responsibility over the foregoing is what nationhood is all about.

Turtle Island supported a number of nations whose cultures varied. In the Stó:lō origin story, opportunism is seen as unconscious. Flora, fauna and humans begin as energy. Thought/power/hidden being/emotion came with our physical being. As energy, we were causing problems in the sky world for one another. Eventually, things came to such a pass that raven and eagle called the sky world to the first great gathering. A conscious decision to take on physical being was made. From this came our transformation from energy to human, animal, plant, water and stone. Stone alone was innocent in all of this and so it alone does not have to go through the life/death transformation process. Stone just is.

This story is told without judgment. We as humans were creating the most havoc therefore we were seen as the most opportunistic, thus we had a greater responsibility to come to grips with the impact and effect of consequences. We were given tools by great thinkers over time, thinkers who had learned from life, who transformed what they had learned into raven stories of transformation and growth. Our ancestors recited them to us during the long winter months of leisure. This kind of opportunism is seen as neutral most of the time; sometimes it is positive, other times negative, and so it is hard to judge it. It is a constant, not a variable. What is variable is our capacity for altering our being.

Humans can temper this inherent opportunism in any direction. This direction is acknowledged without judgment or condemnation in our origin story. In our first war story, the story of the war between the bird and animal kingdom, the personal opportunism of the bat met with dire consequences. This first war was inspired by hardship, which led to violence and opportunistic lifestyles of murder, infanticide and cannibalism. The opportunism of the collective was rooted in the survival of the few.

Bat's opportunism, however, took individualistic shape during the process of resolution. There is recognition that opportunism has little place in the process of resolution of conflict. Wrapped around the recognition of this capacity is an understanding of the conditions under which the optimum capacity for human positive expression and contribution is delineated. Survival is a problem for all beings. But this problem also offers us the choice to take advantage of it, push up our best thinking collectively to solve it, or stay stuck in it, by employing collective thinking (good will) to ensure we are on the winning side of the problem. This war is seen pragmatically as an obstacle to the most beneficial human expression, direction and interaction.

We are not against war per se under any and all circumstances. War is the inability of humans to come to a creative collective resolution. War is an expression of the under-development of human beings. War is seen as defensive, not aggressive, as fear-based, not for the purpose of conquest. It is seen as an obstacle to the positive internal development of nations that engage in it. Hence after engagement in war, the men who killed were stood at the edge of the forest and cleaned themselves off before re-entering the village. Internal peace was primary. Wars occurred over jurisdiction, sometimes trade, and during hardship when survival was threatened and one nation invaded the territory of another in order to ensure the survival of their clan. In a war, the usual governance is abrogated and all systems focus on winning the war and contributing to the war effort. The cleaning off ceremony calls upon the warriors and the villagers to restore the humanistic peace functions in the community, i.e., to restore the power of women.

We respect other nations that are prepared to go to war to ensure the survival of their people. What we do not respect is conquest-based war. Processes for demarcating territorial survival areas were developed by men. The jurisdiction of each nation is a negotiated space. Culture and governing structures maintain these spaces; conquest interrupts the negotiation of space. Language, diplomacy and discipline are required to respect that space.

If you have hard truths to offer up to someone make sure the voice is soft, the language beautiful and that you protect the dignity of the other. When the storm clears, make sure you all see sunshine. This voice was muted through our disconnection from our communities, so now we employ the European rule of *if you can't say anything nice, don't say anything at all* or *get rid of him/her.* For the former, all hell can break loose and the receivers lock their throats — the chest tightens and the arms cross, the legs shake, tongues are bitten to avoid saying anything at all. It doesn't occur to anyone that maybe we ought to reclaim the language of peace, exploration and resolution.

The laws that governed Indigenous peoples were recognized and embraced by each citizen as the basis for mature decision-making and we all wanted to be seen as mature. These laws were rooted in the social praxis and experience of each nation. Each nation carefully structured the lives of their children to ensure they measured up to expected conduct. Each child became a deep thinking child with a consciousness that was fair, just, sharing and caring. Oracy, the stories of behaviour and consequence, was the major disciplinary force that was exacted upon the children. Women were in charge of this process from beginning to end. Women maintained the systemic commitment to earth and life.

Access to food, clothing, and shelter were absolute. Rather than deny children food for undisciplined behaviour, children who were ill-disciplined were viewed as inadequately fed — herbal teas were administered to restore the good health they were entitled to. Physical prowess, agility and strength were seen not as matters of individual idolatry or competition, but as the necessary conditions for emotional, mental, spiritual and physical well being each individual was entitled to. Women governed the distribution of all goods.

The earth was seen as a living entity, not as an object of conquest and exploitation. The rhythms of the earth — its natural capacity for self-rejuvenation — were recognized. We did not live all year round in the same place. If during one season the tide rose and during another it fell we accounted for that and altered our behaviour to accommodate the waters. Likewise we did not live on the flood plains — we moved back from them. We did not expect the river to move. We studied animal and plant behaviour and aligned ourselves with them. We ate seasonally in accordance with the rhythms of the earth. We were careful to preserve what was not available to us all year round in a way that was the least intrusive upon the earth, the being and the rhythms established by those beings that sustained us. Respect for the earth and respect for women were bound together, and organized women governors wielded the power to enforce this.

Culturally, the earth itself was the only being women accommodated. Women did not accommodate the desires of children. Our beliefs and our lifestyle arose from those beliefs called upon us to utilize every part of the plant and animal we killed in an effort to support ourselves without destroying the relationship of the being to the earth. The material culture that arose out of these beliefs was largely biodegradable. Waste was returned to the earth; it was not dumped in landfill sites. The laws governing production precluded the invention of items that might disrupt the rhythm of the earth. Our creativity was structured within very narrow guidelines of respect, consideration of beauty, of architecture without waste. We took mature trees, not all the trees; we turned them to houses and beautiful story poles to adorn these houses. All our tools, clothing, and utensils were contrived from these mature trees. The cutting down of these mature trees led to further plant and life development and made space for younger trees to become mature. Women had the power and authority to make sure this conduct was adhered to.

We did not sell these trees to foreigners; we expected foreigners to house themselves from what was available to them in the same way that we did. The house was made beautiful from within the context of our non-intrusive survival. Taste — aesthetics — was disciplined by making the most of the least. We had useless baubles just like any other culture, but they were made from the waste that existed in the territory. We did not haul goods from other places to create jewelry. There is nothing useless about a carved set of flutes, hair combs, spoons, feast bowls, but once you have one, the need ends. It was inconceivable for us to create art out of new materials. It was inconceivable that we could invent electricity because the damming of rivers ran counter to our spiritual belief that the river itself was alive, and hence had a perfect right to be. It was inconceivable that we could take it upon ourselves to dam a river because the flooding was a nuisance. Better to move our homes further upland, away from the river's swelling banks. Many of the agrarian peoples noted that flooding was ultimately beneficial to their gardens. The longhouses were in the centre of the villages, the gardens surrounded the houses, and the river was at least a mile from the edge of the fields. Women and men maintained the gardens.

Our entire medical practice centred on the specific nature of plant and animal life and was governed not by symptoms of illness, which appear in decrepit bodies, but rather through symptoms that appear before the body becomes decrepit. What good does it do to study decrepitness? The slightest change in character was fed. Restlessness, impatience, change in breath, voice, behaviour, all were regarded as signs of impending illness. Emotional problems are symptoms of an unhealthy, weak body. Medical theory was largely developed by women.

A crying baby is a hungry baby, hungry for food, physical attention, emotional support, and spiritual or intellectual stimulation. Thus, special attention was paid to the food its mother received during nursing. The allo-mothering systems – the aunts, grandmother's cousins, uncles, cousins and siblings – the partner and other community members assisted in attending to the child, and thus ensured the mother's well-being. Mother and child were attended to physically and medicinally with a myriad of teas that prevented the development of pre-menstrual syndrome and took care of post-partum depression, both curses of the twentieth century. The development of young boys into manhood was attended to with a higher consumption of protein, additional physical exercise, guided risk-taking ventures and increased interaction with the men of the village. The health and peace of the nation rested on the accepted authority and knowledge of its women and children.

Youth was considered a time of decision-making about the specific contributions to community and wellness that the individual would make as an adult. It took the entire efforts of the

145

village to coordinate, manage and regulate the above processes. In particular it took the women, who were educated and healthy, who had been vested with the belief and authority of the village, to ensure that this happened.

The earth is not a stupid insensitive lump floating numbly throughout space to be conquered, pillaged, and plundered at will, but rather an intelligent being with its own journey, its own way of resolving illness within itself. We see her as a woman. It is up to humans to become familiar with the patterned behaviour of the earth and ally ourselves with these patterns to augment our life or suffer the consequences.

The structure of authority was an extension of the above belief systems. The relationship between male and female was seen as requiring balance. The relationship between earth and all beings was seen as requiring nurtured balance. The climate of the earth and the conditions of water and land were indicators of balance or imbalance. We strived to live within the limits of this balance. Jurisdiction between men and women was parceled out in accordance with the balance we saw in the natural world. Men had jurisdiction over the external world insofar as they promoted and nurtured balanced engagement of the natural world. Women had jurisdiction over harvesting of food in so far as they nurtured the balanced engagement of the foods.

It was incumbent upon the village to ensure that men and women acquired the knowledge of the plant, animal and sky world to plan the preservation, distribution and consumption of food. Food was not seen as consumed for comfort or aesthetics, but was rather a matter of necessity. Despite the fact that such goods as sugar cane, cocoa, coffee, and chocolate derive from North American plants, until the twentieth century Indigenous people did not consume them as sweets. Permission to choose what you ate at any given moment existed within the confines of necessity for good health and high energy.

Consultation between men and women took place about the location of wild foods and the protection of the women by the men during the harvesting of food. The ceremonious governing of the pre-harvesting generally fell within the realms of those who had direct jurisdiction over the lands and waters from which the food was harvested. Before harvesting, the affect of the harvest on the being was considered.

It is a direct invasion of the general health and well-being of our communities and a violation of our eco-principles to eat according to taste. A body that eats for taste is not a sane, rational or strong body. We have no ceremony for passing from healthful necessity and austerity-driven eating to the right to eat purely for taste, or for emotional comfort. We have no ceremony for women who wish to abdicate their authority over food preparation, distribution or consumption. We have no stories extolling the virtues of sugar, drug, or alcohol consumption. We have no ceremony for extolling the virtues of male domination over female jurisdiction over food and home. We have no ceremony entitling children to eat as they please. There are no teachings to support the foregoing and no stories advising it.

The loss of women's authority is directly connected to the loss of male jurisdiction and their restriction to the village of their husbands advanced by the reservation system and the Indian Act. Their loss of access to tribal territory, their loss of their role as caretakers of the nation, and their loss of their right as mothers to determine their villages' wellness destroyed the social fabric of our world.

Our knowledge was passed on by word of mouth. It was during the course of our daily interaction that we taught our children. Through their daily lives, through the hearing of stories, their

147

participation in ceremonies, feasts and song and dance, our children acquired the knowledge base necessary to wield the authority they were to acquire later in life. The process of pro-active, inter-village learning continued long after adulthood. The connection between good behaviour, personal wellness, and a thriving natural environment remained unbroken until residential school and compulsory public education. The outlawing of our culture disrupted family, clan and political systems necessary to pass on knowledge. The loss of access to land bases from which to access food was contingent on the loss of female authority.

So thorough was the erosion of female authority that few women today can make decisions within their home free of consulting even the smallest child without reprisal. So thorough has the erosion of male authority been that most men now cannot secure food, shelter and livelihood without permission from Canadian authorities. If women resumed their original roles and took up their hereditary authority, we could bring an end to the colonial misery we are currently in. Men too would have to find a way to reclaim their authority and establish good relation with their communities.

Human beings cannot live without self-determination: we still do not have the right to assume responsibility for our homelands, nor do we have access to the wealth of these homelands or the right to secure life for our families from the earth's bounty without some kind of permission from Canada. Humans cannot live without choice and jurisdiction, and we lack that. The rate of death among us is directly related to the absence of choice and jurisdiction. The absence of wellness in our villages in our daily lives attests to this.

At the same time that disease was killing us, white men appropriated the cultural knowledge of women. It was not extinguished among us until compulsory education in industrial training schools limited our knowledge base by severing the students from their teachers. During this time, white men wrote down much of our original medicinal knowledge. While our children's knowledge base atrophied, practicing medicine within our communities was outlawed. The colonizer still has the authority to determine who may practise medicine in our communities today; they still retain the authority to determine what medicine is and what it is not. Jurisdiction over the quality of our common life was the singular most powerful usurpation of power by the colonizer. In fact, many working women find that they have more authority outside the home on the job than they do inside the home.

I am an Indigenous feminist.

Unlike those who dismiss Indigenous feminists for being influenced from outside our world (as though men were not), I believe feminism is a response to the Canadian-state orchestrated invasion of our areas of jurisdiction by Indigenous men. The establishment of the chief electoral system that initially did not allow women to participate is not connected to community, but rather it is connected to the federal government. Unlike those who condemn women for operating outside our culture, I understand that they are operating from within the current reality. Indigenous feminism seeks the restoration of matriarchal authority and the restoration of male responsibility to these matriarchal structures to reinstate respect and support for the women within them. The dismissal of Indigenous feminists silences the whole.

The desire to explore our past jurisdiction is going to flag if we anticipate meeting with negative results. We are experiencing a strange development in our communities. There has been an odd comingling of men and women around state-orchestrated male power and internally orchestrated versions of original society that is male focused. Men know a great deal about diplomatic relations with non-Indigenous people. Reviving original male power without restoring original female power leads to a distortion of who we once were, and thus to an imbalance of power. Men may know a lot about negotiation, politics, war and land struggle, but without access to female knowledge of conduct, they run the risk of dragging their bundles of knowledge into intra-personal familial relations that are outside their bounds of original authority.

In order to be heard and acknowledged women need to pick up the same bundle and engage in similar processes with men. In our communities this has led to the establishment of camps, volatile factions that have negative effects on children. Before we can freely exercise choice as women, we must remove the risk of male opposition. When we speak from our own knowledge, someone must be there to hear us, pick up on the truth of our words, and pursue the trail they point to in an appropriate fashion.

Most of the men and women who are negotiating with the Canadian federal and provincial governments were elected in a blind contest in which the strategies for achieving the vision of our nations and the breadth and extent of authority our nations granted to individual men and women were not discussed. In effecting nationhood in the long run, the relations with the outside world are tertiary, while the relations within our nations are primary. To hobnob with the Canadian state officials under Canadian rules of engagement while our nations' children perish is just plain shameless. This is not to say that none of the current chiefs have integrity; rather, it means that their integrity is not discussable; their views are not negotiated with the communities. Thus the conditions of our villages — despair and inequity, the lack of female and child safety — are not priority issues, and so they do not figure into the budget Canada hands our nations.

A British Columbian Indigenous provincial leader once battered his common-law wife so badly she had to be hospitalized for three months. He escaped charges because she was convinced that divorcing him was her best option. His colleagues affirmed his position after one woman called for his resignation. The discussion centred on his contribution to self-government and land claims. No discussion took place on the nature of the government such a man could advocate. Nor was there any discussion about the absence of commitment to ending violence against women in our world. The assumption was that his career, male-based self-government, and male-based land claims took precedence over Indigenous women's safety.

According to a study by the women of the North West Territories, 90% of women and female children experience sexual assault. This means that the sexual assault of girls that begins in childhood does not end in adulthood. Women do not choose a life of sexual assault over their children and themselves; in fact, if they acquire the means to determine the social relations within their communities, the first practice they stop is that of sexual assault. We have fallen into this morass of maltreatment unconsciously. Indigenous and western feminism will go a long way to lifting us out.

We must gather ourselves together as women. We must reclaim our sociological, psychological, medical, and ecological knowledge. We must determine the health standards for our nations and implement them by exercising our hereditary authority.

I challenge men to make real their commitment to the matriarchal and co-lineal structures of the past. *This is a feminist act.*

We must also have equality between the genders outside the home. This too is a feminist act. For Indigenous women feminism is not just about equality outside the home, but also power within our nations. Authority outside the home is limited. If you prescribe to the industrial capitalist system, you may also believe that men have sufficient authority outside the home. I just don't happen to believe this trade off works, and I am not keen on industrial capitalism.

My feminism does not contradict Western feminism. If we choose to engage with the outside world, we will need Western feminist approaches, but the restoration of our nations is going to require a deeper kind of feminism. We need to resist the preponderance of traditional male power in the absence of female authority. We need to object to men who call for government-to-government relations that do little to revive the female governing structures within our nations.

GLOBALIZATION AND INDIGENOUS WRITING

ALTHOUGH GLOBALIZATION HAS LONG BEEN a hot topic, few Indigenous cultural creators have considered its impact on the arts. Common understanding holds that globalization is economically motivated and technologically driven by corporate forces based in a handful of countries. The world's Indigenous people have historically been excluded from access to technology. Modern technology arose out of capitalism, an exclusive club designed to keep at bay those who weren't at the starting line when the conquest of Indigenous populations began. Globalization is culturally imperious in regions that are already dominated by European cultural values, frameworks and education systems. This lines up with the business of literary production, for literature remains tied to imperial concepts that by nature exclude those who are not white, male and upper class. For Indigenous people globalization alters our reality insignificantly.

It is a known fact that the exploitation of Indigenous peoples has benefited the exploiters. We don't have to look far. In North America it is Indigenous people who remain the most exploited people in Canada, the U.S. and Mexico. We are continuously excluded from engaging in trade with one another, free of interference from imperial governments, and we are still restricted from participating fully in the local and global economy. We are forced to accept leftovers from the home countries.

Senegalese El Hadji Guissé, Working Group on Indigenous Populations expert, speaks to this: "those who lived on land rich with oil...moved to arid lands. The destruction of natural habitats and their fundamental rights, their right to live in a healthy environment was destroyed."

I am not looking to the U.S. or any other imperial country for solutions. I do not apologize for having little or no confidence in the law, politics and democratic tradition of a country that murdered 20 million people to establish itself, enslaved 50 million people to birth itself, and denied democracy to over half its population until 80 years ago.

How does this affect Indigenous People?

There are few universities developed by Indigenous people or rooted to Indigenous knowledge and culture. There is no protection of Indigenous knowledge, culture or oral story. There is no protection of Indigenous rights even in the constitution of Canada. Courses taught in Indigenous programs are mostly developed by Western educated people and are often driven by Canada's own self-interests. What is taught in such programs is usually centred on what Canada did to us, which is, properly speaking, about Canadian white male studies.

Most Western stories must have a beginning, middle and end; a protagonist and an antagonist; and a plot that contains conflict. Further, tragedy requires that a person of the upper class must fall to the lower class. In this tradition, hierarchy is perpetuated and maintained despite the resistance of such authors as N. Scott Momaday, Louise Erdrich, Janet Campbell-Hale, Jeannette

Armstrong, Thomas King, Beatrice Culleton, Sherman Alexie, Marilyn Dumont, Drew Hayden Taylor, and Richard Van Camp, to name just a few.

On the other hand, our students have the opportunity to learn about Indigenous history through the Internet, to write about it and to come to terms with original stories from the Indigenous world. They also have the opportunity to learn the music, spoken word, and new song development going on all over the Indigenous world. We are no longer restricted to small tribal origins; today we have access to global knowledge.

In order to learn, children must see themselves in the stories they read or the films they watch; they must hear themselves in the songs they listen to. This will be possible, if our communities take it upon themselves to give their children an Indigenous education.

In most of our societies, kings, knights, or princes did not exist. In our stories, plot was not the point, and the lead character was usually some mythical figure or messenger that was there to assist us in facing ourselves. The imposition of standardized religious and cultural views that adhere to the worship of beings higher than them need not be part of our children's education process. The higher being theory is not the only theory of humanity. Employing protagonists and antagonists that disrupt the concept of respect for every man and woman that underlies many of our stories is not the only road to mastering English. The Internet is making it possible for the world to purchase outside the box.

All aspects of the universe are the subjects of Indigenous story. The fantastic is deployed in our stories to appeal to youth as well as elders. Globalization is opening doors to viewing our stories, even if only on the periphery of the mainstream as Indigenous people throughout the world gain access to the Internet. Indigenous people from many countries are now reading each other.

Because European standards pervade the definitions of what literature is, what constitutes story, what is marketable and what is worthy, there is always a great deal of pressure on Indigenous people to write stories from outside their cultures. It doesn't have to be this way if we begin to think globally. Indigenous society is an ever widening circle that includes myriad possibilities of human folly, human interaction with the environment, and animal and flora concerns, and holds the possibility of reconciliation. We need to become more inclusive in our sense of what is and what is not Indigenous, and break down our own national and tribal barriers.

Story is the foundation of culture, whether that story is oral or written. The opportunity to conjure story is a luxury enjoyed by those who have time on their hands.

While globalization brings to bear the weight of imperialism, and exacerbates the already invisibilized conditions of Indigenous people, we can also turn the tables by connecting to one another and strengthening our sense of self. The Internet and computer technology may have begun as a means of ensuring corporate preponderance, but they are capable of bringing about human collaboration and coalescence.

It is imperative that we use these resources to the fullest. We are pushed to the limits to create the kind of stories that will halt the murder of First Nations' women, the teachers of our culture and previously the governors of our communities. We are driven to reclaim our knowledge and care for our families, which suffer desertion and violence from without and within, while fighting the affects of massive neglect, cultural invasion and continued invizibilization. Although we are not the arbiters of technology, we can access it. Through it we can become the arbiters of culture, education and story once again. This may be difficult to accomplish in rural regions where access to technology is limited, but it is becoming increasingly possible to do so, for example, through libraries. As Indigenous people we need to create community access to computers and the Internet in every village.

Globalization is not necessarily synonymous with the absence of curiosity about anything that is not non-Western. This does not have to be our legacy. Stories, rooted in Indigenous story structure, objectives, form and style, while they may not be attractive to corporate globalized booksellers, can still be available to us. Since the advent of chain and corporate bookstores in Canada small progressive bookstores, feminist-run bookstores, and Indigenous-run bookstores have closed. They have been usurped by Chapters/Indigo that rarely carry Indigenous literature. Indeed, they barely carry Canadian literature. Most of my own books sell on the Internet. The sad commentary on that reality is that in order to purchase from the Internet you must have a credit card, which means you must be employed, which excludes 60% of Indigenous people, the vast majority of whom are young. But this sad reality just makes it all the more important for Indigenous communities to purchase, sell, and make available Indigenous literature and cultural products through small community libraries and band book sales.

This is not a pipe dream. Band offices could transform the role of receptionist mini-bookseller and mini-librarian without disrupting the work of governance. A powwow, a table in the corner, a book case against a wall, all this can provide space to feature different Indigenous writers each month.

Our children are hungry to see themselves portrayed in our literature. Our bands need to see the significance of Indigenous story as a crucial element in the wellness of our children's lives and think beyond just governance and bureaucracy. There is literally thousands of Indigenous writers worldwide. In our local schools, Indigenous books should take preference.

157

Stories are good medicine. Our children need to learn through story and to create story. The possibility of publishing through the Internet should be exploited on behalf of our children. Our youth have plenty of talent but little opportunity to learn from those who came before them. By including Indigenous writers in local schools, creating libraries and conducting book sales, bands could promote the development of this talent. Teachers could assist students in learning to read like a writer as articulated by Maxine Prose in her Pulitzer Prize winning work, *Reading like a Writer*. Or they could use traditional story games: use a story to create a different story. Bands, as solvent councils, could order via the Internet. In this way, the Internet and globalization technology can serve our youth.

Indigenous writers around the globe must conjure ways to get our stories to our children. Projects like the Good Medicine Project, which puts original stories on the web and encourages youth to *tell the story back, different but the same*, could also take place in the classrooms, in our communities, even around our kitchen tables. The foregoing story game is the source of my creative sensibility around original story. Indigenous studies must include Indigenous authors from K-12 and beyond.

Although we cannot find Indigenous literature in urban bookstores since globalization has eradicated many of the small progressive and independent bookstores, publishers do put our work out. We need our communities to become active in purchasing, making available Indigenous stories to our youth and encouraging them to study and write from those who came before. We must insist on libraries in Indigenous communities that privilege Indigenous writing.

It is my sincere hope that indigenous people globally seize the opportunity to broaden their horizons, study one another, and begin to communicate with one another. The world is in trouble.

Globalization is not necessarily the appropriate response. Indeed, capitalism and imperialism need to be undone, but that doesn't look like it is going to happen quickly. In the meantime we need to do the best we can under the circumstances.

As a broader form of the old colonial exploitation systems, globalization cannot address the troubles of the world unless we understand who all the parties are. Indigenous people should be central to any effective change, development and/or solution to the problems of war, internecine or imperial, environmental degradation and social exclusion.

For those of us who refuse to come to the Imperial table empty handed, our literatures are a beginning point to understanding and seeing the world through different sets of eyes. Imperial systems are no longer capable of seeing past the blood lust for wealth if they were ever capable of seeing past that.

It is my desire and my dream that such authors as Linda Tuhiwai Smith, Jeannette Armstrong, Maria Campbell, Marilyn Dumont, Doris Pilkington and a host of Indigenous writers from all over the world will continue to entertain us, educate us and shape us.

ORATORY
COMING TO THEORY

THEORY. If it can't be shown, it can't be understood. Theory is a proposition, proven by demonstrable argument. Argument: evidence, proof. Evidence: demonstrable testimony, demonstration. We are already running into trouble. There are a number of words in the English language with no appreciable definition. Argument is defined as evidence; proof or evidence is defined by demonstration or proof; and theory as a proposition proven by demonstrable evidence. None of these words exist outside of their interconnectedness. Each is defined by the other.

Oratory, on the other hand, is unambiguous in its meaning. Oratory: place of prayer; to persuade. This is a word we can work with. We regard words as coming from original being — a sacred spiritual being. The orator is coming from a place of prayer and as such attempts to be persuasive. Words are not objects to be wasted. They represent the accumulated knowledge, cultural values, and the vision of an entire people or peoples. We believe the proof of a thing or idea is in the doing. Doing requires some form of social interaction, and thus story is the most persuasive and sensible way to preserve the accumulated thoughts and values of a people.

Among European scholars there is an alienated notion that maintains that theory is separate from story, and thus a different set of words is required to "prove" an idea than to show one. Yet if you take the story out of any school textbook the student is left without proof for the positing of any information. Science textbooks refer to story as an example. The component parts of every example are the same: there is a plot line, tension, a climax, and a conclusion. Mathematical problems have the same components. The tension in math is one number versus another, whether they are added or subtracted, multiplied or divided. The tension is resolved into some sort of conclusion that is different from the two numbers representing the original tension. The numbers have names and the plot line (what to do next) is provided by the theorems and formulae that the student accepts by custom (culture). Since nothing can actually disappear or be conjured into existence, the business of subtraction and addition is fiction (story), though it is generally referred to as abstract thought. Numbers lack character (human form). But when we propose them as a problem, confronting real people, they take on character and human content (social interaction): the number of trees cut to make one edition of a newspaper, for example, or the number of hungry children in a Canadian City.

Academicians waste a great deal of effort deleting character, plot, and story from theoretical arguments but, really, they just change the words. By referring to instances and examples, previous human interaction and social events, academics convince themselves of their own objectivity and persuade us that story is no longer the foundation of abstract thought. However, our intellectuals (elders) believe that "$E=MC2$" means nothing outside of human interaction. Likewise, the concept of zero means nothing — pardon the pun. It is represented by a circle devoid of life.

This has no meaning for the living or the dead, but it is useful in teaching young children to interact in a positive social fashion. A child learns that if she doesn't obey the laws of the people, she will suffer great nothingness in her interaction with women and men. As a child I was aware that beans could leave, could change their location, but they could not be taken away completely, so when the teacher asked "If I take two beans away, how many are left?" the answer was still two. If she had asked how many I was short, I would have said two. She wanted nothing or 0 to be the answer, which of course is fiction. When I understood that math was about fiction, I began to excel.

Enough of that talk. There is a story in every line of theory, not in our capacity to theorize. It seems a waste of words to dispassionately delete the characters from the plot line, tension, and conclusion. It takes a great deal of work to erase people from theoretical discussion, and it is painful.

A theoretical proposition advanced by John Stuart Mill in his little essay on utilitarianism seems the foundation of theory, law, politics, sociology and culture in North America: "All men are motivated by pleasure and pain." He also qualifies that pleasure is not about sexual expression or enjoyment. Mill first has to delete his passion from his theory and his life. The great problem with that, of course is that people think being is a passionate thing.

People are extremely disinclined toward celibacy. "The spirit is strong but the flesh is weak," so says Jesus. We believe that the human spirit and the body agree: to be passionate sexual beings is to be alive. People are not all that willing to delete passion from their spirits. At times people can harness this passionate energy and transform it, putting it to work at endeavors other than sexual expression, but to delete passion from our lives leads to a weird kind of sociopathy — heartlessness.

163

Next, Mr. John Mill had to delete certain types of people, those who regard pleasure as a physical thing. Now we have a spirit without passion and a mind without a body. Unfortunately, there is not much left to deal with here because the mind is also physical. What is left is a very cold, calculating and dispassionate Mr. J.S. Mill. It takes a lot of work to delete the emotional and passionate self from story, to dehumanize story into theory, so we don't do it. We humanize theory by fusing humanity's need for common direction – theory – with story.

Finally, not even Mr. Mill is home. What you have left is a calculator with an attitude. No one in the 1990s is going to reduce himself or herself to a calculator when you can trot over to K-Mart and buy one for less than twenty dollars. We tend to resent uncaring attitudes. So we don't practise them. Our orators know that words governing human direction are sacred, prayerful presentations of the human experience, its direction and the need for transformation in the human condition that arises from time to time.

What is the point of presenting the human condition in a language separate from the human experience: passion, emotion, character and condition? "If you want people to have confidence in your cure, speak in a language no one understands – Latin. No one speaks Latin anymore, so it is the one we use" (Dr. Norman Bethune). By presenting theory in a language no one can grasp the speaker or writer retains authority over the thought. By demanding that all thoughts (theory) be presented in this manner in order to be considered theory (thought), the presenter retains the power to make decisions on behalf of others and the gate is shut to ordinary citizens who seek to gain control over their lives.

Recently, there was a conference in Opitsaht (Meares Island) to discuss and shape thoughts on the importance of trees to the environment. Indigenous people and European environmentalists both attended. The morning consisted of presentations made by prominent environmentalists, who droned on about PBM's chloroform counts, soil erosion and so forth, not much of which was understood by the Indigenous people there. All of our people spoke and understood English, but none had any background in Latin outside of the Catholic liturgy, so the presentations by the environmentalists went over our heads. At the end, an old man got up and said he would like to give an Indian point of view. Gratefully, the European environmentalists bent their ears to listen. The old man spoke for three hours in his language, and then sat down.

The Indigenous people in the audience cracked up. The environmentalists were, for the most part, confused, save one. Most of the Europeans missed the point. We all strive to become orators. An orator is someone who has come to grips with the human condition, humanity's relationship to creation and the need for a human direction that will guarantee the peaceful coexistence of human beings with all things under creation and who can present this as story in ordinary and entertaining language. The point of oratory is to create a passionate feeling for life and help people understand the need for change or preservation as the case may be. No brilliance exists outside of the ability of human beings to grasp the brilliance and move with it. Thus we say what we think. No thought is understood outside of humans' interaction with one another, their condition, and their environment. So we present thought through story, human beings doing something, real characters working out the process of thought/feeling and being.

For Indigenous people, academic notions of theoretical presentation lie in the inherent hierarchy maintained by academics, politicians, lawmakers and law keepers and the language they conjure to prevent lay understanding. Power resides with the theorists

165

so long as they use language no one understands. In order to gain the right to theorize, one must attend their institutions for many years, learn the other language, and unlearn the feeling for the human and earth condition – bizarre.

If it cannot be shown, it cannot be understood. Theory is useless outside human application. If only a minority understands theory, then only a minority can execute theory. Thus theorists require a horde of executives who must control the human condition, control our interactions and our relationships. Because human beings have a tendency to resent such control, we need force to maintain the hierarchy of theorists and executives – police, army, courts: the enforcers of law.

Despite all academic criticism to the contrary, my book *I am Woman* is a theoretical text. It was arrived at through my meticulous ploughing the fields of the colonial process – capitalist theory, decolonization, law and philosophy – from the perspective of Indigenous law, philosophy, culture and methodology. My understanding of the process of colonization and de-colonization of Native women is rooted in my theoretical perception of social reality and it is tested in the crucible of human social practice. Stories and poetry bring the reality home and allow the victims to de-victimize their consciousness and push back on colonization. For Indigenous women and a good many white women, *I am Woman* is empowering and transformative.

I am Woman takes the lives of women very seriously. The book walks gently across the ruined cages, the glass of which I shatter on the very first page – "How can one reduce one's loved ones small...minus the colours and the music that moves them..." – to fields of blossoming flowers at the end. The book is filled with story and it is guided by theory presented through story – the language of people. It is a spiraling in on the self that rises above all the myriad obstacles the colonial and patriarchal process presents for women. More. The book spirals out from the self, in a dogged and heartfelt way, to touch the hearts of women.

By talking to my readers as though they were truly there in my heart, both the point of victimization and the value of resistance become clear. The value of resistance is the reclaiming of the sacred and significant self. By using story and poetry I move from the empowerment of my self to the empowerment of every person who sees himself or herself in the story while reading the book. It is personally dangerous for me to live among disempowered oppressed individuals. "When they come to get me, I want to know who is going to be there with me because I am not going willingly," so said a young white woman, speaking on the possibility of organized state violence against the women's movement in this country. I want to know who is going to be there with me, resisting victimization – peacefully or otherwise, but always stubbornly and doggedly struggling to reclaim and hang on to my sacred self.

ORAL POETRY

DESPITE THE FACT that assimilation has witnessed a movement away from old social structures and old cultural forms, the artistic expression of both the written and oral Indigenous arts retains its non-hierarchical and non-coercive character.

In the past oral poetry influenced conduct when people had fallen from the path. Today it is remembered for its beauty but also because our communities came to cherish the reframing of law, philosophy or social governance contained in this poetry. Through a process of consensus between themselves and between the living and the dead these poems became songs that preceded ceremony. Even love songs became committed to memory because our Stó:lō nation understood the attitude of the singer to reflect the attitude of the community toward love. Random love between two individuals outside the community was inconceivable, so our love stories helped us remember the foundational means of building community. The problem facing oral cultures under scholarly examination is that only art that has resulted from community consensus is remembered. In contrast, the tradition of written literature includes the artistic expression as much of those artists who supported the status quo as those who opposed it. But examination of oral culture is limited to what is remembered and treasured or agreed upon; it doesn't include art that expresses dissenting points of view. The value of orally remembered word art is that each story, each poem, builds upon the original song and original story, and serves to deepen the values of the people.

Because the institutional structures of Native societies relied on family and social structures, oral language art was a powerful way to maintain governance of social and personal conduct without the use of force, and thus was foundational to the education process in Indigenous societies. Children were given stories and poetic teachings, rather than direct instructions, to guide their conduct. Further, because force was never used to maintain internal discipline, choice, cooperation and individual obligations were held in high esteem. These conditions led to the development of poetry and stories that did not offer answers to problems, but rather stimulated thought in the listener. Personal response to language art was connected to concepts of choice and tempered by the social value of cooperation. The listener then became central to the story or poem and was engaged in the process of imagining, building, constructing and responding to the speaker's art. The presence of the speaker was as much a part of the poem as the words spoken.

Voice, choice of words, sound, tone, diction, style and rhythm characterize both the poem and the speaker. A huge array of physical metaphors has developed out of the experience of the collective and its relationship to the environment. The concepts and metaphors employed in oral poetry are thus instantly understood and interpreted by the listener. Because our art is community-based, the use of physical metaphor is understood in the context of the wellness of the whole; personal interpretation, then, becomes the way in which individuals can use the poetry as a guide to their contribution to the wellness of the whole.

Once the story or poem was heard, it was discussed by members of the community, evaluated, and committed or not committed to. Two speakers could present the same story from opposing points of view and both could be considered valid, just as the listener's interpretation of the poem was valid despite the fact that it could be different from the views of both speakers and those of the other listeners. At the same time, individual listeners were expected to find a common point of understanding with the whole. This process of interpretation led, on the one hand, to a tremendous diversity of the meanings of a single poem or story and, on the other, to community consensus about its primary value.

Inherent in oral poetry is a non-instructional sub-text. The teaching power of the poem lies as much in its aesthetic beauty as in the poet's philosophical and socio-spiritual logic and her or his ability to achieve oneness with the listeners. Spiritual concatenation between poet and listener is quintessential to the articulation of oral poetry, and the poem's achievement of this concatenation rests on the spirit.

The spirituality of the poetry of Indigenous people is extremely misunderstood. Oral poetry spoken to white scholars prior to our mastery of the English language was often mistranslated when European intellectuals attempted to fuse their extrinsic sense of the spiritual and of poetics with the poetry of Indigenous people. At the same time, when they dealt with someone whose English was deficient, they did not bother to query deeper into the story or poem. Thus, more often than not, concepts, for example, of sun or war gods posed huge obstacles to understanding the meanings of individual poems, resulting in simplistic interpretations of Indigenous spirituality.

The fact that all things possess spirit, creation is sacred, the human experiences oneness with all creation, and transformation is integral to being alive — all this was simplistically applied to all circumstances, rather than explored in the context of the body politic and culture of Indigenous people. If all creation is sacred, then words as created entities for facilitating oneness are also sacred. If oneness with all creation is valued, then words are intended to achieve oneness. Thus the speaker seeks oneness with her/his audience. Through artistic presentation of thought, emotions, law, philosophy, and spirit, the speaker orchestrates the community process of concatenation. Voice, diction, tone, style, rhythm, and physical metaphor express the spirit of the poet, elicit response from the listener's spirit, and conjoin all into a single and powerful sense of oneness with creation. Thus the sound of language, the choice and meaning of words, and the attitude of the poet must all be carefully considered before the poetry achieves its goal.

The influence of the speaker is dependent upon his or her commitment to community as a spiritual concept, and her or his exceptional capacity to inspire within each listener the desire for the good life. The remembered poems become treasured moments of community concatenation. Concatenation between poet and audience has no co-relative among Europeans.

The object of Western poetry is not concatenation between the self and listener but rather self-expression. Concatenation cannot be understood mechanically, that is, in terms of formulae, standard practices, or basic characteristics; it cannot be achieved outside the context of community, though it can be discussed within a wedge of understanding.

In order to understand original poetry, Indigenous speakers gather together to engage the oratory around the poem and the circumstances that birthed it, but also to engage each other in discovering the poem's old and newly accrued meanings. They do so in a manner that facilitates concatenation with one another. In this way the process that leads to the discovery of the poem's meanings and to consensus between the speakers and concatenation births understanding, the results of which can be committed to.

The poet elicits the imagination of the community, the heart of the nation, and the spirit of the present, the past and the future. Poems move people from where they are to where they need to go to ensure community development. They activate the listener's community-based thought process without prescribing a response. Modern Indigenous poetry needs to be understood in relation to the positioning of community with regard to the good life journey that being human is all about. This is the reason why a number of writers insist that they write for their communities.

We believe that words are sacred, that they have power and impact. The words we needed in the 1960s and through the 1990s were those words that would turn us from the trail of destruction that we were on, like the story of the good red road, and lead us back to our original path. Once on the path to the good life, our community needs the old stories, old poems, and the old songs that have charted this journey to the good life for thousands of years. The revival of these songs, poems and stories are critical to understanding who we are and always will be.

The poems that have been spoken many times change with each generation as the mythmakers reform them to serve the moment. Even as we return to the good life's ways, we need to study those poems and songs so that they can guide our concatenation with the newcomers. Our poems show us how to create oneness between the world and ourselves.

173

Both oral poetry and written poetry are word art forms. One need not be privileged over the other. Both are examinable, able to be studied, and understandable. Both have value.

PEACE

PEACE: tranquility, freedom from strife, freedom from warring conditions, freedom from conditions that annoy the mind. We have not had peace for some 281,614 days since Columbus first came here. Worse, our homeland has not experienced peace since this country's inception.

Violence: an organized, unwarranted attack. Attack: an unjust exertion of force.

We know what violent attacks entail: from the slaughter of cod fish (for use as slave food) in the grand banks of Newfoundland and the annihilation of the Beothuks (for sport) to the poisoning of the Great Lakes and the slaughter of the sturgeon and salmon, the main source of food for the Six Nations and the Wyandot peoples; from the reduction of the beaver, mink, wolf, bear and moose from Sudbury to Manitoba to the slaughter of the buffalo across all three prairie provinces; from the near annihilation of the Cree Nation to the war against the Manitoba Nation and the dispersal of the Métis and Native People throughout the prairie provinces; from the burning of the forests in British Columbia and the contamination of our rivers with toxic waste from pulp mills, saw mills to the recent clear-cutting of our forests and the consequent death of our salmon – we know about organized violence.

Passive: submit without resistance, dispassionate, unemotional and unfeeling acceptance.

We know what that is too. For hundreds of years this country and its citizens watched us and our four-legged, winged, plant and sea relatives die without any emotional response.

Creation is not a passive process. Our mother, the earth, knows it is not a passive process; the earth is not a passive mother. She knows birth is active. It takes hurricanes, thunder, lightning and volcanic eruptions to move from winter to spring, to summer, to fall and back to winter. Creation is a struggle. For every four-legged, winged and two-legged sister of mine, creation is a bloody struggle for mother and child. Even seeds must burst through the casing holding the tender sprout safe. While not bloody, it is definitely not a passive process.

Struggle: strenuous and resolute effort.

We know that this is true, too. It took great effort to live the way we did centuries ago. It took emotional, physical and spiritual effort to discipline the self to live within the laws of waste. The struggle to survive the death of the earth and the disease that European plagues brought here took a huge effort on our part. In fact, for a while it looked as is we would not make it.

Thousands of citizens have decried violence in the resistance struggle of our people. If violence is an organized, unjust and unwarranted attack, we have never organized ourselves to gratuitously attack anyone, unjustly or otherwise. Ours is a peaceful struggle, not a passive one. We are aware of Canadian society's propensity to violence perpetrated against us.

Imagine your mother on a table, a host of angels yelling, "Push, push, bear down, woman, bear down," and she says, "I am not going to participate in this, it's bloody, it's painful, it's violent, and it'll tear my body." You would have died had your mother abhorred the effort to birth you.

The people who tell us to be passive in the face of organized violence are the same people who will hack up a tree because it is obstructing their view. I am not a passive woman. I was there, bearing down and shedding blood in the creation process of my children, and I will be there should anyone obstruct my right to nurture them. Does that make me violent? No. It makes me a profound lover of creation. I will be there should anyone decide to invade my tree relatives in the Stein, and I will be there for the Mohawks at Oka, should the police run amok again and organize themselves to attack them. I don't confuse peace with passivity. I don't confuse defense with aggression.

There is no peace in this country. We are absolutely opposed to a bunch of cowboys in a D9 Cat running hi diddle diddle over the hill, playing *Texas Chainsaw Massacre* with our relatives. Creation is not passive; it is sacred. Every life on this planet is sacred. I swear if lighting struck those clear-cutting, those corporate executives would accuse mother earth of violence. They are the bearers of violence, but they accuse of violence those who resist them. Psychologists see this blame the victim instead of the perpetrator approach as a transfer of the dysfunction from the perpetrator/ predator to the object of their dysfunction.

We are absolutely opposed to everyone organized with machine guns and assault rifles invading another people's territory to play *shoot em up cowboy*. It takes great effort on our part, when faced with hunger, not to leave the barricades and run all over the town of Oka to play *shoot em up cowboy*. Despite the abuse directed at us, the rock throwing, the police invasions, the beatings, we still believe that all life is sacred, that all creation is sacred. And we believe violence is lawless because we are opposed to violence.

But, we are not complacent. We cannot sit idly by in front of the television and watch the Sûreté du Québec invade Indigenous territory and unjustly assault our people. Such unwarranted actions are always unjust and violent.

Violence: to distort basic meaning and understanding.

To expect us to submit to the organized violence of would-be golfers or that of logging corporations, to the garbage disposal needs of settlers who fill our back yards with waste, or to multinational oil or other corporations that seek to strip, mine, clear-cut, or play games on the graves of our ancestors is to distort the meaning of violence and profane our sense of the sacred. We are being asked to sacrifice sacred creation, our children's future and our lineage, and we cannot do that.

Peaceful struggle is all about expending strenuous effort to live our lives free from strife, free from war, free from conditions that annoy the mind. It annoys my mind to think about clear-cutting; it annoys my mind to consider the invasion and death of the people of Oka. It annoys my mind to imagine golfers tromping on the graves of Mohawk grandmothers, children and loved ones. So I struggle to put a stop to it. I walk, I picket, and I block the road, and I speak because I cannot watch a people or any of the earth's relatives die an unjust death.

I am a caretaker. Every single Indigenous person here is a caretaker. Caretaker. Take care. Take care of creation. Creation is not inactive. To take care of creation is an active process, an imaginative process, and a process full of wonderment. It requires strenuous effort, it means healing ourselves of what we call "amber elbow disease." It cannot be done by people who are intoxicated, seeking the pleasure of parties. It cannot be done by disempowered people. It cannot be done by people who cannot imagine a different world, who cannot dream of a life of peace in which all creation is respected and cared for everywhere on this earth.

It cannot be done by people who have a hierarchy in their minds about who is worthy of life. All life is sacred. There is no human life, animal life, bug life, plant life, star life, more sacred than the next. Murder takes all kinds of forms, but if you think, if you can imagine, you can trace the source of murder that is going on today. It leads to a corporate system of violence. No single individual is responsible for the re-creation of a new way of looking at creation. We are all responsible. No caretaker can sit idly by while this assault goes on. We cannot watch sacred life die.

Struggle is hard work. It demands great care and a sacred sense of creation. It requires that we get beyond our me-first sense of strife. We have to rid ourselves of the bitterness of having had this country's citizenry watch us die with great complacency. It does not mean we hide the details of the story of their inertia in the face of our death. It does not mean we pretend all people are good people. What other people choose to do is irrelevant. We, each and every one of us here, own our bodies. We own our minds. We own our actions. To rise above bitterness, ineffective and random acts of rage, is to become conscious, emotionally balanced caretakers, people whose life is guided by the sacredness of creation, the wonderment of life. This is hard work.

Our struggle is a struggle for peace, not just a struggle against violence.

Peace: harmony. Peace: freedom. Peace: tranquility.

Rape is not tranquil. Bitterness is not harmonious. Being locked to someone else's perception of ourselves is not freedom. Freedom is a state of mind. We are free to choose. We may choose to be complacent, we may choose to watch a people die or we may choose to stop the slaughter — actively. Freedom is personal and significant. Freedom and peace require a deep sense of justice and great love.

When mercenaries for multinational corporations wind up their chainsaws on our hillsides to hack at the ankles of my mother's other children, the tree people, it disturbs my harmony. It annoys my mind. I refuse to be passive about the Stein Valley being clear-cut and I refuse to be passive about clear-cutting Mohawks who defend graves. I am not passive about nurturing my children. I worked, I sweated, and I stayed up nights as a tired youth to walk them to health and wellness. I stayed home on weekends when other young parents were tipping back the amber in pubs all across this nation. I was not complacent and I will never be complacent about creation.

If we are all dead, we cannot have peace. If we are allowed to die because the good citizens of this country did nothing, they will be left with their violence. They will be left with the memory not of resolute struggle, great effort for peace, but with the memory of unspirited, unemotional, uncaring inactivity in the face of our genocide. My spirit is not passive. Injustice annoys my mind and disturbs my spirit. I will be that way for all eternity. We have done all the unjust dying a people should have to do. This land has done all the unjust dying she should have to do. Don't be a passive soldier for corporate or military murder. With peace and harmony in your heart go out and spend great effort, strenuous effort, to change the story of Canada. Be active, be resolute, be caring, and we shall eventually have peace.

MAPPING OUR WAY THROUGH HISTORY

REFLECTIONS ON KNUD RASMUSSEN'S *JOURNALS*

MAPS are orders marching men to old places already seen.

Maps conjure memories of spoil, of plunder and innocence.

Maps are journeys to illusions no one has learned from.

Maps are critical revisits with visions, vistas, and never before seen repeats.

Maps direct intentions, call attention, and direct us to previous being.

Maps scatter reflection, leading us to delude our well-being.

Maps flatten surfaces, pictograph time, distance, even height, reducing critical illusions to trails of ink and colour.

Maps are pretentious,

arrogantly purporting to know where everything is.

Pretending power where none is.

Maps are finite.

Maps are always old.

Maps never lead to uncharted places.

Maps flip our attention from being to place,

from metaphysical time to streets, roads and clocks

and cheat our prospective response to depth.

I know so little about the Inuit, and know so few of Nunavut's citizens that I felt somewhat fraudulent about commenting on the film, *The Journals of Knud Rasmussen*, until I watched it. Years ago at a History/Anthropology conference at Laval University, hosted by historian Dr. Laurier Turgeon, I met a professor who had studied early cartography in North America. He told me that the earliest maps were drawn by Indigenous people for the explorers. This made sense. I could not imagine the explorers landing on a continent the size of North America and just wandering aimlessly discovering this or that. They travelled from one Indigenous village to the next at the directions of Indigenous traders. He mentioned that the best cartographers were Inuit, while the worst were my father's people, Salish. This made some kind of crazy sense to me too. There are huge mountains, long rapid rivers and a few glacial lakes in Salish territory; we did not fancy traversing the mountains, but rather chose to scoot by water from coastal village to coastal village. Villages are clearings on large flat plains between the mountains. By canoe you simply keep going until you hit the clearing, not much map-making skill to that. But the Inuit live in the Arctic, at the edge of the mountainous world from which I hail. It would take some great map-making skills to chart a course across tundra that is covered in snow and to my inadequate Salish eye appears flat.

In fact, it would take an amazing pair of eyes to see difference on the snow-covered tundra. What I did not see was that maps are also internal. The world of the intangible, hidden being can be mapped through an event, a story, by someone with a keen sense of insight and some deep well of understanding about the human soul. *The Journals of Knud Rasmussen* is such a map. It charts the journey of cultural collision and finally the madness born of social implosion that the process of colonization has been, not just for the Inuit but also for all of us.

Our connection to others was minimalist, trade-based. Salish people traded with other Salish people, fished and cultivated the natural world in Salish territory. It was odd to step outside our culture, to discover the culture of others. So the internal workings of our world carried on from one generation to the next, with that kind of slow plodding human development that adds rafters to the house naturally with little to shock or paralyze or dismember our world.

The arrival of Knud Rasmussen altered the relations and the dynamics inside the Shaman's family. It changed what Inuit naturally do. Rasmussen wanted to hear stories. The Shaman agreed; in so doing, he altered the way his family related to the very stories that sustained them. Rasmussen was asking him to download his Shamanic knowledge, without any purpose but to inform Rasmussen. It was a call to "hold court" for Rasmussen, as one reviewer so unkindly put it. Meanwhile the family needed to continue to be a family, and the education of Rasmussen, the downloading of story, was not the way the Inuit naturally related to one another. Rasmussen's presence was an interruption in the continuance of family and community. The film maps the journey of not just the Shaman, nor just that of Rasmussen, but of the death of cultural belief and community. We watch as family cohesion and continuance perish.

The power relations shift from the Shaman to Rasmussen, as Rasmussen becomes the centre of attention. The objectives of some of the younger members of the Shaman's family shift, too.

What we see and what we pay homage and attention to is mapped by our communities' objectives, objectives held together by the power relations among us and supported by our beliefs. Attending to something or someone embodies the according of power by the group to that something or someone. The shifting of power from the Shaman to Rasmussen pulls the cultural rug out from under the community's feet. We get to see the shift through the interactions within the family, and imagine the cultural rug slipping out from under our ancestors' feet. We get to see the interest invested by the family in Rasmussen's desires and remember the investment of our elders in men like Rasmussen. We feel that old disarray that occurs in our bodies, the sort of disengagement from one another that is deep and nameless. This investment in someone so different, so foreign, is what corrodes the original map to the internal world of the Inuit. It is so clear and visible through the giggles of the women as they respond primarily to Rasmussen.

The Shaman once held a position of centrality in his family, but Rasmussen usurps the Shaman's place in his own world. The glue holding the Shaman's tenuous connection to being, to power, to place and cohesion is melting, just as the snow of the igloo too will melt. That the film captures all this — visually, actually and dramatically — is amazing.

We get to see the map to madness in the context of social change and shifting power relations. We see the confidence, the cohesion and the beliefs of a community implode as the journey to an altered dynamic plays itself out.

I don't know much about Inuit culture, but it occurs to me that it is unlikely that they ever sat in a circle and downloaded stories and cultural information for others before Rasmussen came with his odd request. While the family was being entertained by the very idea, this downloading of stories also altered its belief systems. Indigenous people did not have complex systems of police, armies and courts to ensure the continuation of their societies. They relied wholly on their beliefs, the trust and respect they invested in those beliefs, and the positions of authority that held them up.

What the film makes clear is that the way we do things is the foundation of belief in one another. To accord Rasmussen his request required a shift in belief, that is, Rasmussen became important, more important than the natural being of this family. The direction that the Shaman initiated by granting Rasmussen his request elevated Rasmussen to a plane higher than that of the Shaman and the community without, however, the Shaman understanding or responding to this shift. As a result of this shift, the Inuit were thrown off course, off their own cultural and sociological map; rudderless, they fractured. The Shaman has no prior experience, no prior knowledge to help him bring his family back to their original being.

He dislocates himself; it is this dislocation that directs him to madness. Colonialism dislocated all of us in some way or other. This dislocation is at the heart of the aimless madness we endure until we finally return to our original being before we completely lose our sense of direction. Because the film maps this journey, Indigenous people get to see how we got so off course, how we lost our sense of direction, how we became socially maddened, fractured and divided.

What also becomes clear is the map to relocation, to re-directing and re-rooting ourselves in a completely different context. This is a map through the internal world of dismemberment and implosion. This is a map through the internal world of cultural collision and cultural loss. This is also a map to re-memberment, to re-membering our origins. I love that this map plays out the subtle — and not so subtle — relations and the alteration of dynamics from the moment Rasmussen enters the igloo. Formalism dominates, Rasmussen becomes a favoured and honoured guest, stories become something to be given, to be orated, and to be told out of the usual Inuit context so long as Rasmussen chooses to listen and record.

185

The Shaman loses his position of influence, of arbitration, of map-making familial directions. The community's respect and acclaim for the Shaman diminishes as he shifts his attention to Rasmussen.

The film is all about mapping. I love that the filmmakers took it upon themselves to map Rasmussen's journals through their own eyes, to play out the experiences that Rasmussen recorded. We don't hear much from Rasmussen himself. I had anticipated that we would. I had already braced myself for the omnipotent narrator, Knud Rasmussen, intervening in the unfolding drama, but this never happens. The story is conjured for the Inuit, not for Rasmussen, and that makes it one of the most singularly powerful and important films for Indigenous people that I know of. We need to be able to see through our own eyes what happened and we need to chart the journey through our familial experience, so that we can see how we are to be a people again, not a trail of broken treaties, not an oppressed group of struggling nations, but a people, believing in what we see and know, creating life from what we believe and building communities from our creativity. We need to know that this is possible, and *The Journals of Knud Rasmussen* is not simply a movie about Rasmussen from an Inuit perspective, but a map through the impact of an historic moment in Inuit history that was and will always be an Inuit moment.

If we fail to see that, then we fail ourselves.

In a chapter earlier in this book, "Who Gets to Draw the Maps: In and Out of British Columbia," I stated that Indigenous people are at a critical juncture in our history, a sociological juncture, and as such we need to return to the beginning of where we wandered off our own maps. After watching *The Journals of Knud Rasmussen* I know that we need to identify the moment in which the diversion occurred, capture it in story, and create the sort of mythology that will put us back in charge of our own sociological map-making.

I don't know the men who made this film, but I can imagine them. I see them as men who come into the world loaded with their own cultural capital, free of the sense of victimization that cripples our communities into a crazy kind of paralysis. I am awed and inspired by the filmmakers who can take a very European document like Rasmussen's journals and create a specifically Inuit film out of them that also serves every Indigenous community. I am further awed and inspired that it shows non-Indigenous people exactly how the madness in our world came about. The next time someone asks, "What happened? Why are Aboriginal people so violent?" I will simply say, watch *The Journals of Knud Rasmussen*.

THE
OF

THE LOST DAYS
OF COLUMBUS

I WONDER SOMETIMES if Christopher imagined the impact his voyage to Turtle Island would have on the geography, culture, demography, economy and sociology of the entire world. I imagine him sitting in some parlour in Italy, a vigorous and youthful male with a huge sense of adventure, studying the Greek classical scientists, some of whom imagined the world to be round, while he considered his contemporaries, some of whom believed it was flat. Which way was the tide moving at the time? I suspect it was in the direction of roundness. Someone, after all, financed his trip — a woman in fact. No ordinary woman, but a Queen. Queen Isabella put up the cash to realize his dream. But this is not his/story or her/story, it's mine.

I would like to say that what was going on in Europe in 1492 had nothing to do with me. I would like to avoid the ostentatious pomp and ceremony around Columbus' quincentennial celebrations. I would prefer not to have to write this piece. Unfortunately, Christopher's voyage did change the world and I inherited the results. I need to write this down.

The ashes of our ancient fires burn low these days. Indigenous people everywhere in the world of late have been hustling to catch up, to somehow find a place in Canada. At the same time we have been struggling to identify and articulate in English the thin lines of cultural connection to our past. Culture is an elusive butterfly. She is wide open to interpretation and she depends on the consciousness of the community, the nation and the individual, to exist. The human variable is an unreliable one. Consciousness is a state of being enjoyed by reasonably healthy people. The colonial legacy I have inherited is neither reasonable nor healthy.

In my living memory, my mother, recently deceased, worked fourteen to sixteen hours a day at very hard physical labour to feed and clothe seven children. We were waifs then. Abandoned, the State would now say, and it would remove us from this state of abandonment and neglect to place us in foster homes, likely never to see each other again. Thank goodness we weren't considered Indians then. My mom, you see, was Métis.

But that just posed an additional heartache for me. You see, her people were among the first throwaways in our community. When I get up to the podium, neither Indigenous people nor my white audience identifies me as Métis. This title has meaning only when I consider my homeland. It is a vaporous thing for me – this notion of homeland.

It didn't take long for white settlers to outnumber us. Preference was given to them, and my ancestors – the grandmothers – packed up their children and their meagre belongings and left. The men they married, if they had done well, stayed behind. Many of them returned to Europe and brought "real" wives home to Canada. Not far down the road we began a new settlement and initiated what became a vigorous trade between whites and Indians, with us in the middle. More settlers came, and we had to move again.

Our children travelled inland to secure the trade routes and the trade items Europe wanted. Often they returned with partners — Indigenous partners. By 1885, in Manitoba the term Métis reflected not just Indian and white bloodlines, but also Indigenous genetic diversity. We are Huron, Mohawk, Micmac, Anishnawbe (Ojibway), Cree, Salish, Chilcoten, Irish, Scottish, Welsh, French, Basque and Chinese by blood. These are the bloodlines of my own children. It is only when my relationships with Indigenous people or white people become intimate that anyone comes to know I am Métis.

I know it everyday. It lurks in the language of white folks, *you half-breeds only want to drink, fuck and fight,* and the language of reservation Indians, *you aren't really Indigenous, are you,* and the language of the Indian government and political tribal councils, *if we are desperate we will hire a Métis.* And we can only have a homeland *at the permission of local tribal councils,* which historically have not granted us that.

When Columbus' antecedents first came, they fathered children. They rarely claimed them. Nowadays, Indigenous men are our fathers. They rarely claim us. I am told Bill C-31 was supposed to resolve this dilemma. It does so for those whose grandmothers were counted in the early days of Canada when Indians were still pure-blooded, or at least that is the story. Counting the Indians and registering them is a recent historical phenomenon — initiated sometime after 1871. Care and vigour to keep the Métis separate from whites and Indians were applied after the unsuccessful 1885 Métis liberation war. This was also the last time Indians, whites, and Métis fought together to realize a dream. That war was initiated by us, and the principles of equality, land protection, and Indigenous democracy for both men and women were articulated jointly by both Métis and Indigenous people. For a short time, we had a homeland. After the rebellion, the moving trail began again.

I was born on the West Coast. It is the end of the trail for me. I cannot and will not consent to be thrown into the sea. As my mother lay dying, I sat in the living room of a dear friend in Toronto, speaking to someone I had just met but about whom I had heard a great deal over the years. A respected man. A sovereignty advocate. *Métis are not Indigenous*, he said earnestly, meaning me. I plummeted. A downward spiral began into the world of tears all Métis women have shed each and every time we were cast away by white men or Indigenous men and now by our own Métis men who are divorcing us at alarming rates. Underneath it all a moment of peace provided by understanding gently rocked. I let the peace and understanding grow in silence.

Columbus came from a throwaway world, a get-rid-of-them culture. We don't. The Métis trail forced our mothers to stead-fastly hold on to the inclusionary culture of our original societies: *Everything — stone, flora, fauna, human — has a perfect right to be.* My mother's words float about the room. I once told her with a good deal of bitterness in my voice that Indigenous people don't like us and asked her why she worked so hard for their sovereignty and salvation. "I don't," she said. I thought at the time this was a lie she had persuaded herself of to save face. My mother, you see, worked tirelessly to halt the mad Child Apprehension Program directed at Indigenous families. She worked to keep Indigenous children in their homes, with their original families and, failing that, at least with their original communities. Single-handedly she reduced the Indigenous child apprehension rate in Vancouver from 49% to 10%. She was sad she hadn't done better. She began her mission at a time when Indigenous people themselves were reluctant to take on their relatives' children. For her it was a clear question of sovereignty and cultural integrity.

Mother sat in the oak chair of my kitchen quietly for some

time before answering in that rare voice I loved so dearly. With great softness and reverence she said, "It doesn't change our obligations to humanity and earth one bit. We are responsible for the caretaking of this earth. Not just a tiny piece of it in some remote reservation, but all of it. That no one but us feels this way doesn't change a thing." When she died I wept, "It isn't enough, momma, it isn't enough."

Christopher brought with him his throwaway culture. When we bought their trade goods, someone should have reminded us not to take the culture along with them. This country was peopled by Europeans who were evicted from their homeland or forced out by economic recession. Today we call such people refugees. They come in every colour, race, shape and size. They are the unwanted. We have integrated, at every level of society, distaste for these castaways. "F.O.B.'s" (Fresh off the Boat), "Chinamen," "Ragheads," "Hindus," "Spics," "Wops," "Wogs," all form a part of the English language now.

But these people form just a small part of the earth's children we throw away. We toss "things" away after we have called them into being. We chuck whole forests of trees, what we call paper, into huge dumping grounds. We toss stones welded into new shapes and forms into dumping grounds. We cast oil, earth's energy source transformed into plastic baubles, into these dumping grounds. We rename it all garbage, but these materials all had beginnings as natural beings, as earth, stone, flora, or fauna. The very word garbage arises from the culture Columbus was born into and brought here.

Racism, sexism and tribalism are predicated on the existence of another kind of garbage – human garbage. They are rooted in the throwaway culture. There is no place called away. Every inch of soil in this world is a place. There is no human garbage either. Every single living human being has a place in this world.

The throwaway culture did not begin with the Métis. It began with patriarchy in Europe centuries ago by throwing away women and other individuals who could not conform to the rigours of patriarchy. We know who these other people are, and a whole language was developed for them. The faggots, dykes, queers were the first to experience being tossed out of their communities eons ago by emerging patriarchal societies far away from here. An entire sector of science is devoted to justifying why these people with their different sexual preference should be thrown away.

I used to think that this was a European problem, not mine. But after reflecting on Columbus and the impact his voyage had on Indigenous society, I no longer can afford to be apathetic about these people. I gamble here. I am no different from the next throwaway kid. Faggot and dyke formed an insidious part of my dictionary when I was young, just as half-breed bitch was part of my brother's language. I am forced to take another look. In the light of my own throwaway condition I am forced to reconsider those whom I once threw away or tried to.

It dawned on me one morning while looking at my children. Who gave us the authority to throw anyone away? Who gave them the authority to throw me away? Who gave reservation-defined Indians the authority to re-define me? Who gave us the authority to reduce the natural world to exploitable products to be thrown away once we had no use for them? It wasn't Columbus. It was the people he worked for, those with guns, money and power.

"They are so few in number," this Indigenous man said to me the other night, but they are held up by our internalization of their attitudes. We — the half-breeds, the dykes, the faggots, the ragheads, the Chinamen, the honkies, the white trash, the gooks, spics, wops, squaws, bucks and niggers — by our silence and our disunity grant them authority; by our acquiescence to divisions among us, we wield the weapons of their authority, we execute the will of a minority, a very small and very sick minority. The same minority that financed Chris's voyage, who threw away their own people, who destroyed the natural environment in their own homelands and pirated the world, buying, selling and murdering life all over this planet. Whole armies of us, the foolish and self-betrayed, girded up our loins and marched about, clear-cutting logs, over-fishing, making war on both human and non-human earth beings. In the end we lost our humanity, we lost a sense of spirit, and we inherited the crippled throwaway culture of Chris's bosses.

I return Christopher to those who would adore him. I give him back to those who cling stubbornly to throwaway ways. I return to my mother's ashes, which people and nourish a small scarlet maple in the home she created for us. I hear her sing the anthem of her ancestry, "Red River Valley," and in my memory I repeat her words: "It doesn't change a thing — we still have obligations to earth and all her children."

"Come sit beside me if you love me / do not hasten to bid me adieu." New meanings are born in the words of her song — a song huge in its social implications.

I have no idea what the world really looked like in 1492. The written accounts were kept by those who would alter our ways, stamp out our cultural connections and annihilate all that was not patriarchal, sexist and racist. It no longer seems relevant. I refuse to throw away life. I grant no one the authority to destroy anyone's life or toss it away. I extend permission to no one to throw away stone, flora or fauna in dumping grounds, which are no longer places.

There are a growing number of people in Canada who share this attitude, who sit next to me and push back on the throwaway culture. These people are the harbingers of a new Canada, a nation of people who promise to be 10,000 times more beautiful than anything we have seen before (Ho Chi Minh). We are all huddled about in kitchens across the country, separated by distance, unified by sentiment, searching for that small moment of peace; the moment that comes with understanding, trying to figure out how in the world anyone could celebrate the past 500 years of history and the man who initiated it all — Columbus. We all know that some day this half millennium will be referred to as the lost days of Columbus, and we look forward to that day.

TOWARD A NATIONAL
LITERATURE
"A BODY OF WRITING"

APPARENTLY, we have a literary tradition. Some refer to oratory as our literature, in some sort of attempt to equalize the two, but that muddies the water and is not necessarily helpful. Literature, according to *The Canadian Oxford Dictionary*, means "A body of writing." If this is so, then most of Europe's English literary tradition is primarily ships' logs, transfers of payment, debt records, accounts payable or receivable, trade transactions, and all the mercantilist, tribute reconciliations, along with the legal and public policy and bureaucratic writings, that accompany the process of establishing and maintaining an imperial world. Along with that go the modern print media, which today include advertising, junk mail, film scripts of all sorts, popular magazines and books, political platforms, debt reduction schemes, followed by the fastest growing body of writing in North America — pornography. But most of the world of academia and much of the public do not share the dictionary definition of literature. Well-crafted novels, poetry, short stories, plays, and the like are generally what come to mind when the word literature is used. Such writing actually makes up a tiny part of the vast bodies of writing in this society, so I wonder about the necessity for the door-closing practice currently known as literary criticism.

If the dictionary definition is used, then our literary tradition is the converse of imperialism. It largely consists of band council resolutions, which are still sent to the mother country for approval, program descriptions, grant applications, and the reports required to substantiate the receipt, use, and continuation of grants, transfer payments, and the like. All these documents form the bulk of the tons of paper consumed in the short writing history of Indigenous people in North America. I am sure that many readers of this collection are not concerned with the above as literature, except to insist that we rise above it.

We have an oral story or performance art and poetic tradition that precedes our literary tradition, some of which is comprised of what we actually think about when we hear the word literature: story, poetry, and drama. While First Nations oratory, oral story, poetry, and drama are thousands of years old, our literary tradition is very new. There is among the Cherokee some writing from the nineteenth century onward (see *Sequoyah's Gift: A Portrait of the Cherokee Leader* by Janet Klausner and Duane H. King), some of which has become recognized as the foundation of our Native literary tradition. In Canada, many First Nations writers recognize E. Pauline Johnson as the mother of Indigenous literature north of the 49th parallel and, following her, the works of Mourning Dove and D'Arcy McNickle, on either side of the 49th parallel respectively, both authors with Salish relatives.

The advent of residential schools created a dearth of any sort of literacy for Indigenous people in Canada, though there were novels written about us during the era of residential schools from non-Native award-winning writers. These included the creation of Aboriginal characters who bear no resemblance to who we are and who we will always be, and have no connection whatsoever to our journey through this long dance of colonialism. In 1892, E. Pauline Johnson wrote a critique of the treatment of First Nations women in her article "A Strong Race Opinion: On the Indian Girl in Modern Fiction," in which she protested the obvious racism in the novels about First Nations women.

It was not until Indigenous people began to attend public school and learned to express themselves in writing that the treatment of Indigenous people in literature began to change. In the past fifty years of Indigenous history, we have experienced a veritable explosion in the literary arts, beginning in the 1960s with the publication of poetry in a number of community newspapers, such as *Akwesasne Notes* and *Native Alliance for Red Power (NARP)*; contemporary oratory of the political and social sort in *The First Citizen*, a private newspaper edited by Floyd Favel; and organizational publications such as *The Indian Voice* and *B.C. Indian Homemakers Association*. Short stories began appearing in the 1970s in *Tawow*, published by the Department of Indian and Northern Affairs. Following that were the autobiographies *Halfbreed* by Maria Campbell, and *Bobbi Lee: Indian Rebel* that I wrote. Two landmark novels marked the beginning of the explosion of fiction writing, Jeannette Armstrong's *Slash* and Beatrice Culleton's *In Search of April Raintree*. The 1990s was the decade for playwrights: Tomson Highway founded Native Earth and launched *The Rez Sisters*; Drew Hayden Taylor launched *Baby Blues*; and these two were soon joined by Columpa Bobb's *Dinky*, Ian Ross's *fareWel*, Joseph A. Dandurand's *No Totem for My Story*, and Marie Humber Clements' *Accidental Women*. It is now nearly impossible to keep up with Indigenous literary publications, as the numbers of published Indigenous authors has increased geometrically, verifying that we do not have a problem learning English. We do, however, have a problem being included in the education process.

199

While we have not been short of the sort of bureaucratic writing that cripples Aboriginal communities, keeping us locked to government granting, policy shifting, and economic goodwill begging, we are still short of the above sort of literary production. But this is changing as new writers such as Eden Robinson, Richard Van Camp, Cherie Dimaline, Michael Paul-Martin, Kateri Akiwenzie-Damm, Louise Halfe, Marilyn Dumont, and Marie Annehart Baker have burst onto the literary scene.

We are also short of the sort of writing rooted in our oracy. Indigenous people have not had the opportunity to study the process of mythmaking linked with oratory and the function of mythmaking that reflects our various national perspectives. The opportunity to study and apply scholarly research and analysis to Indigenous oral cultural foundations at universities and in public schools does not exist. Universities and research funders are less than willing to provide the funds necessary to assist us in moving from oracy to literacy. This inhibits new authors from creating the concomitant literary products necessary to facilitate the rejuvenation of our original cultural bases. We are not necessarily lacking people committed to literary creation that relies on our original oratorical cultural foundations and that can lead us in the direction of liberation, but we are lacking the opportunity to study these foundations. Our emancipation from our colonial condition, which is connected to and can accommodate modernization, is dependent upon the scholarly study and reclamation of original story. The transmission of original knowledge in written form and the development of fiction from original story depend on our ability to rectify the above deficiencies.

The orchestrated fragmentation of our world aborted the knowledge transmission from Indigenous knowledge keepers to their children. The interaction between Indigenous knowledge and citizens is a major aspect of our education. Much of our knowledge was appropriated by anthropologists, museums, archivists and universities. These institutions must commit to the restoration of our knowledge, medicine, song, story and art objects.

Our cultural skeletons remembered by the elders who escaped capture and the disconnected thin memories of children who were told stories and oral history need to come together to create an aggregate body of knowledge that we can study. Some of our knowledge lives on in archives as notes and translations constructed and documented by priests and anthropologists who, nevertheless, viewed our knowledge as being divorced from the intimacy of community interaction that produced that knowledge in the first place. This knowledge needs to be re-examined in the light of our understanding of who we are.

The transmission of knowledge during the cultural prohibition laws required clandestine organization and the careful selection of children who would not talk or tell. Knowledge was parcelled out to children without them knowing who else was receiving this kind of secret national education. The removal of children by the state, first to residential schools and now as apprehended wards of the state, continues. No children meant no cultural transmission and no cultural development.

This all had to occur before the child was six, and so many of the children grew up not having a scholarly sense of the nature or substantive experience of the knowledge they held.

Because the children were disconnected from other children, these bodies of knowledge became scattered and separated. A narrow sense of what constituted knowledge in the individual keepers was often the result. Because the articulation of knowledge associated with understanding and creating story was not recorded by those who chose to document original story, the process of story creation and the theoretical foundations of story creation are not well known.

Indigenous people deserve the institutional support to reclaim story and develop the process for the ordered aggregation, synthesis, and transmission of First Nations oratory. Those with traditional knowledge possess bits and pieces of knowledge, but we still need to aggregate the whole. Some of these keepers have entitled themselves to call the shots on the door to access. All sorts of rules about knowledge acquisition have surfaced, requiring students to prove worthiness, which may or may not be connected to past forms of transmission. Knowledge is our children's birthright, not something they must earn.

The dismantling of the social power that served the original society very nearly destroyed us. False ideas about non-industrial societies being simplistic, primitive, lesser, static, lacking in dynamics, science, medicine, or significant knowledge prevail. Notions of progress as a linear movement of passing time dominate. For these reasons all things Indigenous must be examined anew. Our scholars must take the time to study their national knowledge, pre-colonial to modern. What stories do we have in common? What are our historical links? What knowledge sharing and cultural exchange occurred in our original societies?

These conditions facilitated the cultural, economic, and intellectual collapse of Indigenous peoples and the social, intellectual, and cultural reproduction and knowledge transmission systems. Our modern oratory centres on the reconstruction of those systems of transmission in the modern context: school.

The disconnection of Indigenous peoples from their families and cultural gatherings scattered the fragments of Indigenous knowledge. Cultural prohibition laws led to the creation of clandestine societies. The threat to our societies has diminished.

We need not be secretive about our knowledge. We need to openly advocate the study of our original oratorical texts.

"We are about story and nothing else" (Thomas King, *The Truth About Stories*).

Our oratory (spoken word) covered all areas of knowledge: history, sociology, political science, medical knowledge, aquaculture and horticulture, law, science, as well as stories. Stories, however, are much more fun, seemingly innocuous, less harmful, and much more entertaining than science or medicine. Stories do not indicate the sort of knowledge attached to genius, at least not in quite the way that science and medicine do in Western society, so, to some degree, stories survived the virulence of colonial attack. Western society values science. Because Canadian society is unable to recognize any intelligence among Indigenous societies, it refuses to recognize those aspects of Indigenous society that would force it to value Indigenous people. It is as if the devaluation of all things Indigenous travels along with their colonial hold on our lands. The pattern of colonialism continues to obsessively devaluate all things Indigenous.

Although our knowledge was scattered, it was not destroyed. There are still Indigenous keepers that can recite the oratory that reveal the range of environmental science held by their nation and the connection between all beings in their specific bioregion. There are those who can deliver the understanding Indigenous people had of the interconnectedness of plants, animals, rivers, soil, water, sky, and humans in a way that can be transmogrified and transliterated into a studyable science that is key to our renewal.

To study this knowledge in a systemic way we must first gather, synthesize, and transfer this knowledge. Both of these processes are vital to our survival. This systematization of knowledge is required before writers can write from within their culture. Unless we write from within our culture and from our original knowledge, we cannot grow culturally, and the current problems of social anomie will continue unabated. Further, the systems of transmission have been destroyed, and the conditions that made this knowledge viable have changed. We need both the institutional venues and the time to engage in national discourse about our original knowledge and the method of rendering it relevant to the modern world. We need to understand the difference between oratory as knowledge and oratory as story.

In the past, our societies contained processes through which scholarly debate around law, politics, environmental science, national management of resources, and story (as well as other knowledge) took place. Those institutions barely exist now. They are, however, being revived through the work of Indigenous women across Canada.* Without full understanding of the above and its praxis, literary criticism of Indigenous story cannot naturally arise out of our full oratorical foundations, nor can we call it Indigenous criticism.

Stories are tied to history, and serve the direction the communities need to take in the context of human catastrophes. They don't exist separate from the everyday business of the nation. They are child-rearing tools, not just educational subjects. Thus, we discuss not what the author was trying to say, but rather look for ourselves in the story, and determine how we make it right with creation. This kind of discourse is about the lessons, the teachings, meanings and the conduct that we must arrive at personally and collectively to make the story work for us and to work with the story. Our discourse centres on oratory, which remains largely unacknowledged in the realms of politics, laws, sociology, history and medicine.

* Andrea Smith is currently collaborating, with a number of First Nation Women scholars, to create a discourse and witness process for the book, *Indigenous Feminism: Without Apology.*

Western literary criticism fails to make any kind of full, fair, or just sense of Indigenous work. Its orientation — its *raison d'être* — is to diminish Indigeneity, to confine writers to canons that narrow the field of participation to those arising from the mother country. Indigenous thinkers tend to evaluate stories in connection with their specific historical continuum, which is a very different kind of discourse. Salish people treasure *Ravensong* as a story that shows who we are and always will be — *siem*. They study it in a specifically Salish way. Is this story connected to our oratorical body of knowledge, our sense of Raven the transformer, and could it happen, even if it didn't? Raven called us into being and stole light that we might see both the darkness and the brightness of our humanity, that we might study shadow land and daylight and reach backward and forward for our humanity.

All understanding, all critical thinking, no matter what the subject, is achieved through continuous study and discourse within the cultural context of the student. Europeans study their literature, their folk tales, their archetypes, symbolism, and metaphor on a continuous and critical basis. Excellence is attached to authors whose literary works have advanced the literary canon and upped the stakes and stature of their literature without questioning the canon and without altering the foundations of society. The apple is not intended to fall far from the tree. Defining and critiquing story are cultural acts. Canada, in its arrogance, continues to apply pressure on non-Western writers to master the inherited canon and to abide by the Euro-traditional models of story. This insistence helps to maintain the Canadian white-settler primacy in defining and re-creating our literary tradition.

In schools our children are kept busy studying the stories, culture, knowledge, and science of European society in Canada. While some time is allocated to Indigenous story and storytelling, the sensibility of Indigenous story is simplified and dumbed down. Limited to this dumbed-down, simplified cultural remains, young writers get the feeling that these simple little children's tales comprise all we ever had.

Europeans developed several schools of thought surrounding literary criticism, schools that serve to perpetuate the status quo and further the development of the social structures from which they arise. Aristotelian theories, hermeneutics, structuralism, and now post-colonial theories have shaped their literary criticism. We have not had the same opportunity to engage in discussions about Indigenous story, theories of study, or criticism. Euro-colonial teaching and notions of literature are not the only way to come to understand literature and story. Indigenous people must be able to attain scholarly credentials from Indigenous theoretical principles. Indigenous myth-making principles need to shape Indigenous discourse on Indigenous story. The flip side of this is a commitment to dispelling the notion that pre-colonial theories of literary creation cannot arise out of Indigenous society and dispelling, too, the very racist superstition that Indigenous people had no theories until Europe brought them *enlightenment.*

Theorists are comprised of individuals with a broad and solid foundation in their own society's knowledge that exercise unique brilliance and apply analysis and imagination to received knowledge to devise structurally sound hypotheses for understanding the development, advancement, and augmentation of existing foundations. We have words in our languages for such people, and we have specific processes for conducting such discourses. A careful and connected study of old and recent Indigenous literary products will show that our original story base is worthy of study. This cannot be done by individuals who apply themselves to studying another society's knowledge, history and social foundations through their own imported theories. It cannot be done by those who merely live within the culture either. It can only be done by those who live within the culture *and* who have studied its foundations, the oldest texts, and engaged in discussion with elders and scholars. There is much to be gained by studying our newer literary products through theoretical principles that are integral to our culture, along with other theories. Whereas colonial education in and of itself is deficient as First Nations literary criticism, this combined approach has the potential to develop a critical discourse that respects the foundations of our literature.

Today we have many scholars studying Indigenous writing, many of them Europeans or with a European education, armed with colonial definitions and post-colonial theories. These scholars are not expected to pay attention to the study of the original culture from which the Indigenous authors they study arise. Certainly, they are not expected to concern themselves with original oratorical principles of study. In contrast, an Indigenous graduate of literature automatically becomes an expert in Salish, Ojibway, Oji-Cree, Iroquoian, and Cherokee writing, without having to know much about the nations and the national story or oratorical traditions of those nations. Few Indigenous writers are in a position to comb through the oratory, story, drama, and poetry in their original forms in order to glean the principles of Indigenous story creation.

The body of Salish oratory in its totality and original form, free of interpretive teachings, constitutes our sacred texts. In order for criticism to arise naturally from within our cultures, discourse must serve the same function that it has always served. In Euro-society, literary criticism heightens the competition between writers and controls the entry of new writers to preserve the original canon. In my society, story creates discourse around healthy communal doubt, which inspires us to face ourselves, to grow and transform ourselves through the augmentation of the house by adding rafters to it; it calls us to create myth from new and transformed beings. The process of gathering together to find what is new and what is being born, learning as an ensemble, is the appropriate process of learning for Indigenous people.

From this discourse, new writers can then create a whole new series of transformation myths set in the modern or contemporary context. The new transformation myths still encourage us to clear old obstacles, and point us all in the direction of the good life. It is the responsibility of every Stó:lō to enter the world, to go out and create new stories so that we don't return to our ancestors boring. In one of our creation myths, we struggle to reach some sort of awareness of the impact of behaviour on hidden being (mind, spirit, and heart) so we can return to our ancestors and teach about consequences.

The deployment of the historic and the continued use of original processes is part of the responsibility of the mythmaker. The original processes of myth creation required that the mythmaker use the original processes in the interest of the nation. The clans, community, were the basis for interaction with the mythmaker. The nation was the ultimate judge of the success or failure of the student in the mastery of text and story. In Salish Raven stories, transformation is not only at the centre of our oratorical story tradition; it is the objective of life itself.

Salish people were referred to as natural poets by E. Pauline Johnson (*Legends of Vancouver*), natural sociologists, and great rememberers. We are still, by and large, an oratorical society. I do not consider this a backward thing, nor do I believe that my stories are illegitimate little bastards because they follow the responsibilities, principles, and objectives of oratory and oral myth making from a Stó:lō perspective.

In the first leg of decolonization, the process of cultural rec-lamation by intellectuals born of the people and the disciplined study of original oral history and story paves the way for the cre-ation of a new body of writers. Alongside this, a growing social and political activism and economic struggle directed at independence must occur. Reclaiming knowledge must become recognized as a legitimate course of study.

The citizens of the imperial centres fought and won certain privileges hitherto only accorded to the upper echelons: literacy and education, cultural reproduction rights, and human rights are all part of the gains made by Euro-settler workers and educated citizens. These privileges depend on the continuance of imperial-ism as a global socio-economic order, which serves, first, the upper classes and, second, Europeans and their descendants. Although we are witnessing the corrosion of these privileges certain forms stub-bornly remain. Even while imperialism implodes and can barely afford its own citizens, the re-establishment of economic rape priv-ileges in all its former colonies is being fought for militarily, while the Canadian population doesn't seem to mind.

What does all this have to do with literature?

Reclaiming original knowledge, reconstructing original sys-tems, and rebuilding them costs money. Canadian advantage, which includes theft of our territorial sources of wealth and appro-priation of knowledge, has left us impoverished. The attitude that this condition is a fait accompli needs to be challenged. We are entitled to rebuild our national economy from original bases. We are further entitled to exact war reparations from the former col-onizer. This has not been put on the agenda except by Indigenous writers. Instead, we have been presented with a single option: emulate Euro type story-telling and literary criticism. That is, con-tinue to study dead white people, become competent, get a PhD, and borrow a better structure, better knowledge, and better framework from Europeans than the framework we last used.

I am not advocating abandoning all Euro-based scholarly pursuits, but rather building from literature and literary discourse through oratorical knowledge and story that are still functioning in our nations and re-examining the Euro-knowledge filters used to analyse original oratory. Some Indigenous scholars have been studying oratory or orality, our original systems. There is some exciting work being written on the subject, but we have a long way to go.

In his landmark work *The Truth about Stories*, Thomas King states that "We are all about story and nothing else." I confess I know very little about Cherokee knowledge. I do know this, however, that when I was sick or about to give birth, I wished to get well or deliver a healthy baby. To do this I did not search for the best storyteller in my nation; I searched for the best medical personnel: a herbologist, a body mechanic, a diagnostician, a therapist, or midwife, as the case required. As a gardener, a fisherwoman, a shellfish cultivator, I know that we have oral knowledge about the science of agriculture or aquaculture directed at the production of all of the above.

Stories arise out of social engagement or praxis. What is absent from the above statement is the recognition that we came to the table full banquet, that we had bodies of knowledge, that each and every one of us was familiar, in varying degrees, with those bodies of knowledge, and that there were positions of competence measured through very definite governing processes. Schools of thought were attached to the specific bodies of knowledge; some of our elders are familiar with the concepts that guided the various knowledge systems. Medical knowledge, psychological knowledge, mediation systems, governance knowledge, and how we see the business of social transformation are all legitimate aspects of story, as are trade, environmentalism, midwifery, and management knowledge.

Stories acquired over time in our very long history here embody and reflect the author's knowledge. Knowledge, although a part of story, requires a separate process of study. Oratory as knowledge is worthy of study and reclamation both for the world and us. Oral transference and the development of processes of coming to understand a subject and coming to reconcile ourselves to story are legitimate fields of inquiry. Reclaiming our national bodies of knowledge is a pre-condition for the development of national literary criticism. We need to appreciate the full scope of oratory and its function in our contemporary world, or we will be in danger of participating in the very colonial practice of reducing Indigenous culture to simplistic, narrowed wedges of being.

On the development of Stó:lō literature

The creation and re-creation of literary culture is a function of education. Education is the system by which a nation develops and transfers knowledge. The study of literature is the business of examining story, poetry, and drama in the above context. The creation of literature results from the study of original oratory, from imagining its connection to original story. Writing story is connected to the context we inherit. The painting of character and story under an individual or family's unique circumstances reflects our social conditions (colonialism). We have stories that are both oral and modern. We must be clear that story is the end run of the process of oratorical study of original oratory in the context of colonialism. In the Stó:lō tradition, the original knowledge exists independent of story and story co-exists with the original knowledge.

Storylines are kept by individuals assigned to carry particular story. The business of story creation by Stó:lō nationalists require that the mythmakers engage in discourse with the intellectuals of the nation whom they recognize as understanding the context we inherit. The mythmakers, with the aid of the keepers of story, decide which of the stories are most likely required to guide our conduct, and then they create the new myth from the old, independently of the keepers with whom they consulted. If the storier is a woman, the focus is a Ravenesque social transformation story, as women are responsible for the social relations within the nation. Stó:lō story, poetry, and song express people's spiritual connections to the earth; they embrace the human journey from the past to the present and strive to prepare us for the future in a way that keeps the nation connected to the earth and all living beings without dictating direction or personal conduct.

Art is a reflection of Stó:lō national and social being, expressed as an imagined state of human collaboration with the world. Whole systems of engagement, of relationship, of agreement of knowledge and the stories that went with them can be revived and studied. To eliminate the transferring of original knowledge would diminish the nation's capacity for the creation and re-creation of life, liberty, economy, political communion, and social interaction among the people. Elimination narrows the frame within which mythmakers create story and the sense of what stories need telling. It narrows the rememberers' sense of significant story, and it narrows, too, the field of study for those who would become national mythmakers — those who seek to create fiction. It further narrows the field for those who choose to become critics of the mythmakers, but it does not eliminate the need for its re-creation.

Our ability to look inward and face ourselves, our inability to research and restore our knowledge in its broadest and most complete sense is part of the past. Re-examining knowledge transfer and collaborating globally with other Indigenous people will assist our future. Capitulating to the conditions that preserve the Western canon will not just hamper us, but will paralyze us. Those who capitulate limit their growth and transformation, which constitute the foundation of Stó:lō individual and social being.

We are operating from a diminished capacity to imagine the future not because we are not capable of brilliance but because the knowledge we were to inherit has been seriously diminished, scattered, or altered. The result is that we gaze continuously at colonization and its encumbrances and engage in its criticism in the hope that somehow the means by which we can decolonize ourselves from ourselves will show itself to us or in the hope that the colonizer will see the error of his ways and pave the road to decolonization with some magic program.

The angle from which we gaze ought to come from within our original knowledge and systems of study, not from beneath the colonizer, as the vision produced will not be much more than the colonizer's posterior.

The term oral tradition is a diminished term. We feel obligated to use it when speaking English to refer to the various bodies of knowledge once maintained in Aboriginal societies. What exactly does it say beyond the obvious, that traditionally we spoke? Intellectual heritage, literature, and theoretical frameworks are all terms used to defer to Euro-knowledge, while oral tradition, which is widely employed as a nonsensical term that denotes nothing but speaking, is a term used by us to refer to our bodies of knowledge transferred through complex oral processes. The term does not imply a systemic means by which to embrace complex systems of knowledge and their development in the same way that European terms do. Oral tradition as a term does not spark images of systemic

213

being, organized transference, serious study, and measurement of competence; rather, as its usage by Euro-scholars, it creates a diminished image of elders telling stories, endlessly chatting with one another, an image that minimizes the importance of these carriers of knowledge. The reality of a process of educating, reproducing and transferring organized bodies of knowledge through a complex system of designated rememberers is thus seriously negated. Our original economic, political, and national knowledge to promote our well being, our very existence as independent peoples, is savaged and erased. The oral tradition as a reduced form of spoken word has come to denote everything that is said, even in simple broken English.

Many literary creators advocate orality as a means of collaboratively creating and re-creating knowledge of science, medicine, politics, literature, and art. Hence, when Arnold Krupat and others exclude fiction as oracy or hint that the literature of Lee Maracle is not conversive (Brill de Ramirez) or authentic Indigenous writing, two things are accomplished: one is the reduction of oracy to some form of broken English style poetics as advanced by Wendy Wickwire and others, and the second is our recolonization.

More than critique what they did to us, I want to know how we have developed story, science, governance, sociology, psychology, health, and well being, and how that knowledge has been transferred. The place from which we look at the world determines, in part, the result. Standing on some bridge hoping to legitimize Canada and experience a share of whatever leftovers Canada has to offer the Stó:lō nation is undignified.

Stó:lō stories talk about naming things from the position of collaboration and future engagement with the subject being named. Thus, Snauq'w becomes our gardens as a result of several generations of scientific, social, spiritual, and storied engagement with the beings that were part of the garden and that, as a result of our having studied them and engaged in an agreement of continuous growth and development with them, sustained us. The beings in the garden became part of our nation, holding the same rights, privileges, and obligations as the human Stó:lō.

When Europeans named things, they did so from the position of conquest, hence the use of the now nearly dead Roman conquerors' language, Latin. The colonizers' propensity to rename things is the least of our worries. How did the Iroquois, Cree, and others name things, and what their relationship to other people on this Island is? What are their laws governing relationship, oratory, story creation, and being? Where do our stories intersect and commune?

As a Stó:lō mythmaker, I am required to engage Salish peoples and their nation's relations in spirit-to-spirit relations and reproduce myths from original knowledge in the context I inherit, to find freedom in this context, and to transform the journey into future stories of conduct that will uphold that knowledge. This is a sociological, political, economic, medicinal, and psychological responsibility, and it travels with mythmaking.

Our stories belong in and to our future. The processes of story creation belong to the future too. Maintaining the story structure of our longhouses must be one of our choices. Studying the structure of our oracy in the way we have always studied it — collectively and personally from the vantage point of Stó:lō philosophy and oracy — travels with that choice. The original agreements between the Stó:lō and the Salish world, between the Salish world and other beings of this Island, are still valid. The system by which we arrived at story still exists as a theoretical framework, and there are people who engage this framework. The story we are studying today is the story of imperialism, its coming into being and its going out of being from the place of Salish independent being. Over

215

two hundred years before the Europeans appeared on the West Coast we abrogated slavery. The abrogation of slavery required discourse and imagined story creation. These stories are significant as they address the business of overcoming masterhood, and they are stories that the colonizer needs to hear.

I was given a fierce mask and a soft mask, a fish weir and a war club. I have inherent story, knowledge, and governance and I am governed by my inheritance. As a member of an ex-slave-owning society, I strive to engage the world in a reproductive and mutually beneficial manner. Let us re-create story in the way that our ancestors did through the study of old story, through the structural, mythical, and artful creation and reproduction of original story — different, but the same.

Indigenous people are bound together by circumstance. In our literary journey let us add new rafters to our old longhouse and include the stories of others as we march to freedom. This essay is Raven coming out of the House to Salish-speak to those with whom we are not yet familiar, but to whom we are inextricably bound. The engagement of other nations in the process of decolonization is an important story. There can be no new society outside of the global examination of Indigenous systems of being and story. Inside our texts, inside our oracy and our literature, is the necessary cultural knowledge that can address our liberation, and I believe that we are ultimately responsible for our liberation.

We need to systematize our sense of knowledge acquisition in the service of our nations. This is my contribution to this process.

DANCING MY WAY
TO ORALITY

"Everything begins with song"

Bruce Miller, (Skokomish) Evergreen College, Salish orality instructor,
Evergreen, Washington, April, 2002

MY MEMORIES OF ORALITY begin when I first learned to speak.
The first three years after speaking were intense as my elders
seemed desperate to squeeze as much oral story and teachings
into my pre-school life as was possible. I would soon attend a
foreign school and would likely be there for some twelve years.
If things went well, I might attend university, which meant adding on another round of years, separating me from what would
have been my Salish education were I born in another time. So I
suppose the desperation was connected to that, though I cannot
be sure as my first teachers have long since passed onto the other
world and I never asked them while I was young. I remembered
little of that first education as it was happening, but my Ta'ah
(my great-grandmother) assured me that I would remember when
I needed to know. I believed her, so I did not worry about what I
remembered until much later when I began to write. I wanted to
write from my own origins and story base. My first attempts at

writing met disaster. Others with different sensibilities taught me. They thought my stories quite fine, but they didn't sound like me.

My earlier stories remind me of taking piano lessons and hitting the keys with some accuracy, but not being able to make the piano talk the way I heard the instrument's sound in my mind. Oral cultures are all about sound, rhythm, and the dance of language that story is all about. It is not just what is said, but how. It is about how the words link themselves together when spoken to create a symphony of sound that the body can feel and hear. At college I learned that story must have a conflict, a plot, a main protagonist and an antagonist and I realized that our stories don't have that. It seems we are always lacking – lacking food, lacking housing, health – and now I had to deal with our lack of plot, conflict, protagonist and antagonist. Not so recently, someone accused me of having an ego. I have to say this is true. My ego has always refused to completely accept that we are lacking. I wanted my stories to be songs: songs of war, of peace, of hope, of overcoming adversity, calamity and disaster, but I wasn't sure that I wanted a protagonist and an antagonist. Even when I include conflict, I try to render it as a general tension in the community. My ego drove me back to the longhouse, to elder storytellers. It forced me to remember those first stories and to think about the lessons they gave me. It drove me back to song, because that is where this long dance of life begins.

We come to the table full banquet:

Our songs are partly words and partly vocables that the old and the young can all sing. The stories reflect the sound, the meaning of words and evocable songs, that is, the story is a common one, one that can be told and understood by the old and the young alike. These are the story lines that form the bases for the myths we create, which may not always be appropriate for the young. When we re-tell old stories in the context we inherit they become fictional guides. In this way we find freedom from oppression; we create dreams from obstacles, and derive hope from besiegement. Our stories in their mythological form are dramatic; they are accompanied by song, dance, masks and the natural world's hold on our best being. We sing and the rhythm of the song matches the rhythm of the work we engage, the sound, the beauty of the words, while the vocables match the delicacy or strength of subject. To realize all this we search our inner selves for our personal song, our song of spirit, of strength of commitment, our devotion to community and our selves. Our stories reflect our personal and common search for inner peace in the context of our realization of community. Whether we are successful or not, this is our intent.

In the same way, I search for the rhythm in my contemporary story, the drama that aligns itself with the old myths, and recreate this search for inner peace in the realization of community. I clear old obstacles.

Song is our first language:

Songs are the unadorned emotionality of our community and our selves in relation to community. They are the springboard from which our words begin. We seek resonance when we speak. We struggle for rhythm; we invert and infix words into a sentence because they sound better that way. We construct metaphorical extravaganzas rich in poetics because the subject is so difficult and requires so much beauty that we are obliged to do so. Normally, a story is told by a number of people in the longhouse, and so sometimes the voice changes and the story shifts just slightly because maybe an elder is talking the story, so I shift and write in the voice of the elders translating and transforming English into a shape that is purely Salish. Sometimes it is a warrior speaking, club rattling — quiver full of arrows shaking in the wind as the enemy approaches — and the language becomes forceful, powerful, a huge tsunami to be attended to. My language shifts again to the sound of the rattling of the club or the quiver of the arrows, or the howling of the wind. I never let go of the song in the story.

We are mask dancers:

Sometimes the story sits still and silent as the (mask) dancers perform a section of the story, particularly if raven or wolf or blue jay is speaking. I shift again to recreate the scene, the dialogue and the drama. These brief scenes change the direction of the story; lend weight to the unfolding tension between the characters and their dilemmas, whether internal or external. Raven's interlude needs to be heard, attended to, and sometimes we utterly fail to hear her song. My characters sometimes miss the song too, or perhaps the listener is too young to understand the song and so the teaching weighs heavy as the listener recoils from its lack of meaning. I shift again to negotiate between masked Raven and the characters in the story. I layer them with enough masks to make it through the story. The masking, unmasking and quick changes make them artists too.

Stories are our governors:

I embrace the laws I inherit. I hold close the teachings I have arrived at through my consideration of original story, and I speak to the pages, carefully culling meaning from my years of contemplation while trying not to insult my listeners. All the while I remember that listeners and readers are interpreters, and that to interpret on their behalf is an encroachment on their freedom to derive their own meaning from story. In the longhouse, the listeners add to the story when they notice a gap or a pause, and our elders are happy because they know that we are listening. So when I write,

I am careful not to talk too much story. I pare down the narrative without depriving my listeners of the language they will need to play with my characters. In the longhouse there are gaps in the storytelling process. Not everything is fleshed out; enough must be said to spark the listeners' desire to contribute to the story. I have listened to others tell me that, while reading *Daughters are Forever*, they would read a little bit out loud and the listeners would all say, that's right, that's just like ... that's how we are *siem* ... how we remember, thus building on the text in their own way, on their own paths. More than knowing that they understood, this tells me they were listening because they interrupted my story to add to it. I also know my gaps were judiciously located and well placed. I know the listeners were already getting ready to govern themselves according to my story, because they knew the story, it was their story, our story, and we were all there in the longhouse, calling out the story together as we have done for centuries.

There must be enough governance to empower the listeners to shift the direction they are travelling. So all the scenes are open-ended; they direct the listeners to consider their own journey through this long dance of colonization and de-colonization. Governance is about spirit-to-spirit relationship about travelling to the good life, about holding up the spirit of all things (*Haitchka siem*). They are about our energy harnessed from the cosmic spirit world, the living world, the natural world and the world of our ancestors, and using this energy to guide us to good being, good conduct and the purity of emotional and spiritual investment that will lead us to this spirit-to spirit-relationship. So I must create the sort of characters in whom this commitment is present, whose collaboration aims for this original intention. Whether they fail or succeed does not matter; the possibility of success, however, must be present in the unraveling of the story.

Be careful which side you feed:

I am wolf. Wolves are capable of collaboration, planning the hunt and collectively sustaining ourselves. We are also capable of chewing off our own foot if trapped and attacking anyone who undertakes to release us from the trap. As wolves, we must be careful which wolf spirit we feed. All humans have a dialectical internal dynamic: we are both capable of generosity and parasitic conduct, and we need to pay attention to which side of our humanity we feed. I must create enough characters in my stories to show collaboration, to show parasitism, to show attention to our humanity.

If you have hard things to say let your language tread softly:

Soft language is poetry; it intervenes in the story as the subject presents difficult or hard circumstances. I weave in and out of poetics and prose narrative, although I struggle to retain the essential prose of novel writing. I am now negotiating my way through three disparate genres of writing in the Western tradition: drama, poetry and story narrative underpinned by song, by dance and accompanied by sociological intent.

Our stories are call songs, inviting response:

I need to write the responsiveness to catastrophe and daily life of the characters in such a way that they are able to embrace their own song free of the intervening judgment of the storier. Further, the characters bound to the good life must respond with the whole community and its future in mind to the behaviour of the members of the community. In the tension of our story there are some characters who are off path – the path to the good life – and those who are on path. The journey of each character embraces the sacred right of choice each one has to respond to story (behaviour through calamity, catastrophe) in their own way. Each one delivers an aspect of the whole picture of the journey through the catastrophe or calamity and the response of each human to it. I first need to create the whole in my mind – centre on the wheel and spiral through the journey from as many directions as I am able – and then create characters based on the separate journey to the centre of the circle.

The shape of the house matches the structure of society:

I am longhouse. The front entrance is always for the living invited to the ceremony story. The back door is the spirit door, the entrance of the cosmic spirit world, the natural spirit world, the ancestral spirit world and the spirit world of our unborn. The storyteller is obligated to the generations (human, cosmic, natural or otherwise) that came before and those that will come after (our grandchildren). I am a link in this long chain of myth makers urging the living to the path of the good life.

As a writer, I embrace the above, cognizant that this is a ceremony, that each character is familiar with both doors. The listeners sit on three sides of the house. They sit above the speaker. The storier must look up at them. Respect is reflected by the physical positioning of the speaker, storier, and dramatist below the people. I come through my work struggling to delete, rearrange, and reframe that which sets me above the people. In the structure of the longhouse, the story is always bigger than the storyteller. The story is accompanied by dancers, singers, masks, comics, clowns and the audience. The storyteller is small. I did dig around in my story, my history and sense of being, and I strived to create "communitism" from separation, spiritedness from despair, generosity from impoverishment, heroics from fear, and I strive to do so today as though I were full myself of all the dichotomous types of being I inherited.

223

Stories are ceremonies inviting prayerful being:

If you see yourself in this story come and make it right with creation. We do not ask for things when we pray; instead, we sing our history, our story; we appeal to the spirit world because we are pitiful and we are pitiful because we cannot always see ourselves. Because we know we march about our pragmatic lives somewhat blind, when we hear story we know to look for ourselves in it. We look for all aspects of ourselves, and those parts of us that are off the path become amusing to us as we see the characters fumble in the dark, or parade their arrogant misfit behaviour before the community, or trip on their own self-righteousness, so we recall our own fumbling, misfitting, parading of arrogance. I have done all those things, and it must be clear to the audience that it is this parade of arrogant and misfitting tripping and fumbling that has conjured the myth I am telling. Then we must face ourselves and alter our conduct accordingly. As a writer I must also write as though it is this misfitting, tripping, fumbling and parading that in the end has brought me my greatest joy because it revealed the journey to the good life. I must write as though I have embraced my ugly inside and struggled with my own transformation. No one expects me to be successful, but they do expect that I make this effort to face my tripping, parading, and fumbling and struggle to make it right with creation after having faced myself.

Our stories are oral and our language clean:

I don't use a single word in a story that I have not spoken many times. So when I want to write a story like *Ravensong*, I first consult elders of my choosing who understand what I am meaning to say to see if I have the oral teaching right, then I spend upwards of a year speaking to my elders, consulting with them and talking about it. Once the English I need to use has become clear, I begin to track the original stories attached to the dilemma or pattern of events and the journey out. We do not need to look at our colonial history to understand how we fell off the path. We have been off the path before. Our teachings, our ceremonies, our counseling methodologies, our oratory on governance, conduct and spirit-to-spirit relations are all born of our having met with disaster, reacted badly, and from our efforts to reclaim our original path. Our stories are full of pathfinders. I retreat to original story to conjure the myths of colonialism. I am cognizant that as a storyteller I am adjunct to speaker with a distinct position and responsibility in our governing system and that the cleanest language is required. Clean language comes from clean living. If there is unclean language in the story then the listeners will know I am not perfect, I am not completely clean, and they will forgive because they can see the effort made in the story to present "in the cleanest language I know." To know is to have faced the unclean. This, we know, takes a lifetime of retracing old story, facing ourselves and altering conduct. Storiers are not required to wait until the end of their journey to begin telling stories. In our writing, we must find a way to show that we understand the heroic journey to clean language and continuous transformation because we are continuously facing ourselves and cleaning up the language in our everyday lives.

We are transformers:

We are transformers. We arrived through transformation and our stories are documents of the historical transformations we have experienced. We are expected to carry on the tradition of continuous transformation by re-creating new stories that are connected to our history of story and transformation. We are expected to live our lives as story. We breathe story, tell and re-tell story, we alter our being over and over again throughout our lives based on the creation and recreation of story. The stories we tell address the transformations we have and have not made in our own lives.

Raven stole the light:

Colonialism has a soft underbelly. On the one hand, there are the spikes that injure and wound; on the other, colonialism brought us together in large urban centres that we might hear each other's stories and learn from them. Here is what I have faced about *Raven steals the light.* When Raven stole the light she created this beautiful shadow land. We are seekers, we seek to look upon the light and appreciate it, but we are further called to remember that Raven likes shiny things and when he saw something shiny he pecked and pecked at it with delight until it lost its shine. In the dark shadows of calamity, disaster, and oppression is colonialism's soft underbelly. Inside the shadows we can find our own light. But first we must steal the light of colonialism ourselves, then in shadow land shine it on the very colonial darkness from whence came the light. Colonialism is an invasive human condition that binds all humans together. To alter these bindings, we must courageously study its shadow land and bring it into the light. Our rejection of white people in their totality is contrary to our inclusive history. *Ravensong's* Stacey is a good person with not so good biases. If a reader does not get that, it is because they think bad people are biased or racist. But this is not the case at all as many good people continue to allow us to die. The exorbitant death of Indigenous people is the result of plain racism. This severely weakens the bindings between us and changes the omnipotent oppressiveness of colonial conditions. We don't have to get all tied in knots because of some racist remark. With a snip and a tug the bindings are cut loose and we are no longer threatened by shadow land. We are standing in the shadows giving off our own brilliant light. This is what I gained from the story: it is not the story that matters but how the story serves the listener. This is what is most important.

As transformers we are not afraid to add rafters to our house:

Religions invite traditionalism, be they Christian, Muslim, Pagan, Dalai Lama Buddhists or any other religion. Religions often hold up tradition as though this were their goal. For me this is a short-sighted goal. The goal is self-governed conduct that values all life as sacred. To this end, I let go of tradition when it calls for slaves, polygamy, unequal treatment of women, homophobia, race-based emotionality and retention of colonial structures, but this letting go does not require me to switch my allegiance from Stó:lō to some other paradigm. We have added many new rafters to our houses. All of the transformations that took place over the thousands of years of our story have added a rafter or two to our houses. Each calamity or disaster or falling out we endured led to the need for change, for a new rafter, a new song, dance, ceremony, new sets of teachings and stories. I studied the western novel and story writing so that I could add this rafter to my house, and I move in and out of the Longhouse and Western-based story at will. I am not only seeking my transformation and the transformation of my current relations, but I am also seeking connection and relation with those who are privileged by colonialism. This requires that I include those privileged by colonialism in my stories, striving to cement relations with the characters as well as those who present the face of colonialism. It doesn't require that my characters be successful; still, I must write those who are willing to make the effort to transform and I must create the colonial face of those whose reactive being shows the spikes of colonialism. I strive to do so from a place not of force or arrogance but from a place of choice.

227

Choice is sacred:

We are more or less educated in the teachings and stories of our nations and we select what we commit to remember. We create by selecting from this knowledge base, though we may think we create from the whole. For example, Thomas King is a Longhouse (Cherokee) storier; he creates very different stories from me, though we tackle very similar subjects, have some very common teachings – our origin story is almost the same, so much so that some Stó:lō people believe that the Iroquoian speaking peoples have pirated our origin story – but we have taken very different story telling aspects to commit to and applied different ways of imagining story. This is not unlike European storiers who are taught English story structure, plot, metaphor, etc. and yet when the pen hits the page something completely unique is born. Storiers are aware that choice is sacred, that story creation, while hooked to social origins, is a uniquely personal ceremony and the product, the story, will be always different if some other person crafts it. That is not to say that our stories have nothing in common. European-crafted story enjoys common elements with many Indigenous stories, but an individual storier makes choices that render the stories intensely individual. Stories arise from the cultural base of the storiers' origins, but the individuality of the storier personalizes and alters the presentation of each story. Freedom of expression and the sacredness of choice bind all storiers, European and Indigenous, together.

Haitchka, Gloria.

ORATORY ON ORATORY

Seeing Ourselves Through Story vs. Western Models

In the study of literature, Western instructors often pose the question, "What was the author thinking, doing, intending?" Salish thinkers and philosophers (orators) regard such questions as invasive, and do not grant themselves the right to ask them, much less answer, in the absence of the author. Such questions are meaningless in terms of the function of story in our society. The point of hearing (and now reading) story is to study it in and of itself, to examine the context in which it is told, to understand the obstacles to being that it presents, and then to see ourselves through the story, that is, transform ourselves in accordance with our agreement with and understanding of the story. The answer to the question governing the author's intent leads to the transformation of the author, not that of the listener or reader. We encourage growth and transformation in other humans, but we do not see it as our purpose to assist them in the process of maturation. The objective is mature, transformative governance.

This invasiveness marks the nature of the Diaspora. It is rooted in the Western notion that society can guess what is going on in someone's mind by what they write. In their successful global conquest, the mother countries, the Diaspora I am talking about here, collectively and individually, granted themselves the right to claim discovery, and then proceeded to define, delineate, and demarcate the cultural, intellectual, economic, spiritual, and physical being for the entire world. The institutions of this Diaspora usurped the authority of, and established exclusive dominion over, the standards for all sorts of things, including education and literary creation. This global positioning of privilege and dominion affects the Diaspora's attitude toward those outside its privileged location. Its right to speculate on what is in the mind, body, heart, and spirit of others is an unquestioned agreement. The citizens of this Diaspora practise this exclusive right based on the right of their state to arbitrarily determine the nature of their relations with all others, often without due consideration to those others. This has had disastrous results in the world. Disaster is the outcome of invasiveness, to wit, war and environmental destruction.

The structure of a building determines its style; the structure establishes the parameters of its foundation in a limiting way. The type of building constructed tends to be similar to others built before it. This, in turn, limits its function, its use, and its aesthetics. The owner of the building limits entry. Aristotelian definitions of drama and poetry were based on Greek aristocratic supremacy and exclusivity. They reflected Greek culture and Greek social norms. The structure of Aristotelian story reproduces the structure of Aristotle's society: hierarchical, patriarchal, and racist. The compliance by White male writers over centuries with Aristotelian definitions gave birth to a collection of writings that, designated as the canon, governs our present. As Europe set about to establish colonial preponderance over the entire globe, it foisted this canon on the colonies. It erected structures globally to exclude and limit other types of participation.

Today the colonized are free to challenge this House of Lords.

Stó:lō Study Methodology

Study can be contemplative, reflective, dramatic, responsive, analytical, dynamic, collaborative, and inspiring. It is capable of sparking and moving people toward social transformation, dissolving inequities, eradicating dangerous assumptions, and altering oppressive conditions. It is also capable of rationalizing those same oppressive conditions and upholding inequity by ignoring underlying assumptions that may prove dangerous to position. Depending on the direction from which we choose to examine the subject and the position we hold as examiners, serious study can maintain or threaten the status quo. The motivation for our examination (gatekeeping or a desire for relationship) guides the process of examination. The objective of the examiner narrows or broadens the thoroughness of the examiner's search. If we are colonized, study can direct us toward freedom, and it can be liberating. If we are colonizers, it can direct us toward our humanity, and this too is liberating. If we fail to master study, to question the direction from which looking occurs, or to ponder the motive for seeing and studying, then study becomes reactive, reproductive, and colonial.

In a certain sense, fiction/myth, story, is real: it is historic and reflects life; it is conditioned by the desire to mirror a character's relationships with the world. Salish study looks for the obstacles to growth and transformation, both in the external and the internal worlds. Once an understanding is achieved, the mythmakers story it up in a way that they hope leads humans toward social maturity and growth. The assumption here is that growth and maturity are capable of inspiring intervention and will lead to the transformation of the dichotomous social arrangements in Canada.

For First Nations people, study is directed at that which is not seen, not known, at what is cherished and hidden. In the discovery of the unknown lies growth. At the bare minimum, consciousness of who we are ought to occur. This takes some humility and, of course, some witnesses who know you. Study, then, is a collective and collaborative process: collective not in the sense that one wants to come to a common position, but collective in that many participate; and collaborative in that we all wish to come to a good mind about what is cherished and hidden. The good mind ranges from clarity, consciousness, to the end goal of a good life. In order to see what is not known, personal agendas must be articulated and set aside. We engage witnesses to assist students in ensuring that we have truly set aside our agendas. The light must be bent in a direction that is not obvious, that is in the shadow.

In shadow land we experience the discomfort of the unknown. Healers are present to ensure that this discomfort is processed and pushed past, and that we don't make fear-based, discomfort-based decisions about the unknown. Each of us is called upon to open our eyes to see what we have not dared hitherto to look at. Study is about searching for what lies beneath the obvious, unmasking the journey of a phenomenon coming into being, and engaging ourselves in imagining its passing out of being.

Mythmakers, storiers, are present to bear witness, see, and understand the subject under study, and serve as adjuncts to the process, so that they may story up each round of discourse in a way that governs the new conduct required to grow from the new knowledge discovered. We assume that individuals have different viewpoints: in fact, the more variance in viewpoints, the better. There is no arguing or challenging someone's viewpoint. We are certain that there is a place for oppositional points of view, as all views are seen as an aspect of the whole. We are interested in clearly stating what we see and looking for the key to the unknown in the voices and words of others. We are listening — our imaginations fully engaged – to what is said, what is not said, and what is connected to what is not said. The words spoken by others direct the listener to imagine and think. Rememberers attend to the words spoken with care, so that the oratory can be repeated later. They commit to recalling without judgement every word spoken. The speakers use words sparingly with poetic force, vision, and poignancy, so the rememberers will have an easy time of recall. Once the first round of deliberations is up, we imagine the story that will encourage us to look again, to peel back each layer and gain deeper understanding.

The next round is to imagine what direction each of the pathways arising from each person's contribution leads. This is a query round, sometimes a round of mini-stories, to assist in our search. It is a round in which we attempt to look beyond ourselves, to gauge the future, and to reassess the masks we wear in the present. The moment we hear something we have not heard before, whether we believe it has value or not, we build on it as a way of arriving at understanding. We flesh out this new idea, and then we story that up.

Every deliberation leads to discovery, new relationships, new directions, and, of course, new story because we build on what we have not heard or said before. Once the new thought is understood, then the storiers, the mythmakers, the poets, and the dramatists conjure story in a way that will assist the whole in establishing a relationship to the new. They are expected to do so with freedom and choice in mind; the stories then must be lean narratives, narratives that enable the listener to contribute to the narrative and make choices about the direction he or she chooses to take in the light of this new phenomenon.

Orators are our knowledge bearers, teachers, scientists, environmentalists, agriculturists, aquaculturists, historians, and rememberers. For a people whose culture rests on becoming, not

233

becoming is tragic. In order to blossom, we must be free to see, to study in a culturally appropriate manner. See is relentless, powerful or hampering, imprisoning or liberating. What we look at and what we do not look at is no accident. It is established by the place of the seers in the social fabric, the positions they hold and the journeys to their particular place. Position also shapes what is looked at and what is ignored. Culture abrogates personal responsibility for systemic being, or it calls us to question being and place and culture itself. It grants us a means by which to rationalize our position and place in relation to, or it challenges us to question the arrangement and assignment of place. If we enjoy a position of privilege, we may engage ourselves in personalizing the journey of the story and resent the challenge to place. In seeing our selves through story, we become part of the journey. Those who turn a blind eye to Canadian First Nations literature will not see the rock upon which the place and privilege of each member of the Diaspora rests.

When studying a subject, we first face our attitudes, our beliefs, and our agendas. We face the filters through which our specific cultural and personal origins affect clear and clean vision. Even though we may not be aware of our blinders, our masks, and our filters, we have them. These blinders, masks, and filters pervert the attention we pay or don't pay to the condition or being of others. Attention is a device driving us to implode – or explode or desire – transformation, or to exchange desire for the mundane and the old, driving us to plod along blind to the new and different in the world. We articulate the way in which we rationalize our place and identify how this colours our vision. It is not enough to articulate the masks through which we see. For see to be thorough, the seekers must engage their search in a conscious process of removing the masks and dropping the filters through which they are peering; we struggle to set them aside, to ensure that we are looking at the being and the phenomena free of our personal history. We believe that our attitudes, our beliefs, and our agendas are the ordinary, everyday masks we wear that facilitate the reproduction of social and cultural being in a static way. Stasis promotes decadence. The goal is to study something with transformation and growth in mind. These masks are not all that useful in establishing new relationships. Unless we bend the light in the direction of our attitudes, beliefs, and agendas, we will not be able to drop the mask, let go of our original vision, and expand it to "include" the vision of others in our scope of see. Oratory is braided to the processes of see, to study, to unmasking our attitudes; it requires the mythmakers to remove the filters that colour and taint vision. Our stories reflect all of these processes.

See has a methodology that is emotive, spiritual, intellectual, and physical. It can be affirming and mundane, as though it sought the repainting of the same picture, as though it were moved to repeat history, as though it were its own force holding the old social conditions and relations in place. In its possession of force, it may draw us to look again, to re-search, to play, to fiction ourselves in dreams of transformation or to escape the very force of looking. Intentions are masks constructed of experience; they hide cruel intent arising out of wounded and violated vulnerability, or surrender, or unrequited love. Force is a volcano waiting to explode. In the dichotomized world of Diaspora and chronic invasion, we are all equally capable of marching in these directions.

Story becomes a means of intervention preventing humans from re-traversing dangerous and dehumanizing paths. Oratory, then, is responsive. It challenges the state of being of the people who are being "storied up." It is transformative. It pulls up the sort of characters who can best "story" the subject, the obstacles, and the characters, which impede transformation and/or freedom.

235

The Object of Study

The object of study from a Salish perspective is ultimately the creation of oratory that will lead us onto a path of continuous growth and transformation, and that will enable us to engage all life in the type of spirit-to-spirit relationship that leads all parties to the good life. We did not have the concepts of law, order, and compliance that require systems of force to uphold them. Our concept of the good life was rooted in recognition of the perfect right to be for all beings. We do so from the emotional, spiritual, intellectual, and physical perspective that all beings enjoy a perfect right to be as they are. We believe that each being owns a sense of distance between itself and human beings, a survival right, and a value to the totality of life, even if we don't know what that value is.

Study is tempered by humans studying the space between the beings in the relationships humans are engaged by. From the snow flea on a glacier to barracudas and sharks, the small beings and the invisible beings, all beings have a perfect right to be. We respect the barracuda, but we recognize that the charming smile of this predator is dangerous, and so we maintain a good distance from his territory, and we don't swim with sharks. Principles of fair exchange govern all of our relationships. We pick berries in such a way that the berries are assured of continued renewal, and we are cautious to leave some for the bears. We study from the perspective that, as the variable beings on earth, it is humans that need to transform and alter their conduct to engage in relationship with other beings and phenomena. Relationship engagement is disciplined by conjuring the least intrusive and invasive conduct possible, respecting the distance and reproductive rights of other beings, and ensuring the greatest freedom of beings to be as they are and always will be. This requires that we study the life of beings and phenomena in our world from their perspective, and not from the perspective of our needs.

The goal of study is to see a being or phenomenon in and of itself and for itself with the purpose of engaging it in a relationship that is mutually beneficial. First, we need to know *who we are* and the possible obstacles to understanding that our history may present. In the course of study, we deliberately engage people with different kinds of knowledge, points of view, and different understandings, people whose journeys are dissimilar to ours, who may have witnessed the phenomena under study from their own perspective. Should we discover discomfort during the process, we track back the source of discomfort from inside ourselves, inside our journey, our history, and face our fears and ourselves, face our discomfort and disconnect it from the subject under study. Then we story this up. We express the governing impact our history has on the way we see. We story up the blinders and the filters we inherit from our history. In this way, we develop an intimate appraisal of our emotional responses to history, to movement, to the dynamics and conduct of others in relation to ourselves. If we cannot let go of our history's impact, we abstain from the process. We imagine our desire, our capacity for transformation, and our place in the universe next to the being we try to relate to, gauge its importance to us, measure our desire for relationship with it, and discuss it with our peers as story/oratory. We must study, and engage ourselves in the pursuit of study, in the interest of both ourselves and the subject of study. We are in varying degrees successful or not in this endeavour, but it is the goal of our study.

We know that standards, norms, and experiences can become obstacles to clear perception, and we take the time to clear the norms that reduce us to seeing through some kind of collective fog, filtered through old standards.

This Is the First Story That Needs to Be Told

On one hand, we recognize that humans have the capacity to be concatenate, to link with all beings and phenomena, to be conscious, to be aware of our personal motives, to be curious, to be open to the discovery of others, and to be creative, to make the links and connections happen in a mutually beneficial way. On the other hand, we recognize that humans are very much like viruses; given the opportunity, they will colonize another being, unless disciplined to travel in another direction toward relationship and away from conquest. Opportunism is an inherent part of our spirit. This opportunistic behaviour has both an upside and a downside. On the upside, opportunism creates a sense of doubt and desire that leads us to question ourselves and the world around us, calls us on our motivations, calls us to create new things from the world around us so that, when we feel uncomfortable, we can be inspired to track our discomfort and engage in personal and social transformation.

As variables in the grand scheme of creation, in our origin stories we enter the world as both fragile and resilient beings. Like viruses, we are difficult to contain. In fact, our resilience defies containment. Freedom is always on our agenda. Like viruses, we appear to have an edge on the animal beings. A wolf, for instance, cannot alter its being and become, say, a truck driver, a doctor, or a lawyer, while a doctor or a lawyer could in theory lead a wolf 's life; he or she could live in very harsh circumstances, sleep under the stars with a minimum of protection from nature (like a fur coat), and sustain himself for some time on field mice, the primary diet of a wolf. This is not to say that wolves are not as intelligent, emotional, spiritual, character-driven, social, or complex as we are; it is just a fact that a wolf would not succeed at a contemporary law school, and it would be dangerous for a wolf to undertake to drive a truck. As variables that are fragile, and yet capable of great opportunistic destruction, we are called upon to pay attention to our relationship with others, to engage the world and all its beings in a responsive and responsible manner that is cognizant of the perfect right of other beings to be in relationship to us. We are not entitled to use the information gathered about the impossibility of the wolf becoming a lawyer to demean the wolf's being, or to give us the right to murder him. This is the exploitative work of invaders. This will not result in a future relationship with the wolf.

Conquest is neither the object of study nor the desire of relationship. We long ago relinquished invasion as a way of being. In so doing, we have come to see that if we see the story of a social formation as an inherently oppressive phenomenon, we are called upon to story up its oppressive features and the impact of these features on the myriad of characters from our world in the hope that our citizens will catalyze social transformation from within the story. This opportunism can sometimes drive us to sink into discomfort, pirate the things around us, retreat into blind denial, and entrench ourselves in the defeat of the business of personal growth in exchange for participation in conquest and colonization.

This Is the Business of Oratory

Even in the worst catastrophe, there is something unknown and cherished to be discovered. We are certain that all life and death contain something cherished that can be observed; if we listen, if we look for its internal dynamic, watch its behaviour, and commit to its being, we may discover it. Once we discover it, we can establish a relationship with it. Despite the distance maintained between the barracuda and ourselves, we still have a relationship with it. That relationship is one of cherishing the distance between predator and prey; in this way, the barracuda becomes a teacher, and the relationship is one of student and teacher. The space is deep green water. We determine the nature of relationship, and the mythmakers create oratory as story so that each person can conduct himself or herself in a complementary fashion. We can know that we are successful only if both the being and ourselves flourish, or if the phenomenon (e.g., colonialism) is transformed into something all agree is better than before.

This Is the Desire of Oratory

Salish people created the frameworks and language within which we may view the world in the way I'm outlining here to ensure the greatest absence of destruction, invasion, imposition, and obstruction in our engagement of the world, while still availing ourselves of the resources required for our specific continuance. These frameworks prevent us from becoming conquerors, and lead us away from systems of slavery and toward spirit-to-spirit relationships based on a profound understanding of ourselves. They did not lead us away from war, but we are sure they will in the end.

We set the unknown but cherished thing at the centre of a study circle. Each of the students is an expert gathered at the outer edges of the circle. Each person forms a wedge of vision observing the space directed toward discovery of the unknown. Each observer brings an angle of perception that, when rallied, engaged, and exchanged, brings vital observations, which will assist us in considering the internal dynamics that might govern the behaviour of the being in the least judgemental way possible. We do not believe we can fully understand the being/phenomena under study. We recognize that we are not able to walk inside the body/

mind/heart/spirit of the being/phenomenon; we cannot know the thoughts/thinking, emotions/emotionality, and spirit/spirituality of the being or phenomenon. In our ordinary travels through the mundane tasks of life, we rarely look deeply at the world around us. In the course of study, we pay attention to ordinary beings and bend the light in the direction of the unseen, of the shadows inherent in any being. Inside shadow land lies the dynamics of hidden being. We can see its behaviour, gauge its patterns, note the direction of its movement, and come to grips with it in relation to us. We can see its journey, and render it as story. We can study this journey and try to understand ourselves in relation to its story so that we can peacefully coexist.

We then story up the nature of safe engagement in mutually beneficial relations.

We attempt to story another being/phenomenon's behaviour and commit to its journey, its coming into being and going out of being, to this story. We then alter our conduct, our behaviour, to facilitate a common journey alongside of the being/phenomenon without interrupting its physical or cultural continuum, and we story that up. We commit ourselves to social structures, which lend themselves to creative, re-creative formation and transformation. This is how oratory is born. Oratory is a painting; it is about the freedom between beings and about cherishing the distance between them; it is about relationship, and as such it is about life. Oratory is comprised of the complex relations between disparate characters in their concatenation or their lack of it. It is the story of patterned events. Oratory is a human story in relation to the story of other beings, and so it is fiction, for it takes place in, while engaging, the imagination of ourselves in relation to all beings. Oratory informs the stories of our nations in relation to beings of all life.

The Study of Oratory Requires That We Peel Back the Layers

The process of study is based on story. Stories are about characters, and we believe that character is inherent and unalterable. Those who would alter character do so under threat of creating disastrous consequences; therefore we challenge conduct, not character. The conduct we challenge is, of course, the conduct of ourselves as humans. Under each pattern of conduct is a layer of history. We strive to protect the dignity, movement, and space of those under study. Thus we search and research the history of their conduct and deal with their history as influence. We attach conduct to the influence of history, inspiring the character to alter conduct if that conduct impedes relationship. This is our meaning of respect. We engage in the process without the expectation of agreement or amicability, without preset standards. This is the meaning of openness, which is a prerequisite to learning. No being is reduced to the conquered. No being is extorted by others or demeaned to a lesser place of being through humiliating practices. All phenomena are valid and acceptable, part of the picture, and it is in the creation of a whole picture, a totality, that the work of study begins as story, that becomes part of the body of our oratory. We do not leave the world of flora and fauna out of the process. The origin stories of the trees, the flora and fauna, and so forth are articulated during the process as needed.

We first see how the character moves, see how it conducts itself, how it marks its own sense of movement, its sense of time and being, its sense of territoriality, its organizational structure. We connect its conduct to its being, and then we connect its movement to its desire, its sense of time to its longevity, and its behaviour to its condition, history, and environment; and we story that up. Until we have a vast body of patterned movement and conduct observed through many sets of eyes, we make no deductions. *Ravensong* presents characters in the condition of patterned colonial movement. This is what oratory or a novel is all about to me. It is also one of the options accorded literary creation in the Euro-tradition. To include oratory as novel in the world of literature does not detract from western definitions.

This process of study is a collective process. It is not oriented toward collectivizing the thinking of those who participate in it. It requires many different sets of eyes, many different minds whose histories are known yet different, whose journeys have led them along adjunct but disparate paths, whose understandings and whose emotions/spirit/mind/body are determined to be travelling in the direction of relationship and good will. We gather people together who are the most capable of seeing and articulating what they see. Together, we paint a whole picture, as complete a picture as our collective can create. We engage one another through the images created by those sitting in the circle. The images must be sincerely and genuinely presented points of view – images, observations, and understandings, not biases. Should a bias arise, we are called upon to set it aside, and identify our ability to rise above our history and conditions and state our capacity for making, or not making, judgements based on some previous past.

The desire is to find the connections, to create the webs between the disparate points of view, images, and stories, and to ensure that the end of the journey is the spiralling down to a moment of peace and recognition. These connections are seen as the creation of windows of opportunity for seeing the future and for transformation. What the speakers/storiers do share is a common sense of direction and a common commitment to moving in the direction of discovering the unknown. We know that, if we examine something from one subjective angle (all human observation and thought are

243

presumed to be subjective), then we will understand only an aspect of the being under study, and we are very likely to engage in huge errors, leap to absurd conclusions based on subjective assumptions, and so forth. This is a process that shows we have come to cherish what is new and struggling to be born.

Discourse Is Creative

This discourse of study engages the work of our creative imagination. The first round articulates the direction from which the viewer perceives. The second round engages with what is seen of the physical behaviour, the coming into being and the going out of being of the being/phenomenon. The third round articulates the being/phenomenon's interaction, its relations with other beings (water, flora, fauna, human, stars, night, day, etc.). Next comes the articulation of its characteristics — its personalities, quirks, oddities — and of its difference from the human condition. Then follows a discussion about what was cherished and hidden, but is now seen in the light of our different perspectives, from our separate, and now shared, observations. Where do we intersect and connect? How do we commune with this being/phenomenon? How do we interact in the least obtrusive way possible? This process requires a facilitator/teacher who has no personal stake in guiding the outcome, but rather is committed to the purity of process and maximizing the participation of each contributor.

We are successful in varying degrees, but we are all clear that that is the process to which we commit.

Conventions Governing Process

There are conventions governing the language of this process. Words are sacred, they are breath, breath is wind, and wind is power. Wind is earth's bellows transforming land, water, sea, and weather. Breath is human wind, our bellows urging us in the direction of transformation and relationship forming. In the end, life is lived through wind's breath. Hard truths require soft language – poetics; journeys are the language of story. The physical coming into being and going out of being is the language of drama; relationship is the language of poetic story. Everyone commits to remembering what others have said, which means brevity is critical. The story conjured is lean, the poetry as pure as the speaker can render it, and the drama short, open-ended scenes linked to the being/phenomenon. Relationship between listeners and the subjects of story becomes possible if the listeners can study the story, see themselves in the story, and transform themselves or their society. Some of the speakers' stories have to do with what lies underneath the past – storied observations presented – and enable the new storiers, the mythmakers, to deepen the story, broaden it, and find intersecting, connecting moments between human and the being/phenomenon.

We conjure the story in such a way that the best human conduct will show itself through it. How do we shape the story so listeners are inspired to consider conduct that will explicitly direct them to the specifics of transformation without narrowing or defining what may be learned? Without limiting the myriad of directions the transformation of all listeners might take? Every story is a guide fleshed out by the listeners in their consideration of future. Story impacts on the shape of the future the listener hears, and she or he completes the story from his or her own direction. The process of study must give listeners the option of determining the alteration of their personal conduct in an atmosphere of freedom. They must be free to make change in accordance with the limits of their character. At the same time, the direction of the whole nation must serve the longevity of relationship with the beings/phenomena generations into the future. If the story does not do this, then how do we story this up? The story calls upon listeners to lend their imagination and voice to it, contribute to its unfolding, and reshape their conduct based on their personal understanding of the relationship or the absence of relationship.

The story must represent the obstacles to the future that are inherent in the story experienced by the listener. Its lean, poetic, dramatic, and narrative structure is deliberate. The circle of listeners provides the flesh of the narratives. Their villages carried history, story, romance, social being, cultural life, creativity, and growth and transformation from the village to the nation and back to the village. They did so in the language of the listeners. The more attitudes storied, the more perspectives presented, the more choices the listeners have. Thus I think it is funny when someone criticizes *Ravensong*, saying the character of Celia is insufficiently exploited; from the Salish perspective of oratory, this is a compliment.

The final step is to recognize a rememberer as guardian/keeper of the story. No elections are held, nor are appointments made or any agendas drawn up. This process is as fluid as the tide. We know when the story is born. The rememberer knows when she or he has committed to its telling. In the modern world, a book assumes the position of rememberer.

The end result is a powerful story, a long lasting relationship, and characters that foster beauty, hope, heart, and song.

Students are responsible for identifying what they know of the subject of study before tackling the business of study. The instructor is responsible for facilitating the student's study. Thus study becomes a process of personal exploration of the truths within the layers of hidden being, peering past the obvious and ferreting out the unseen. Students pull on the threads that feed the story (Diaspora, sexism, racism, patriarchy, homophobia, etc.)

and that constructed the cultural fabric. They seek the invisible threads that bind them to the characters in the story, and unravel these threads. Students travel on the story's journey to the centre where peace and recognition lie within them. When students have come to a place of peace with the journey, reconciled themselves to themselves, then and only then do they really know something. At that moment, they can remove their blinders, what keeps their feet on the ground, and see sacred black, eyes closed, light cut out, and their point of coming into being and the point of going out of being, and begin a new journey. We need to draw upon the tangled web of colonial being, thread by thread – watch as each thread unfurls, untangles, shows its soft underbelly, its vulnerability, its strength, its resilience, its defiance, its imposition, its stubbornness – rediscover Canada and First Nations people.

We desire to find the fullest, richest, and most interesting and mutually beneficial relationship possible in the least obtrusive and most congenial way possible, to engage the being/phenomenon – its history, its condition, and its conduct in relation to ourselves. This does not require that we shy from the obstacles in the path to relationship. Quite the contrary, obstacles need to be seen, and the hope of story is that the listeners will come together to clear the obstacles to future relationship. We imagine that this desire for relationship might be driven by our mutual right to be. We seek to satisfy our need for continuum as cultural and social beings alongside others – not under them or over them, but exactly like them, alongside them, different, known and cherished by them. This means that the current Diaspora and chronic invasion dynamic interrupting the relationships between us needs to be addressed. We have addressed this obstacle from our side of the table, but Canadians need to face themselves and commit to the transformation of the current relationship between us.

247

Desire is the hothouse motoring our opportunism and our doubt; it also motors our ability to be concatenate, to be creative, to be conscious, and to remain genuinely curious about all life. In our opportunistic self, humans look with a self-motivated affirmative purpose. That which does not serve our interests is not always attended to. Each human enjoys the capacity for transformation and seeks it on one level or another, or does not. In its unconscious opportunistic state, see's objective can be holy or perverse, and the seer has no way of knowing, without advice and counsel from the community, which direction the vision is guiding him or her. Humans bring intent with their vision. Intentions are sometimes dangerously reactionary. We may choose to see phenomena from the angle of perception we inherit. In our conscious state, we may seek that which is beyond our realm of perception, and this produces a visionary perception that can be transformative or reactive. Study is not about isolating parts; it is about seeing things in their separate movement and being, then connecting what we see to our own capacity for concatenation and the limits of the concatenate of the being under examination. At this time in history, Canadians are unable to face themselves, and so the concatenation between us will be limited. This does not mean that concatenation on a limited scale is not preferred to isolation; nor does it mean that examining parts cannot be interesting or that they are unworthy of study and recognition. But examining the parts – the thin wedges of being, of life, of society – is not the only way to study. Nor am I saying that Salish study formations are the only way to learn, the only way to achieve transformation, growth, or maturity. I am saying that we cannot arrive at whole understanding outside of a broadened and deepened framework. We cannot produce the results of study that will lead to the kind of story that will ensure our growth and transformation, lead to human maturity, to life, to freedom. The colonial system, which still rests squarely on our historic path, stultifies the possibility of concatenation between First Nations peoples and Canadians. The composition of an aggregate picture, a dynamic image of genuine being, and the imagining of the journey from separation to connection – these are the subjects of story and study that can produce freedom.

Instructors are not experts filling up passive empty heads. Students are as responsible for learning as their instructors are for facilitating this process. The student and instructor must be able to differentiate between what is clearly the responsibility of the student in the process of study and what is the responsibility of the instructor in the student's learning. Both must be able to see where teaching ends and internal learning begins. Students must be permitted to respond to education in their own voice. At the same time, critics, instructors, and institutions must respect that the picture First Nations authors advance is true, even if they don't see it that way, that it is half the colonial picture, that what you see may be true, but is not what we see. It may be the other half the picture. The moment we share a commonly constructed picture, a story, then we can begin to pull at the fabric holding the picture together, see its construction, and dismantle and recreate the design. Only then can we collectively recreate a community more human than before. This is the business of study in its totality for us.

From a Salish perspective, study ought to move us beyond the relentless reproduction of our cultural bias and remove the filters blinding our ability to see beyond this bias. In relinquishing the obstacles to new paths, we invite ourselves to this open field of fire we could be. Study requires characters that can challenge us to relinquish the mundane, the perverse, and the repetitive. We need to study stories whose characters and spaces will unlock our confinement and take us on a journey up to those planes of freedom.

The spiritual objective of study is to transform the way we see, to broaden the field of vision, to inspire us to "turn around," to drink in the images both of the world and the imagination. When we speak to this process, this too is oratory. When we gather thoughts, examine the conditions of our story, represent it as theory, and unveil the processes inherent in the journey of story – all this becomes the speaker's map to orating the future, and this too is oratory.

Discourse, theory, cognizance, and the transference of knowledge are parts of a creative, oratorical, dramatic, process through which our narrative history and story – oratory – were crafted, understood, and transferred systemically, both locally and nationally. This is what has created the body of knowledge of the nation and shaped the oral tradition, which then the listeners use to govern themselves. Oratory has ensured continuous growth and transformation: a powerful sense of justice, a broad framework for seeing, and a method of study and representation. Holistic thinking and being are the result. *The study of Native literature, then, is a written and oratorical collaborative process of seeing the self and society through story, in which the instructor is the facilitator.*

"DIFFERENT BUT THE SAME"

ONE OF THE MANY STORIES that Stó:lō author Lee Maracle shared with me during the editorial process that led to *Memory Serves: Oratories* was about a story her grandfather told her when she was a child. When he finished his telling, he said, "Now you tell it back to me, different but the same." Different but the same, a phrase that occurs more than once in this book, encapsulates the spirit and letter as much of Maracle's oratories as the revision and editorial processes that have turned them into what she calls in her Preface "a new kind of prose, what is fashioned when oratory is written down" (xii).

Oratory is an ongoing and dynamic process of transmitting inherited knowledge and values that have been safeguarded and expanded through generations of Indigenous culture. Or, as Donald M. Bahr defines it, oratory is speech "by a mortal person to mortal people" that "argues a position on what is good for the community" (107). The emphasis placed on "the good life" in *Memory Serves* leaves no doubt as to the goal of Indigenous oratory: to provide direction so "that we are all travelling toward the good mind," to offer guidance so that we can "restore our human journey to the good life" (11). Oratory's objective may be "unambiguous" (161) but the

251

journey it points toward is a challenging one, often stalled, perhaps even entirely aborted, for the humans who walk the path usually encounter various emotional, spiritual, political and material obstacles. Oratory provides a map that makes this journey possible, that shows the ways in which the river of life – Stó:lō in Halkomelen means "river" – can be crossed. "Without language," Maracle writes, "humans cannot think or consider the context of their life ... cannot reflect on their historical journey ... and create a vision of the future"; oratory makes it possible for them to "view obstacles as surmountable" (125). As the embodiment of collective memory, oratory can help those who "stand unsure at the edge of the river" paddle "through the rapids" (114) by reminding them to remember their communal heritage and thus stay the course.

Turning oratory into a written document reinforces memory by creating a more permanent record of it. Moreover, the printed format makes this repository of oral knowledge widely accessible to a broader group of people, offering, as Maracle says, "another way to be, to think, to know" (xiv), one that can help bring Indigenous and non-Indigenous communities closer together by showing the latter the benefit of engaging with the world in a holistic manner.

The conversion of orally delivered oratory into printed form does not always involve direct transcription. It is not necessarily a matter of transferring content from one system of communication to another, of transposing voiced speech beyond its moment of articulation into material inscription. Rather, rendering oratory in written form often entails a complex process of re-vision that parallels the relay of traditional oratory through various voices and protocols. Jo-ann Archibald, another Stó:lō author, writes that "[w]henever Indigenous oral tradition is presented in textual form, the text limits the level of understanding because it cannot portray the storyteller's gestures, tone, rhythm, and personality" (17). This

252

is certainly the case, but the absence of the vocal, acoustical, and gestural elements of oral delivery does not mean that the oratory's meaning is distorted as a matter of course. Because the meaning, value, and function of oratory do not derive from or depend upon a single authorial source, and because oratory, if it does not veer away from the heritage it represents, still maintains its links to orality, converting oratory into textual form does not inevitably warp its import. It is different, but it is also the same.

Creating a written record of oratory, as Maracle has done, produces yet another modality of the transmission and sharing of Indigenous knowledge, alongside the poetry, fiction, drama and criticism that Indigenous authors have been publishing for a long time now. Written oratory does not signal the kind of shift from oral literacy to written literacy that could be seen as orality's surrender to the hegemony of writing in Western culture. Nor is Indigenous oratory an extension of the European traditions of oracy; after all, as Bahr puts it, "Europeans brought oratory to Indians and, somewhat to their surprise, received oratory back from them" (107). Nor should orality be taken to be the feature par excellence of Indigenous cultures. Such notions would only serve to define Indigenous orality in Western terms, thus reifying the "colonialist conception of Indigenous discursive practices" that has "shape[d] the ways in which Indigenous cultures" (Teuton 170) have been studied until recently. Instead, embodying formal elements of Indigenous oral storytelling and directly addressing the oral tradition it comes from, written oratory unsettles the binary of the oral versus the scribal; it creates a space where orality and writing intercross and bolster each other. This comingling of inscription and orality incorporates the materiality of both expressions of language without devaluing one or the other. Despite the "movement away from old social structures and old cultural forms," Maracle writes,

253

"the artistic expression of both the written and oral Indigenous arts retains its non-hierarchical and non-coercive character" (169).

As *Memory Serves* illustrates, written oratory evokes the circle of an attentive audience at the same time that it reaches out to the reader; it re-presents the immediacy of speech but it also relies on the intimacy that develops when a reader holds a book in her hands; it retains the craft of orally delivered oratory yet it also reflects the orator's own craft of writing; it evinces the tradition of oral storytelling but it also engages with the more recent tradition of Indigenous writing. Written oratory, then, opens orality and writing up to one another in ways that simultaneously honour the protocols and values of Indigenous oracy and move Indigenous knowledge forward into the future. To echo Maracle's own words in one of our conversations, written oratory preserves and propels forward Indigenous knowledge "in the same way a river becomes the sea." Far from signaling an intention to arrest the evanescence of speech or a recuperative attempt to rescue what might be deemed to be a vanishing tradition, it animates aspects of orality both through various literary devices and a persistent acknowledgement that its textuality is decidedly embedded in the cultural practice of storytelling. Belying the Western epistemological assumption that speech is fluid and therefore perishable, it posits itself as the twin-other to spoken oratory. If traditional oratory is simultaneously storytelling and event, then one way in which we can understand written oratory is as a textual testimonial to oratory's performativity. Different yet the same, at once referencing and incorporating its twin other, and thus never losing sight of where it comes from, it too is put in the service of communal memory. Despite the relative fixity that writing imposes on meaning, written oratory does not rehearse a people's history as a finished product; instead, it renders it as a living archive of their enduring and continuously unfolding intellectual and spiritual heritage, a compass with which to find the way to the good life.

Maracle's written oratories position her as "a witness," a *si'yam* in Halkomelen, the Stó:lō language, "someone who can capture common thought," who "has [her] people's direction and thought at heart" (xiv). In discourses of bearing witness, especially in the context of trauma studies, the witness is usually cast as a figure burdened by the "solitude" he has to bear, which he must transcend via his testimony of a traumatic event by "speaking *for* others and *to* others" (Felman 15). In Shoshana Felman's words, "[t]o bear witness is to *bear the solitude* of a responsibility, and to *bear the responsibility*, precisely, of that solitude" (15). As Maracle attests, responsibility is key to the orator's role as witness (54), but in the Stó:lō tradition the witness is not relegated to a position outside of what transpires within the circle of knowledge delivery and knowledge sharing. The Stó:lō witness is always already embedded in an interrelational process, one that was traditionally accompanied by specific rituals and ceremony (Carlson et. al. 184–85), a process that makes him a necessary — if silent at times, yet always listening — partaker in communal storytelling. Indeed, "[t]he first task of every [Stó:lō] speaker is to call witnesses ... certain respected guests" who are invited to "'please witness, respectfully watch, and carefully remember the events you are going to hear and see this evening'" (Carlson et. al. 184–85). The Stó:lō witness, then, is not someone who happens upon an event; he is invited to become a witness by virtue of the fact that his presence has already been witnessed by others because of the respect his conduct in life has gained him.

255

When Maracle is told by Indigenous people that "*You just articulated everything I was thinking*"(xiv), she is recognized as a witness. This double act of witnessing — being a witness who pays attention and someone who has already been witnessed as

possessing the acumen necessary to capture common thought —
reveals the interrelational subjectivity of the orator-as-witness and,
by extension, the interrelational process that constitutes oratory
as storytelling. Consequently, bearing witness in this context is
not limited to acts of eye-witnessing as such; not only does it also
involve listening, but "seeing," as Maracle elaborates in "Oratory
on Oratory," is a multifarious act that encompasses what the eye
registers but also (self-)reflection and critical discernment. The
frequency with which the verb "to see" appears in this book may
emphasize the function of the gaze but here seeing is best understood as an instance of synesthesia, a cross-sensory perception
that involves direct and indirect speech, non-verbal sounds, haptic
engagement, indeed an array of synesthetic effects that connects
the viewer's own body to the dynamics of bearing witness.

This is abundantly obvious in the titular oratory in this book
in which Maracle offers a powerful and poetic narrative of her
encounter with Gloria Anzaldúa at the 1988 Third International
Feminist Book Fair in Montreal, an event that was momentous
in Indigenous cultural politics in Canada and, along with other
events around the same time, led to the difficult but necessary
debates about cultural appropriation. Self-identifying as an orator, she declares, *"Before I know what I am about to say, I need to
read my audience"* (17). While relating to the audience she sees
and hears as text, she also offers a highly affective account of the
various tensions in the room but also of the excitement — almost
intoxication — she experiences in recognizing in Gloria Anzaldúa
a kindred spirit. Clasping hands with Jeannette Armstrong under
the table (18), her gazed is fixed on Anzaldúa who is speaking; she
listens to her with her entire body while also *"feel[ing] the openness of each of her cells as Jeannette's words sing inside her."* Her
"[l]istening is an emotional, spiritual and physical act"; it *"is so old,*

so clean, so innocent and so very intense, and so full of the kind of remembering that is required of the women of Turtle Island ... [that it] is sentient, a total body experience" (21). When it is her turn to speak, she senses *"Gloria and Jeannette's listening ... like a blanket — a dome of protection. As it warms, strengthens and blurs the border at the edge of all our cloths the words inside gain power. The warm isn't like the heat wave rattling Montreal, threatening to bleed us of whatever sanity we came here with, but warm in that spirit way"* (22). Maracle's account demonstrates that witnessing in the Stó:lō oratorical context is both an embodied and generative act, an intersubjective process that records how and what she is "called upon to remember" (61) at the same time that she re-stories her tradition while storying her own experiences.

In "Memory Serves" memory and remembering are both distinct and coincident, part of a series of corresponding narratives and rhetorical turns that weave together sensorial and perceptual acts of witnessing. What remains constant in the narrated incident about Anzaldúa, and indeed throughout the book, is the figure of Maracle the orator as both witness and teller who never deviates from the task at hand: "to remember the past and re-determine [her] direction" (8). Acknowledging that for Salish people "re-membering is not a simple act of recall" — "All minds have pathways — dendrites — travelling to all parts of our memory" (14) — she posits her personal memories not as digressions that spread beyond her oratory's structure but as integral elements of materializing communal memory. *"I like realizing this,"* she writes, referring to how she remembers and documents her encounter with Anzaldúa: *"I roll the memory about, taste it; I like the edges of it as it titillates my lips. I swallow, savour it going down; each word commits itself to my memory"* (15). Visceral memories such as this dramatize the actual process of remembering while, at the same time, their centrifugal force helps elucidate the overall structure of oratory, the discursive process of committing to memory. Digressions of this kind not only serve to manifest the *"multiplicity of ways to remember"* but also function as paradigmatic instances of the *"discipline"* (21) the orator has to demonstrate. "Our imaginations," Maracle writes, "cannot discipline themselves outside of some form of social context; some sort of peer pressure is required to convert our wildly operating brain into some framework that will provide us with a reliable sense of order" (95). Discipline here, as I understand it, does not simply refer to the speaker exercising enough self-discipline so that she does not meander too far off course; it also refers to the method the orator must employ so that her oratories as composites of collective knowledge and self-narration achieve "community concatenation" (172).

Indeed, method is of paramount importance in Maracle's oratories, for it helps mould the orator's skills and facilitate her "spiritual concatenation" (171) with other members of her community and "the natural and spiritual world" (48). More specifically, as "Oratory: Coming to theory" makes it apparent, devising a method is equivalent to coming to theory, a process that entails, among other things, braiding together shared and personal memories so that a Stó:lō story about a war or Raven is narrated, as the example above illustrates, in the same context as Maracle's own memories of Anzaldúa. This intermingling of different narrative registers across different temporalities makes it possible for the orator to draw attention to their underlying sameness while expanding on the implications and applications of inherited knowledge.

258

"Salmon is the Hub of Salish Memory" exemplifies this particular way of coming to theory. Here Maracle as orator is at once teller and interpreter: while as teller her goal is to remember and share a story in a manner that respectfully echoes her people's traditional knowledge, her task as interpreter inflects her telling with her own artistic signature and perspective in a fashion that allows her to materialize what she wants to express in concrete terms; as she says, if theory "can't be shown, it can't be understood" (161). In this oratory, the old story of how sockeye came to Salish women to assist them during times of famine is linked to 2001 when "a run of sockeye committed suicide." Maracle's use of suicide in both literal and metaphorical terms enables her to uncover the ethical, political and environmental elements that connect, in her view, the sockeye of the past to the sockeye of the present. To put this otherwise, at the same time that her storying of the present moment is enfolded into Salish memory, she exercises her role as interpreter by associating the salmon's "social suicide" to world events that occurred beyond Salish territory, specifically the 9-11 attack on the Twin Towers in New York City and "suicidal warriors" in Afghanistan (53). The web of relations she establishes epitomizes how storytelling as the foundation of oratory operates as critical discourse. As Maracle writes, it is the orator's particular use of "diction, tone, style, rhythm, and physical metaphor" (172) that grounds her coming to theory in the experiential but also links her telling and interpreting to the oratorical tradition. Her emphasis on the process of coming to theory, as opposed to theory as an abstract system that introduces new critical paradigms or conceptual thought, suggests that coming to theory is not a teleological practice but an inexhaustible process.

The production of oratory, then, be it oral or written, is the result of a reciprocal transaction between the communal and the personal, while its delivery constitutes multiple and diverse acts of bearing witness that cultivate "community concatenation." The orator-as-witness-as-rememberer may often speak in the first person but, precisely because she "consult[s] with others" in order to reach "a clear and common view" of a given event (54), the agency she exercises is always interpellated by her community's ethos. Neither her voice nor her perspective is monologic. Still, the self-reflexiveness that characterizes *Memory Serves* shows that Maracle as orator is not just a spokesperson. As she states clearly, "I have been witnessing for as far back as my memory serves, but this does not make me an expert on our people" (xiv). Her oratories certainly belong to the continuum of Indigenous knowledge, affirming her kinship relations with her community, but they also bear the markers of her storytelling skills and her own individual position.

As a result of Maracle's position as *si'yam* and speaking subject, her oratories are the result of a hybrid compositional and editorial process. They comprise aspects, to borrow Susan Gingell's terms, of both "textualized orature" — "oral work that has been transcribed ... from a live performance, tape recording, compact disk film, or video tape" — and "textualized orality" (286) — writing composed in a fashion that bears oral markers. Initially delivered orally, taped, and transcribed, Maracle re-worked and expanded the transcriptions before gathering them together for this collection. Her oratories, then, are neither literal transcriptions of speeches nor pure instances of textualized orality. During the various stages of the production of *Memory Serves*, Maracle, as she makes it clear in her Preface, followed what Archibald calls "storywork," the intellectual, emotional, and spiritual work required to engage with and practise storytelling for educational purposes, a process that follows, according to Archibald, seven principles as outlined by Stó:lō elders: "respect, responsibility, reciprocity, reverence, holism, interrelatedness, and synergy" (ix). These principles are reflected in Maracle's oratories but I have also tried to remain mindful of them as an editor.

Editing *Memory Serves: Oratories* has been a long, complex, intensive, and highly rewarding process that has involved both unlearning some of my already well-honed editorial practices and learning an entirely new way of engaging with a text. The starting point of this process goes back to the summer of 2006 when I began editing "Oratory as Oratory," the plenary talk Maracle delivered at the first TransCanada conference (Vancouver 2005), included as the last oratory in this book. Because of computer mishaps, Maracle produced two different versions of the original script from which she delivered her talk. Reading, what I called in the early stages of that process, the script of that oratory, and doing so through an editorial lens, posed a range of compelling issues that revolved around one question: how could, or should, I edit "Oratory on Oratory" so that it would fit the academic publication it was intended for while remaining respectful of its particularities? For example, I had asked her to change her use of "see," as in "See has a methodology that is emotive, spiritual, intellectual and physical" (235). But this "see," as I learned, was neither an imperative gone astray nor an instance of an incomplete gerund; rather, it was Maracle's way of translating Halkomelen into English, an instance of translation that bent standard English usage to the conceptual demands of what she sought to convey, what some critics call Indigenizing English. In other words, although I knew the text to be oratory, I was still trying to edit it as a standard essay because it looked like one.

What moved my editorial process forward was storywork, for Maracle's response to my queries invariably involved storytelling. It was during that process of storywork that I realized she had so much more to say than what "Oratory on Oratory" was about, hence my inviting her to collect together her oratories.

It was after we took turns reading aloud to each other "Memory Serves" that the real editing of this volume commenced. This process began after Maracle had already revised some of the oratories following my first set of editorial comments, which addressed the structure of individual oratories but also of the entire book, and identified material that appeared – verbatim or with some variations – in more than one oratory because of the circumstances of their original deliveries. Reading out loud to each other the original written version of this oratory took almost an entire day, not only because at the time it was almost twice the length it is now but also because our reading out loud developed into the dialogic process of storywork, a process that allowed me to witness how Maracle practises community concatenation. She told me stories to explain key concepts and provide context, meanwhile remembering where, when and by whom she was first told a story, often calling a relative or an elder to confirm a story's layered meaning. Laughter and tears (and breaks to eat the food cooked by my mother) were part of the process. Not every oratory included in this book was edited with the two of us sitting side by side, but reading out loud and storying became integral elements of the editorial process: the goal of this process was to turn what had been written for oral delivery into a text that would still maintain its original formal and tonal modalities, its Salish cadences, while also working as a written text intended to be shared by a wide range of readers. We took turns reading out loud entire paragraphs, and then pausing to discuss whether certain statements needed clarification for non-Indigenous readers or argue about commas and the length of sentences, or how to edit out parts that appeared in more than one oratory. Many revisions were made during this process. I took dictation as she rephrased a sentence or typed up my suggested rewrite, and then we read the text out loud again. We agreed that working in this manner was the best way to ensure that the orality of the text was not entirely compromised; furthermore, working with Maracle by my side, seeing her at work as teller and interpreter, gave me the confidence I needed as a non-Indigenous editor to continue working with her text.

There was one unfortunate outcome as a result of this process of oral editing: being prone to bouts of laryngitis, I woke up the morning after our first marathon session on "Memory Serves" unable to speak above a whisper. Losing my voice for about ten days was difficult, but there was, I thought, a beautiful irony in it; I might have lost my voice temporarily but I had gained immense insight into Maracle's way of thinking and writing. I hope that other readers will also find long-lasting inspiration in her oratorories.

Smaro Kamboureli
TORONTO 2015

WORKS CITED

Achibald, Jo-Ann. *Indigenous Storywork: Educating the heart, mind, body, and Spirit.* Vancouver: UBC Press, 2008.

Bahr, Donald M. "Oratory." *Dictionary of Native American literature.* Ed. Andrew M. Wiget. New York: Garland, 1994. 107–117.

Carlson, Keith Thor, ed. *You are asked to Witness: The Sto:lo in Canada's Pacific Coast History.* Chilliwack, BC: Sto:lo Heritage Trust, 1997.

Carlson, Teresa M., Keith Thor Carlson, Brian Thom, and Albert "Sonny" McHalsie. "Spoken Literature: Sto:lo Oral Narratives." In Carlson. 181–96.

Felman, Shoshana. "Education and Crisis, Or the Vicissitudes of Teaching." *Trauma: Explorations in Memory.* Ed. Cathy Carouth. Baltimore: Johns Hopkins University Press, 1995. 13–60.

Gingell, Susan. "Teaching the Talk That Walks on Paper: Oral Traditions and Textualized Orature in the Canadian Literature Classroom." *Home-work: Postcolonialism, Pedagogy, and Canadian Literature.* Ed. Cynthia Sugars. Ottawa: Ottawa University Press, 2004. 285–300.

Teuton, Christopher B. "Indigenous Orality and Oral Literatues." *The Oxford Handbook of Indigenous American Literature.* Eds. James Howard Cox and Daniel Heath Justice. New York: Oxford University Press, 2014. 167–185.

WORKS CONSULTED

Akwesasne Notes. Mohawk Territory, Roosevelt Town, NY: Mohawk Nation at Akwesasne. 1969–1996.

Alfred, Taiaike. *Wasáse: Indigenous Pathways of Action and Freedom*. Peterborough: Broadview Press, 2005.

Archibald, Jo-ann. *Indigenous Storywork: Educating the Heart, Mind, Body, and Spirit*. Vancouver: UBC Press, 2008.

Armstrong, Jeannette C. *Slash*. Penticton: Theytus Books, 1986.

Boaz, Franz. *Indian Myths & Legends from the North Pacific Coast of America: A Translation of Franz Boas' 1895 Edition of Indianische Sagen von der Nord-Pacifischen Küste-Amerikas*. Eds. Randy Bouchard and Dorothy Kennedy. Trans. Dietrich Bertz. Vancouver: Talonbooks, 2006.

Blackburn, Thomas and Kat Anderson, eds. *Before The Wilderness: Environmental Management by Native Californians*. Menlo Park, CA: Ballena Press, 1993.

Bobb, Columpa C. *Dinky*. Native Earth Performing Arts, Native Canadian Centre, Toronto. 16 Feb. 1993. (First performed at the Wasakeejak Festival in 1994.)

Brill de Ramirez, Susan Berry. *Contemporary American Indian Literatures and the Oral Tradition*. Tucson: University of Arizona Press, 1999.

Cabral, Amílcar. *National Liberation and Culture*. Syracuse: Syracuse University Press, 1970.

Campbell, Maria. *Halfbreed*. (1973) Lincoln, NB: University of Nebraska Press, 1988.

Clements, Marie Humber. "The Girl Who Swam Forever." *Footpaths & Bridges: Voices from the Native American Women Playwrights Archive*. Eds. Shirley Huston-Findley and Rebecca Howard. Ann Arbor: University of Michigan Press, 2008. 51–70.

_____. "Age of Iron." Greg Daniels, Margo Kane, and Marie Humber Clements, *DraMétis: Three Métis Plays*. Penticton, BC: Theytus Books, 2001.

_____. *The Unnatural and Accidental Women*. Dir. Donna Spencer and Marie Humber Clements. Firehall Arts Centre, Vancouver, BC. 2000.

Culleton Mosionier, Beatrice. *In Search of April Raintree: Critical Edition*. Ed. Cheryl Suzack. Winnipeg: Portage & Main Press, 1999.

Dandurand, Joseph. *No Totem for My Story*. Native Earth Performing Arts, Toronto. 16 Feb. 1995.

Dimaline, Cherie. *Red Rooms*. Penticton: Theytus Books, 2007.

Dumont, Marilyn. *A Really Good Brown Girl*. London: Brick Books, 1996.

Emerson, Ralph Waldo. *The American Scholar: Self Reliance, Compensation*. Ed. Orren Henry Smith. Ann Arbor, Michigan: University of Michigan Library, 2005.

Ermine, Willie. Personal consultations with. Ethicist. First Nations University of Canada, Saskatoon, SK.

Fanon, Franz, *Wretched of the Earth*. Trans. Richard Wilcox. Foreword Homi K. Bhabha. Preface Jean-Paul Sartre. New York: Grove Press, 2004.

Favel, Floyd, ed. *The First Citizen*. Vancouver: First Citizen Newspaper Ltd., 1969–1975.

Halfe, Louise. *Bear Bones and Feathers*. Regina: Coteau Books, 1994.

Hayden Taylor, Drew. *Toronto at Dreamer's Rock*. Calgary: Fifth House Publishing, 1990.

_____. *alterNatives*. Vancouver: Talonbooks, 2000.

Highway, Tomson. *The Rez Sisters*. Act IV Theatre Company/Native Earth Performing Arts, Native Canadian Centre, Toronto, ON. 1986.

Hoy, Helen. *How Shall I Read These?: Native Women Writers in Canada*. Toronto: University of Toronto Press, 2001.

Johnson, E. Pauline. "A Strong Race Opinion: On The Indian Girl in Modern Literature." *The Toronto Globe*, 22 May, 1892.

Johnson, E. Pauline. *Legends of Vancouver*. Toronto: McClelland, Goodchild & Stewart, 1911.

The Journals of Knud Rasmussen. Dir. Zacharias Kunuk and Norman Cohn. Screenplay by Eugene Ipkamak, et. al. Alliance Atlantis. Film.

King, Martin Luther. *I Have a Dream — 40th Anniversary Edition: Writings and Speeches That Changed the World*. Ed. James M. Washington. San Francisco: HarperCollins, 1992.

King, Thomas. *The Truth About Stories: A Native Narrative*. Toronto: House of Anansi, 2003.

Klausner, Janet and Duane H. King. *Sequoyah's Gift: A Portrait of the Cherokee Leader*. New York: HarperCollins, 1999.

Krupat, Arnold. *The Voice in the Margin: Native American Literature and the Canon*. Berkeley: University of California Press, 1989.

Lawrence, Margaret. *The Diviners*. Toronto: McClelland & Stewart, 1974.

Mao, Tse-Tung. *Selected Works of Mao Zedong*. University Press of the Pacific, 2001.

Marx, Karl and Friedrich Engels. *Economic and Philosophic Manuscripts of 1844*. Trans. Martin Milligan. Amherst, N.Y: Prometheus Books, 1988.

Matthews, James Skitt, ed. *Conversations with Khahtsahlano, 1932-1954*. Vancouver: City Archives, 1955.

McNickle, D'Arcy. *William, the Hawk and Other Stories*. Tucson, AZ: University of Arizona Press, 1992.

Mercredi, Duncan. *The Duke of Windsor: Wolf Sings the Blues*. Winnipeg: Pemmican Publications, 1997.

Mills, C., Wright. *The Sociological Imagination*. New York: Oxford University Press, 1959.

Mootoo, Shani. *Cereus Blooms at Night*. Toronto: McClelland and Stewart, 1996.

Morgan, Lewis H. *League of the Ho-de-no-sau-nee or Iroquois*. Ed. Herbert M. Lloyd. New York: Dodd, Mead and Company, 1922.

Mourning Dove. "Coyote Stories." *Masterpieces of American Indian Literature*. Ed. Willis G. Regier. New York: MJF Books, 1993. 291–438.

NARP Newsletter. Vancouver: Native Alliance for Red Power, 1968 – 1972.

Paul-Martin, Michael. *She Said Sometimes I Hear Things*. Toronto: Seventh Generation Books, 1996.

Robinson, Eden. *Monkey Beach*. Toronto: Vintage Canada, 2001.

Ross, Ian. *fareWel*. Winnipeg: J.G. Shillingford Publishing, 1998.

Ryga, George. *The Ecstasy of Rita Joe*. Vancouver: Talonbooks, 1970.

Smith, Andrea. *Conquest: Sexual Violence and American Indian Genocide*. Cambridge, MA: South End Press, 2005.

Steinem, Gloria, *Revolution from Within: A Book of Self-Esteem*. Boston: Little, Brown and Co., 1992

Tawow. Ed. Jean Goodwill. Ottawa: Dept. of Indian and Northern Affairs, 1970–1973.

Teuton, Sean Kicummah. *Red Land, Red Power: Grounding Knowledge in the American Indian Novel*. Durham: Duke University Press, 2008.

The Indian Voice. Newsletter of the Indian Homemakers Association of B.C. Vancouver: Canadian Indian Voice Society, 1969 – 1975.

Van Camp, Richard. *The Lesser Blessed*. Vancouver: Douglas & McIntyre, 2004.

Wickwire, Wendy. *Write it on Your Heart: The Epic World of an Okanagan Storyteller*. Vancouver: Talonbooks, 1989.

Wheeler, Jordan. *Brothers in Arms*. Winnipeg: Pemmican Publication, 1989.

LEE MARACLE is a member of the Stó:lō nation. Born in Vancouver, she grew up on the North Shore. The author of many critically acclaimed novels, including *Sundogs, Daughters Are Forever, Ravensong* and *Celia's Song,* she has also published short fiction, *Sojourner's Truth and Other Stories* and *First Wives Club: Coast Salish Style.* The granddaughter of the renowned Chief Dan George, she is considered to be a "knowledge keeper" of her people's history, and was one of the founders of the En'owkin Centre, the international school of Indigenous writing in Penticton, B.C. Widely published in anthologies and scholarly journals, she is also the author of *Bent Box,* a poetry book, the young adult novel, *Will's Garden,* and the autobiographical narratives of *Bobbi Lee: Indian Rebel* and *I Am Woman.* She is currently an instructor and student mentor in the Aboriginal Studies Program at the University of Toronto, as well as the Traditional Teacher for First Nations' House at Toronto's Centre for Indigenous Theatre. Maracle's writing and contributions to First Nations communities have been recognized by many awards, including the JT Stewart Award, the Queen's Diamond Jubilee Medal, and the Premier's Award for Excellence in the Arts for Ontario.

SMARO KAMBOURELI is the Avie Bennett Chair in Canadian Literature at the University of Toronto. Her most recent publications are *Critical Collaborations: Indigeneity, Diaspora, Ecology,* co-edited with Christl Verduyn, and *Editing as Cultural Practice,* co-edited with Dean Irvine (forthcoming).